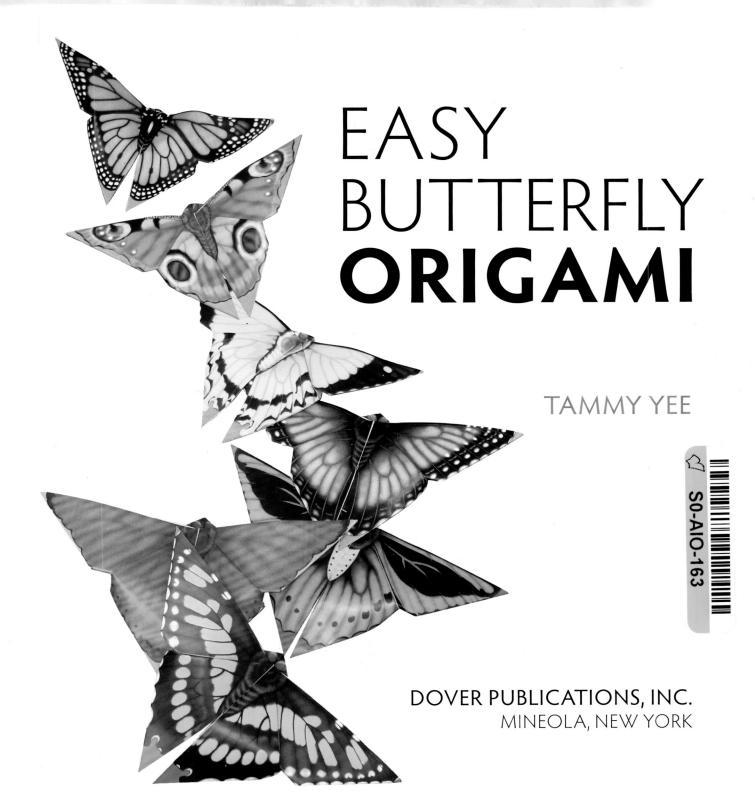

EASY
BUTTERFLY
ORIGAMI

TAMMY YEE

DOVER PUBLICATIONS, INC.
MINEOLA, NEW YORK

Introduction

Butterflies are among the world's most beautiful insects. As pollinators, they play a very important role in nature, but are most often noticed due to their striking colors and patterns. Still, not all butterflies are colorful. Some have drab markings, which provide camouflage as they rest. Others have patterns resembling false eyes or heads to startle or distract predators.

Butterflies undergo metamorphosis, which means that they change in appearance several times as they pass through their life cycle. The life cycle of a butterfly has four stages: egg, larva (caterpillar), pupa (cocoon), and adult. Caterpillars are generally herbivores, but there are a few species that feed on other insects. Adult butterflies do not have jaws to chew, so they must find liquid food, like nectar, that can be sipped through their straw-like mouthpart, called a proboscis.

The origami patterns in this book are designed to accurately portray the variations in each butterfly's dorsal (top) and ventral (bottom) view so that you can truly appreciate the diversity of these remarkable insects.

Bibliographical Note

Easy Butterfly Origami is a new work, first published by Dover Publications, Inc., in 2015.

International Standard Book Number
ISBN-13: 978-0-486-78457-1
ISBN-10: 0-486-78457-6

Printed in China by RR Donnelley
78457604   2019
www.doverpublications.com

Apollo

Black Swallowtail

Blood Red Glider

Blue Morpho

Boulder Copper

Cairns Birdwing

Chestnut Tiger

Claudina

Cleopatra

Colorado Hairstreak

Common Buckeye

Dead Leaf

Emperor of India

Malachite

Malaysian Clipper

Mocker Swallowtail

Monarch

Moth Butterfly

Mountain Alcon Blue

Noble Leafwing

Painted Beauty

Painted Lady

Pansy Daggerwing

Peacock

Purple Spotted Swallowtail

Queen Purple Tip

Red Flasher

Shining Red Charaxes

Tentyris Forester

Tiger Swallowtail

Apollo

DORSAL

VENTRAL

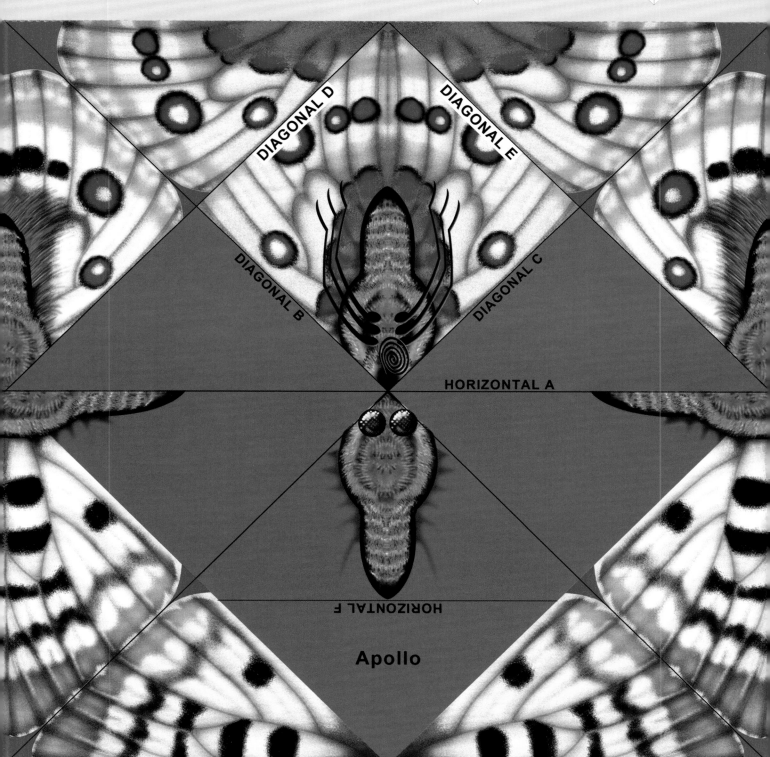

DIAGONAL D

DIAGONAL E

DIAGONAL B

DIAGONAL C

HORIZONTAL A

HORIZONTAL F

Apollo

Apollo
(Parnassius apollo)

The Apollo was once a favorite of butterfly collectors. However, over collection, habitat loss, and acid rain have made this European alpine butterfly increasingly rare. Laws have been enacted to protect this vulnerable species. In Germany, shepherds adjust their schedules to protect the caterpillars from being trampled by grazing sheep.

The Apollo's black, velvety caterpillars are difficult to spot. As they grow and molt, the larvae develop orange markings. These markings offer protection by mimicking the patterns found on pill millipedes, which secrete a foul-smelling odor. Adult butterflies are found in flowery mountain meadows and pastures.

DORSAL

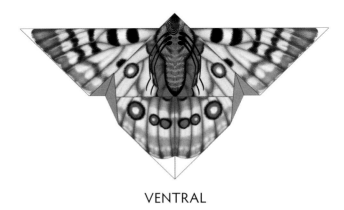

VENTRAL

Black Swallowtail

DIAGONAL D

DIAGONAL E

DIAGONAL B

DIAGONAL C

HORIZONTAL A

HORIZONTAL F

Black Swallowtail

Black Swallowtail
(Papilio polyxenes)

One of North America's most common butterflies, the Black Swallowtail often visits vegetable gardens where parsley, fennel, and dill grow. Males' wings are edged in yellow spots with cloudy blue markings on the hind wings. In females, the blue markings form a wide band. Orange and black eyespots on the hind wings distinguish them from similar-looking butterflies.

Caterpillars change appearance as they grow. Young larvae resemble bird droppings, while older larvae are green with black bands and yellow spots. To deter predators, they release a foul odor from a gland called an *osmeterium*.

DORSAL

VENTRAL

Blood Red Glider

DIAGONAL D

DIAGONAL E

DIAGONAL B

DIAGONAL C

HORIZONTAL A

HORIZONTAL F

Blood Red Glider

Blood Red Glider
(Cymothoe sangaris)

The Blood Red Glider of central Africa is the world's reddest butterfly. Males are crimson (hence the name sangaris, after the Latin word for blood); females are less brightly colored and vary in appearance amongst subspecies. Both males and females have brown undersides to provide camouflage against the jungle floor.

Adults spend much of the day high in the treetops, and descend into the understory to bask in sunlit spots in forest clearings, and to find host-plants on which the females lay their eggs.

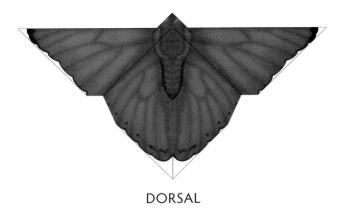

DORSAL

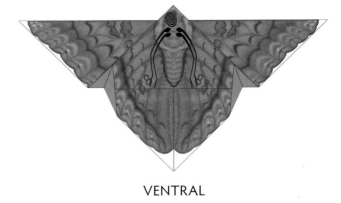

VENTRAL

Blue Morpho

DORSAL

VENTRAL

DIAGONAL D

DIAGONAL E

DIAGONAL B

DIAGONAL C

HORIZONTAL A

HORIZONTAL F

Blue Morpho

Blue Morpho
(Morpho peleides)

With its wings closed, the Blue Morpho is superbly camouflaged. The drab undersides of its wings blend in with dead leaves and tree bark, and large eyespots confuse predators. With its wings open, the butterfly is an iridescent blue. The contrasting colors make it look like it is disappearing and reappearing as it flutters through the forests of Central and South America. The larger and brighter males often chase rivals from their territory.

Caterpillars feed on plants in the pea family and defend themselves by secreting a foul smelling liquid. Adults feed on tree sap and the juices of rotting fruit and carrion.

DORSAL

VENTRAL

Boulder Copper

DIAGONAL D DIAGONAL E

DIAGONAL B DIAGONAL C

HORIZONTAL A

HORIZONTAL F

Boulder Copper

Boulder Copper
(Lycaena boldenarum)

This New Zealand butterfly is easily overlooked because of its tiny (less than one-inch) wingspan and its habit of fluttering close to the ground. But look closely, and you may find it basking with open wings on sunlit rocks. When disturbed, it closes its wings and disappears—its blue-grey underside blends perfectly with rocks and pebbles.

Caterpillars feed on creeping pohuehue and are a favorite food of paper wasps. Adult males have a brilliant purple or fuchsia sheen. Females are orange.

DORSAL

VENTRAL

Cairns Birdwing

DORSAL

VENTRAL

DIAGONAL D

DIAGONAL E

DIAGONAL B

DIAGONAL C

HORIZONTAL A

HORIZONTAL F

Cairns Birdwing

Cairns Birdwing
(Ornithoptera euphorion)

The Cairns Birdwing, named after Euphorion, the winged son of Achilles and Helen of Troy, is Australia's largest butterfly. Females, which are black and white with yellow accents, have six-inch wingspans. The smaller males are green and black. Both have bright red thoraxes and yellow abdomens.

The caterpillars feed on poisonous pipe vines and store the toxins in their spines for protection. Before pupating, they ringbark vines by chewing around the entire circumference of the stem. This makes the leaves droop from lack of water, and ensures that the caterpillar's last meal is packed with concentrated nutrients.

DORSAL

VENTRAL

Chestnut Tiger

DIAGONAL D

DIAGONAL E

DIAGONAL B

DIAGONAL C

HORIZONTAL A

HORIZONTAL F

Chestnut Tiger

Chestnut Tiger
(Parantica sita)

The Chestnut Tiger is found across Asia from the Himalayas to Japan. Like its relative, the North American Monarch, it feeds on milkweeds and migrates in the winter. One butterfly, marked and released in Japan, was recaptured 83 days later in Hong Kong—a flight of 1,500 miles across the ocean!

Although common, Chestnut Tigers are dwindling in places like Hong Kong's Butterfly Valley. Once the winter home of up to 40,000 butterflies, a recent survey found less than 600 individuals. Tracking their migration will help researchers conserve habitats along the route.

DORSAL

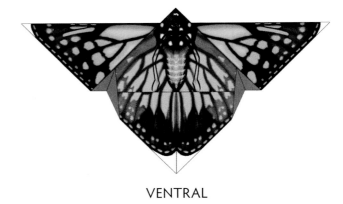

VENTRAL

Claudina

DIAGONAL D

DIAGONAL E

DIAGONAL B

DIAGONAL C

HORIZONTAL A

HORIZONTAL F

Claudina

Claudina
(Agrias claudina)

The Claudina may be one of the world's most spectacular butterflies, but it is rarely seen. It lives high in the canopy of the Amazon rainforest, and can only be coaxed down from the treetops with rotting fruit, dead fish, or animal dung left along forested trails.

Male Claudinas have bright yellow tufts on their hindwings that release chemicals—like butterfly cologne—to attract females.

DORSAL

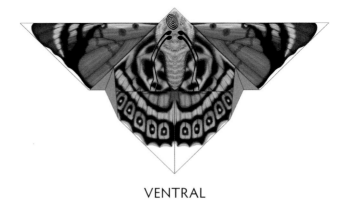

VENTRAL

Cleopatra

DORSAL   VENTRAL

DIAGONAL D   DIAGONAL E

DIAGONAL B   DIAGONAL C

HORIZONTAL A

HORIZONTAL F

Cleopatra

Cleopatra
(Gonepteryx cleopatra)

At rest, the male Cleopatra disguises himself as a young green leaf. In flight, he shows off sunny yellow wings splashed with orange. The females are modest by comparison, having pale yellow-green wings adorned with four orange dots.

Found in open woodlands and scrubby grasslands along the Mediterranean, the Cleopatra can live for up to ten months—ancient in the butterfly world! Adults spend the winter hibernating in evergreens and under bramble leaves.

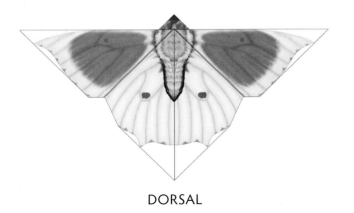

DORSAL

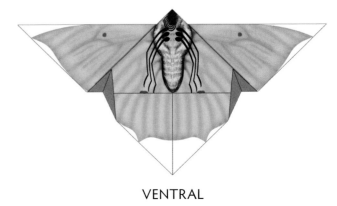

VENTRAL

Colorado Hairstreak

DORSAL

VENTRAL

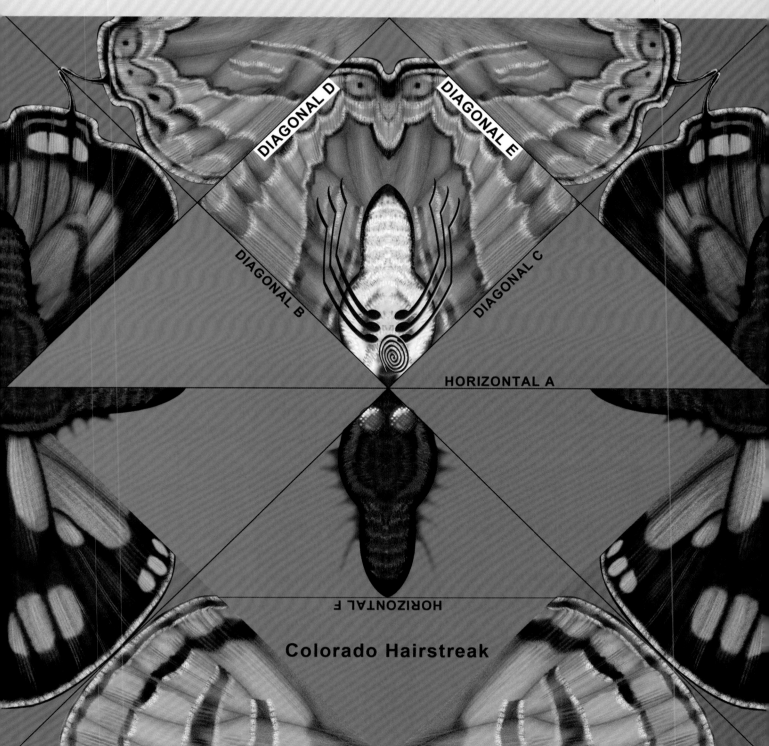

DIAGONAL D

DIAGONAL E

DIAGONAL B

DIAGONAL C

HORIZONTAL A

HORIZONTAL F

Colorado Hairstreak

Colorado Hairstreak
(Hypaurotis crysalus)

The Colorado Hairstreak is a purple butterfly with a distinctive hair-like tail on each hind wing. Found in the Gambel oak woodlands throughout the Southwestern United States and Northern Mexico, it has been designated the official state insect of Colorado.

Unlike most butterflies, the Colorado Hairstreak rarely visits flowers. Instead it flitters in the treetops, feeding on tree sap, raindrops, and aphid honeydew. Females lay eggs on oak twigs. The eggs hibernate through the winter, and caterpillars emerge in the spring.

DORSAL

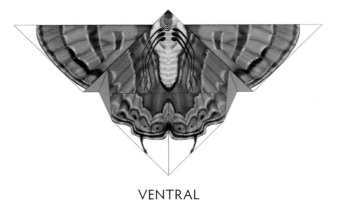

VENTRAL

Common Buckeye

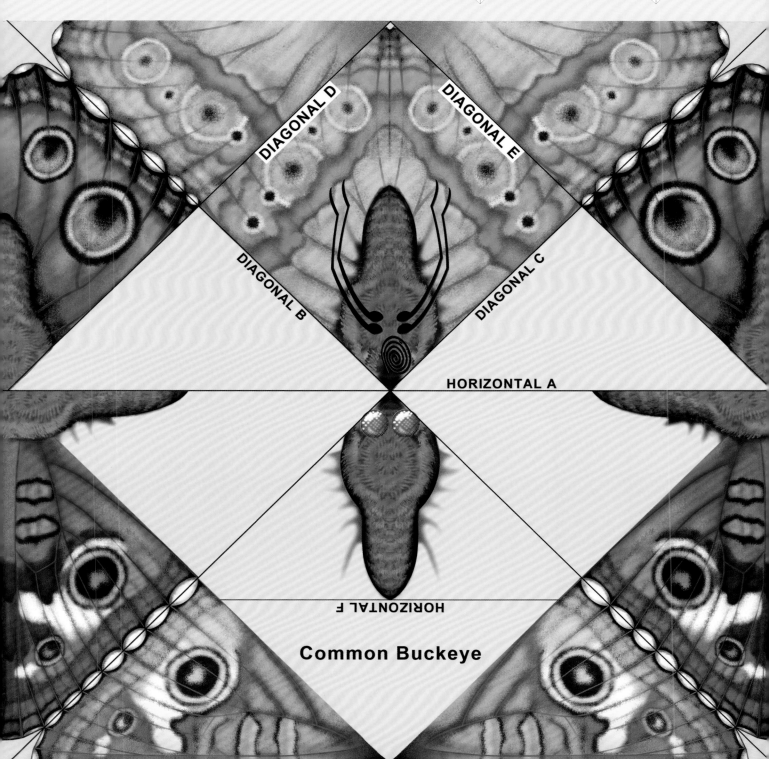

DIAGONAL D

DIAGONAL E

DIAGONAL B

DIAGONAL C

HORIZONTAL A

HORIZONTAL F

Common Buckeye

Common Buckeye
(Junonia coenia)

Buckeyes belong to the large family of brush-footed or four-footed but-terflies, so called because the adults walk on only four legs—their front legs are brush-like stumps that are held close to the body and not used for walking.

Easily identified by their bold eyespots, Buckeyes are found throughout the Southern United States, Mexico, the Caribbean, and along the coasts of Central California and North Carolina. In the summer they migrate north through the Midwest and into Southern Canada.

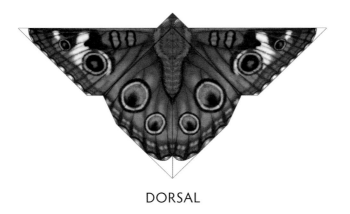

DORSAL

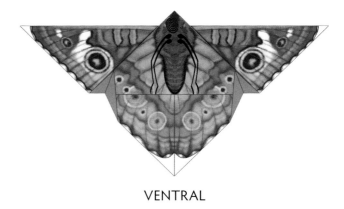

VENTRAL

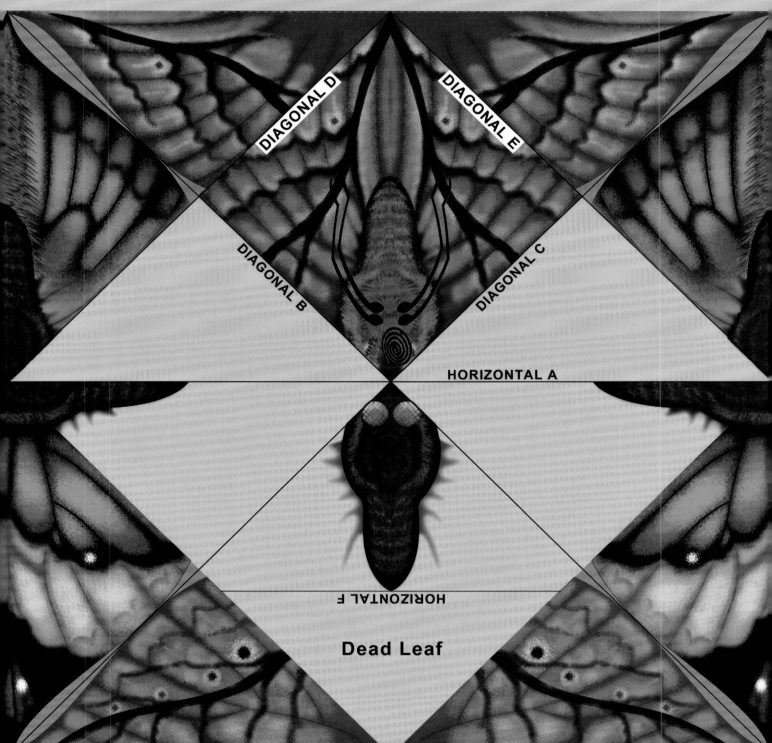

Dead Leaf

DORSAL   VENTRAL

DIAGONAL D   DIAGONAL E

DIAGONAL B   DIAGONAL C

HORIZONTAL A

HORIZONTAL F

Dead Leaf

Dead Leaf
(Kallima inachus)

The Dead Leaf is an astonishing example of camouflage. When closed, the tapered wings reveal brown splotches and striations that perfectly mimic the veins of a tattered leaf.

The Dead Leaf is a strong flier and can be found from India to Japan in dense tropical forests. If threatened, it disappears into the underbrush and hides with its wings closed. Adults feed on rotting fruit and tree sap, and sometimes gather around puddles to sip moisture, salt, and minerals from the mud.

DORSAL

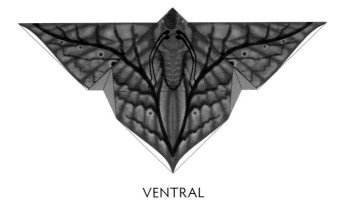

VENTRAL

Emperor of India

DORSAL

VENTRAL

DIAGONAL D

DIAGONAL E

DIAGONAL B

DIAGONAL C

HORIZONTAL A

HORIZONTAL F

Emperor of India

Emperor of India
(Teinopalpus imperialis)

The Emperor of India is a rare and magnificent Swallowtail that lives in the high-altitude forests of the Himalayas. Officially listed as a threatened species by the World Conservation Union (IUCN), it is endangered by over-collecting and the destruction of its forest home by logging, limestone mining, and encroaching development.

The Emperor of India is a fast and powerful flier. Females are larger than males, with wingspans reaching up to five inches across.

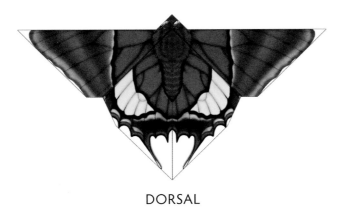

DORSAL

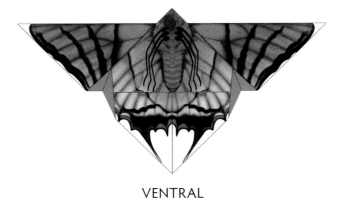

VENTRAL

Malachite

Malachite

Malachite
(Siproeta stelenes)

Named after the green mineral malachite, this highly adaptable butterfly thrives in the forests of Central and South America, and north into the gardens and orchards of Southern Texas and Florida.

The caterpillars are black with red spines. These spines may look fierce, but are soft and harmless; they scare off predators by mimicking the stinging spines of other larvae. Adult butterflies feed on flower nectar, rotting fruit, fluids from carrion, and animal dung.

DORSAL

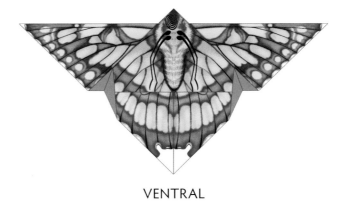

VENTRAL

Malaysian Clipper

DORSAL   VENTRAL

DIAGONAL D

DIAGONAL E

DIAGONAL B

DIAGONAL C

HORIZONTAL A

HORIZONTAL F

Malaysian Clipper

Malaysian Clipper
(Parthenos sylvia)

The Clipper is named after the swift merchant ships of the eighteenth century. It was first described by a Dutch merchant and amateur naturalist named Pieter Cramer. Cramer collected butterflies from trading posts around the world, and the Clipper's white wing markings reminded him of white sails.

Clippers are found throughout South and Southeast Asia. They come in a variety of colors, from golden brown in the Philippines, to jade green in India, and peacock blue in Malaysia. Clippers are popular because they often rest on flowers and foliage with their boldly patterned wings wide open.

DORSAL

VENTRAL

Mocker Swallowtail

DORSAL

VENTRAL

Mocker Swallowtail

Mocker Swallowtail
(Papilio dardanus)

The Mocker Swallowtail, described by biologist Edward Poultan as "the most interesting butterfly in the world," is a well-known example of *Batesian mimicry,* where harmless species defend themselves by imitating the appearance of harmful species. The males all look alike, with yellow wings edged in black. Females however, come in at least fourteen different forms that resemble various poisonous butterflies. The Mocker Swallowtail is native to the forests of sub-Saharan Africa.

DORSAL

VENTRAL

Monarch

DORSAL

VENTRAL

DIAGONAL D

DIAGONAL E

DIAGONAL B

DIAGONAL C

HORIZONTAL A

HORIZONTAL F

Monarch

Monarch
(Danaus plexippus)

Every winter, Monarchs travel up to 3,000 miles from North America to warmer climates in Northern South America—a migration that spans four butterfly generations. They cluster by the thousands in trees along the way to rest and keep warm. Scientists don't fully understand how they find their way, but suspect they are aided by the sun's position and the earth's magnetic pull.

The Monarch's bright markings warn birds and other predators that they are poisonous. This warning strategy is so effective, that the Viceroy butterfly mimics the Monarch's appearance to deter predators.

DORSAL

VENTRAL

Moth Butterfly

DORSAL

VENTRAL

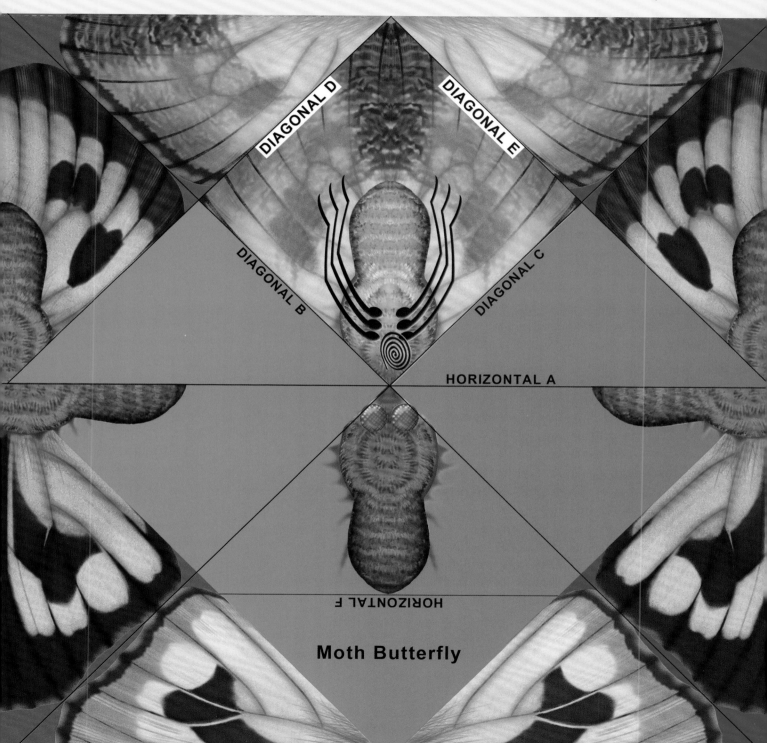

DIAGONAL D

DIAGONAL E

DIAGONAL B

DIAGONAL C

HORIZONTAL A

HORIZONTAL F

Moth Butterfly

Moth Butterfly
(Liphyra brassolis)

The Moth butterfly has a heavy, moth-like body, hence its name. Its odd-looking larvae resemble slugs—it has tough, leathery skin, and its sucker-like feet and flat wide body make it impossible for ants to flip it over to attack the soft underbody. These carnivorous caterpillars eat Green Tree Ant larvae and pupae, and can easily devour the entire brood in a nest. Adult butterflies emerging from their pupae protect themselves from attacking ants by shedding sticky scales from their wings.

Moth butterflies are found in Australia and Southeast Asia.

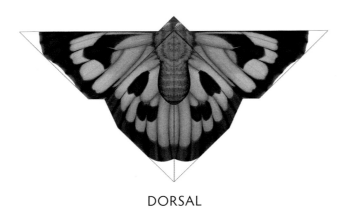

DORSAL

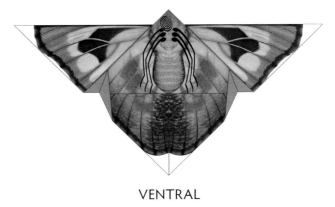

VENTRAL

Mountain Alcon Blue

DORSAL   VENTRAL

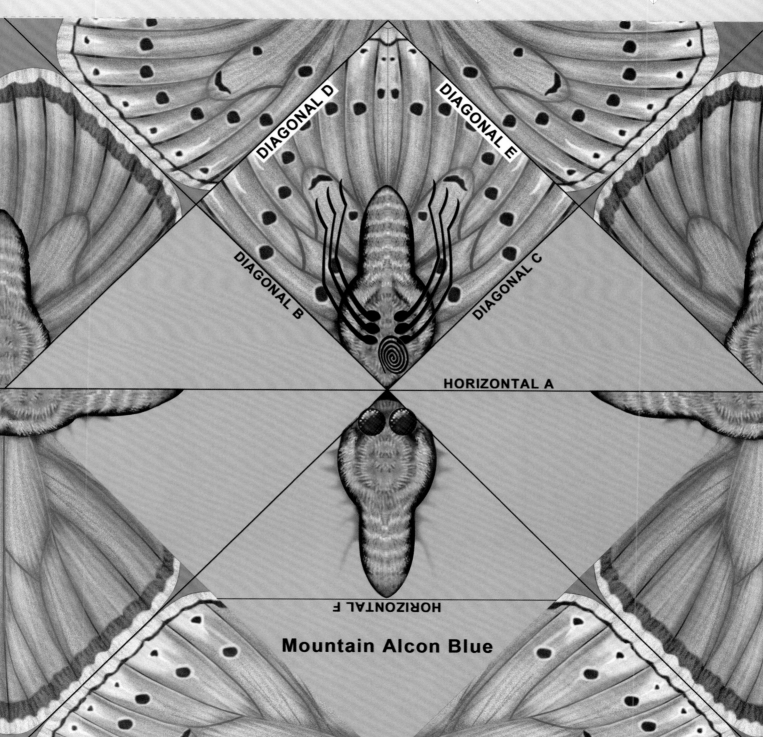

DIAGONAL D

DIAGONAL E

DIAGONAL B

DIAGONAL C

HORIZONTAL A

HORIZONTAL F

Mountain Alcon Blue

Mountain Alcon Blue
(Phengaris rebeli)

The Mountain Alcon Blue has a devious survival strategy: it tricks ants into feeding and protecting its young! Caterpillars use chemical signals to fool ants into carrying them into the nest. Once inside, the caterpillars get preferential treatment. Ants will rescue the caterpillars over their own brood, and during food shortages, they will even sacrifice their own larva to feed them. Studies suggest that the caterpillars also copy the sounds made by queen ants.

The Mountain Alcon Blue is found in temperate grasslands across Europe and is threatened by habitat loss.

DORSAL

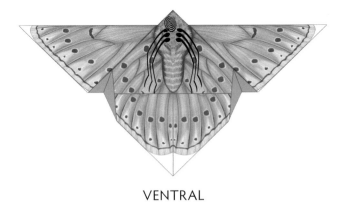

VENTRAL

Noble Leafwing

DIAGONAL D

DIAGONAL E

DIAGONAL B

DIAGONAL C

HORIZONTAL A

HORIZONTAL F

Noble Leafwing

Noble Leafwing
(Fountainea nobilis)

The Noble Leafwing lives in cool, wet forests from Mexico to Peru. In most places the males are deep red-orange and brown, but in Colombia they are iridescent pink and purple. Both males and females have short tails on their hind wings, and brown undersides that have the same patterns as dead leaves. They are well-camouflaged when resting with their wings closed. On cool mornings and in the late afternoon, they sometimes rest with their wings open, to warm themselves in the sun.

Most butterflies in the Leafwing family prefer mineralized mud, tree sap, and rotting fruit over flower nectar.

DORSAL

VENTRAL

Painted Beauty

DORSAL

VENTRAL

DIAGONAL D

DIAGONAL E

DIAGONAL B

DIAGONAL C

HORIZONTAL A

HORIZONTAL F

Painted Beauty

Painted Beauty
(Batesia hypochlora)

Pink is a color that is rarely seen in butterflies. The Painted Beauty flaunts its pink wing patches as it flutters through the Amazon rainforest, as if calling attention to its unique color and bold markings. Some researchers think that this display is a warning signal that the butterfly is foul-tasting. When threatened, caterpillars raise their front ends and wave their heads side to side—a peculiar dance that may deter other insects from eating them.

The Painted Beauty's host plant is the inchi tree. Inchi nuts are prized by native Amazonians for food, medicine, and as a source of edible oil.

DORSAL   VENTRAL

Painted Lady

DORSAL

VENTRAL

DIAGONAL D

DIAGONAL E

DIAGONAL B

DIAGONAL C

HORIZONTAL A

HORIZONTAL F

Painted Lady

Painted Lady
(Vanessa cardui)

The Painted Lady is found on all continents except South America and Antarctica, making it the world's most widespread butterfly. Its migratory behavior and ability to feed from a wide variety of plants contribute to its success. Heavy rains in North Africa can produce massive migrations of Painted Ladies across the Mediterranean, and up into Europe and Britain.

The caterpillars protect themselves by weaving silk nests on leaves. As they grow, they develop spines that look menacing, but are soft and harmless.

DORSAL

VENTRAL

Pansy Daggerwing

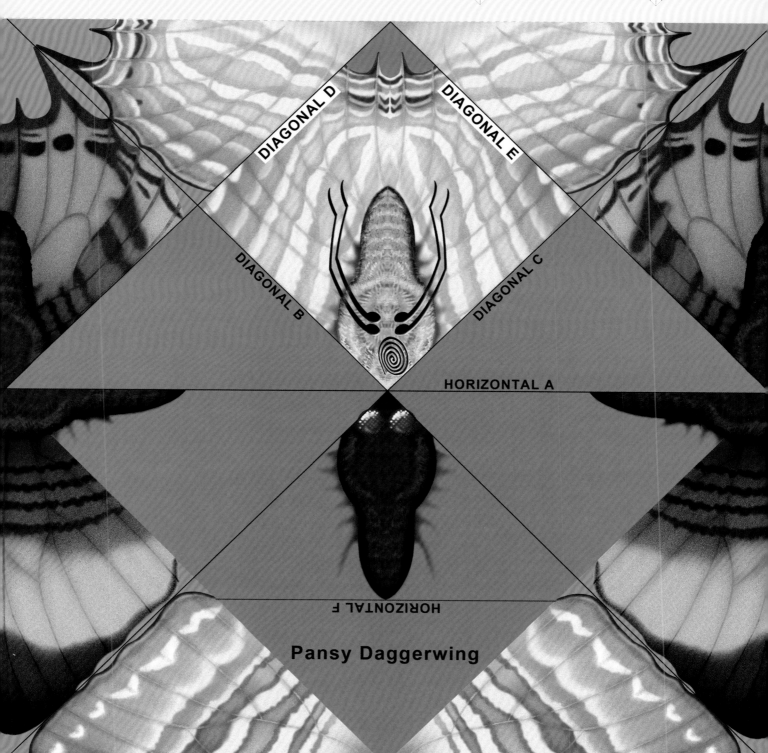

DIAGONAL D

DIAGONAL E

DIAGONAL B

DIAGONAL C

HORIZONTAL A

HORIZONTAL F

Pansy Daggerwing

Pansy Daggerwing
(Marpesia marcella)

The Pansy Daggerwing is found in neotropical cloud forests from Guatemala to Peru. Adult males will sometimes gather in small clusters on mineral-rich soil banks. Females prefer hiding in the lush canopy. Because cloud forests are so mountainous and remote, little else is known about the Pansy Daggerwing's life cycle.

Daggerwings have tails on their hind wings, and are often confused with swallowtail butterflies. However, like other members of the brush-footed butterfly family, adult Daggerwings have only four legs.

DORSAL

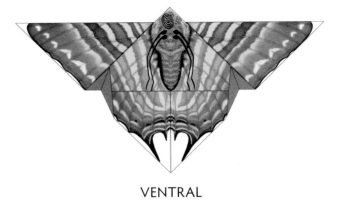

VENTRAL

Peacock

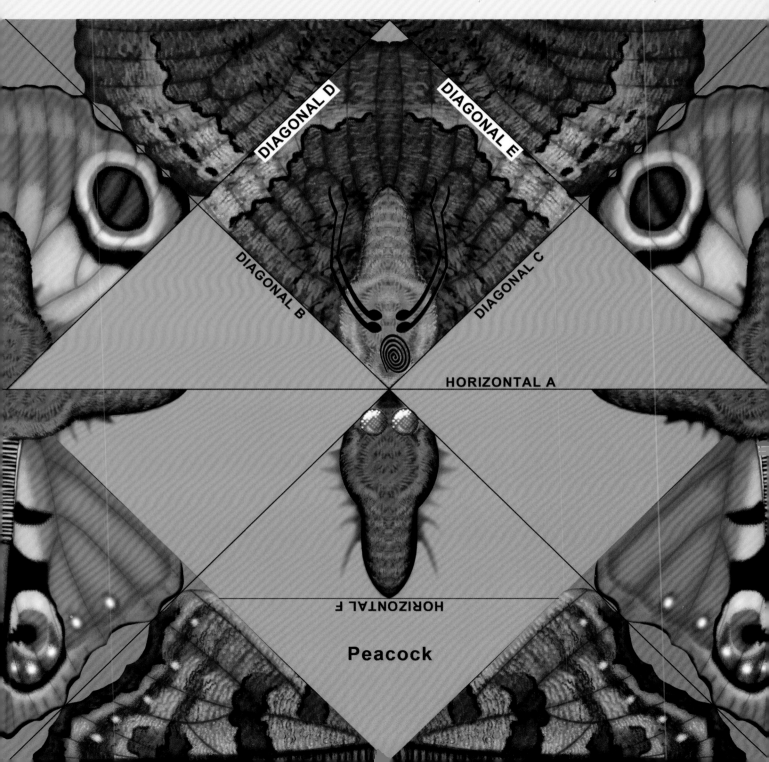

DIAGONAL D

DIAGONAL E

DIAGONAL B

DIAGONAL C

HORIZONTAL A

HORIZONTAL F

Peacock

Peacock
(Inachis io)

The Peacock has a unique defense strategy. When disturbed, it makes a hissing sound by rubbing its wings together, then flicks open its wings to display bold eyespots. These spots startle predators and divert attacks to its main body.

Peacocks are found in temperate regions across Europe and Asia, and are a common sight in European meadows, parks, and gardens. In the winter, adults hibernate in outbuildings, hollow trees, and piles of wood.

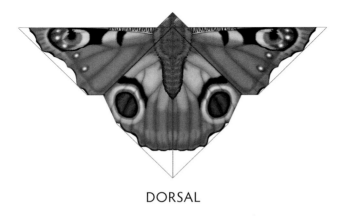

DORSAL

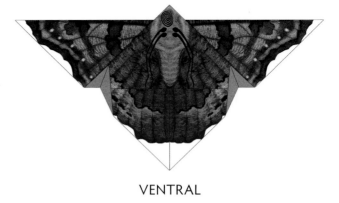

VENTRAL

Purple Spotted Swallowtail

DORSAL

VENTRAL

DIAGONAL D

DIAGONAL E

DIAGONAL B

DIAGONAL C

HORIZONTAL A

HORIZONTAL F

Purple Spotted Swallowtail

Purple Spotted Swallowtail
(Graphium weiskei)

Found only in the misty mountains of Papua New Guinea at elevations of 4,500 to 8,000 feet, the Purple Spotted Swallowtail boasts striking splashes of purple, pink, green, and blue across its wings. With a wingspan of only three inches, it is one of the smallest swallowtails in its family. Extensions or "tails" at the end of each hind wing distract birds from attacking the butterfly's vulnerable head and body.

DORSAL

VENTRAL

Queen Purple Tip

DORSAL

VENTRAL

DIAGONAL D

DIAGONAL E

DIAGONAL B

DIAGONAL C

HORIZONTAL A

HORIZONTAL F

Queen Purple Tip

Queen Purple Tip
(Colotis regina)

The Queen Purple Tip's distinctive white wings look like they've been dipped in purple paint. These butterflies can be found year-round in the arid regions of the Afrotropic ecozone, where caper bushes and shepherd's trees grow on dry hilltops. The males flitter near these host plants, hoping to find females searching for a place to lay their eggs. Queen Purple Tips are quick and agile fliers and have two-inch wingspans. Females have a pinkish tinge to their undersides.

DORSAL

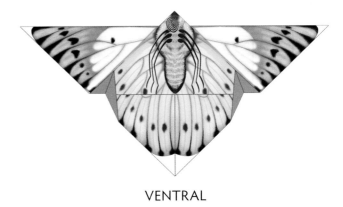

VENTRAL

Red Flasher

DORSAL   VENTRAL

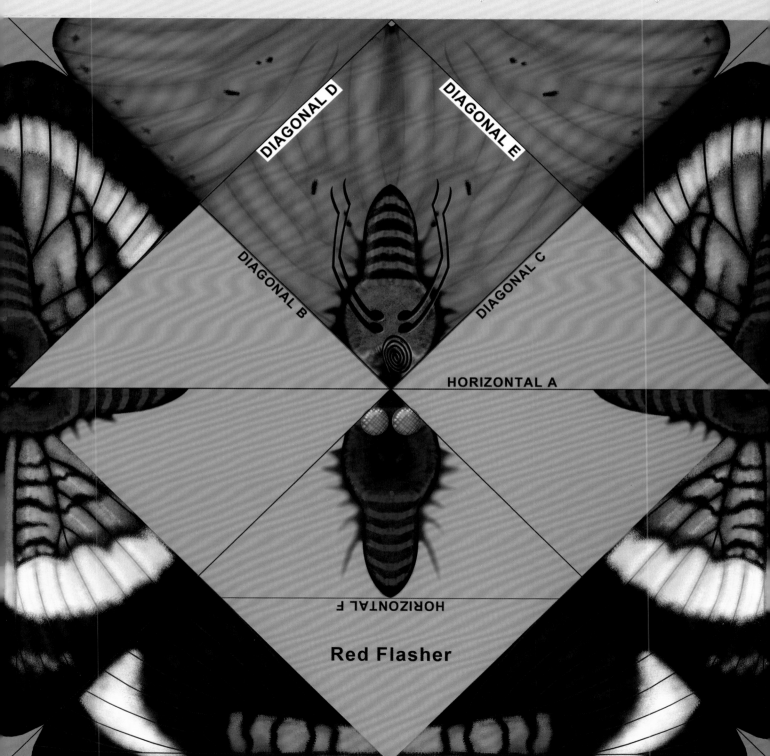

DIAGONAL D

DIAGONAL E

DIAGONAL B

DIAGONAL C

HORIZONTAL A

HORIZONTAL F

Red Flasher

Red Flasher
(Panacea prola)

Red Flashers are found throughout South America, from Columbia to Southern Brazil, where they roost high in the forest canopy. As the day warms, they descend lower into the forest to bask in large groups along mineral-rich riverbanks. The name comes from their habit of flashing their wings to display their bright red undersides. When disturbed, one individual will flash its wings in alarm and prompt a ripple of synchronized wing fanning through the entire group.

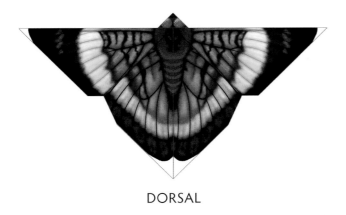

DORSAL

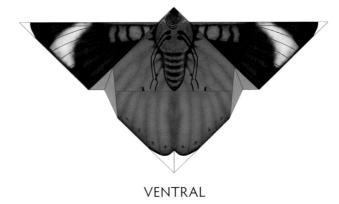

VENTRAL

Shining Red Charaxes

DORSAL
VENTRAL

DORSAL

VENTRAL

DIAGONAL D

DIAGONAL E

DIAGONAL B

DIAGONAL C

HORIZONTAL A

HORIZONTAL F

Shining Red Charaxes

Shining Red Charaxes
(Charaxes zingha)

The Shining Red Charaxes is a strong and aggressive flier that lives in the tropical forests of Africa. Males are highly territorial, often engaging in aerial battle to chase rival males from the vicinity.

The slug-shaped caterpillars have wide, flat heads, with four horn-like protrusions that make them look like tiny green dragons.

DORSAL

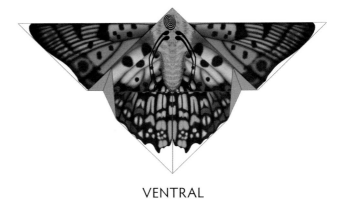

VENTRAL

Tentyris Forester

DORSAL

VENTRAL

DIAGONAL D

DIAGONAL E

DIAGONAL B

DIAGONAL C

HORIZONTAL A

HORIZONTAL F

Tentyris Forester

Tentyris Forester
(Bebearia tentyris)

In the shade, the Tentyris Forester's wings are dull and reddish brown. In the light, the wings shimmer with the colors of sunrise: orange, pink, purple, and blue. This effect, where colors glow and change depending upon the angle of the light, is called *iridescence*. Microscopic scales on the butterfly's wing diffract and scatter light, helping the butterfly to warm itself, signal mates and rivals, and even camouflage itself.

The Tentyris Forester lives in the drier rainforests of Western Africa, from the Ivory Coast to the Congo. Because they adapt well to areas affected by forest degradation, their population remains stable.

DORSAL

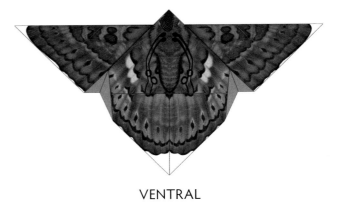

VENTRAL

Tiger Swallowtail

DIAGONAL D

DIAGONAL E

DIAGONAL B

DIAGONAL C

HORIZONTAL A

HORIZONTAL F

Tiger Swallowtail

Tiger Swallowtail
(Papilio glaucus)

The Tiger Swallowtail of North America is easily identified by the four "tiger stripes" running across its yellow forewings. Adult females come in two forms, or morphs: light and dark. Light morph females are more colorful than the males, with a wide blue band and orange spots across the wings. Dark morph females are almost black and gain protection by mimicking poisonous Pipevine Swallowtails.

Caterpillars change appearance as they molt. Young caterpillars resemble bird droppings. Older caterpillars are green with bright eyespots that scare predators; they then turn brown before pupating. They hibernate through the winter in their chrysalises.

DORSAL

VENTRAL

All About Surf Fishing

All About Surf Fishing

A complete guide to fishing the ocean's edges–including bridges, jetties, flats, creeks, and the high surf–with special contributions by Frank Woolner, George Heinold, Milt Rosko, Frank Daignault, Jim Rizzuto, Ken Laver, and Larry Green

Jack Fallon

Winchester Press

Library of Congress Catalog Card Number: 75-9528
ISBN: 0-87691-201-3

Fallon, Jack.
    All about surf fishing.

    Includes index.
    SUMMARY: Discusses the sport of fishing the edges of
the ocean and advises the reader on surfing strategy, fly-fishing,
kite fishing and all the accompanying tackle, lures, baits, and
accessories.
        1. Surf fishing.   [1. Surf fishing.   2. Fishing] I. Wool-
ner, Frank, 1916-   II. Title.
SH457.2.F34   799.1'7   75-9258

Published by Winchester Press
205 East 42nd Street, New York 10017

Printed in the United States of America

Contents

Preface

MANY YEARS AGO a redheaded stringbean with fire in his eyes and a rocket in his rump asked me if I would like to try surf fishing. All night long we prowled and plugged, and we didn't catch a fish. I loved every minute of it.

Arnold Clark's invitation was my "Open Sesame" to a world that I didn't know existed: soft night and hazy days, crystal dawns and incandescent evenings; an ocean pulsating with promise; a no-holds-barred brand of fishing right in the fish's front yard with only a fragile filament pitting my puny prowess against its elemental instincts.

Half a lifetime later, I still haven't found anything quite like it. For soothing the soul, igniting the mind, testing the body, recharging rundown emotional batteries, and just plain having a wonderful time, surf fishing is laps ahead of the competition.

This book is my way of holding the door open to folks whose lives have similar holes that need filling. There's something here for everyone: man, woman, boy, girl, the veteran whose balky legs have blazed their last trail, the tyro whose legs have yet to feel the surf's first cold kiss.

Some of what I say here I have said before in *Salt Water Sportsman, Field & Stream, Fishing World, Massachusetts Out-of-Doors,* and *New Hampshire Outdoors.* For permission to reprint, I am grateful. I also am grateful to a Pantheon of surfmen—Frank Woolner, George Heinold, Milt Rosko, Frank Daignault, Jim Rizzuto, Ken Lauer, Larry Green—for generously disclosing how they got started and what they would do differently if they were starting today; to Jack, Dan, Liz, Matthew, Julie, and Margaret for adding new dimensions; to Peg for sharing; to Himself for putting it all there in the first place; and especially to Mr. and Mrs. J. Stanley Upton, who gave me a quiet sanctuary in which to write and to whom I affectionately dedicate this book.

JACK FALLON
Chelmsford, Mass.
May 21, 1975

An autumn surf can be hostile, but it's often the scene of spectacular feeding binges by migrating fish.

1
Welcome to Surf Fishing

EVENTUALLY EVERY SWEETWATER FISHERMAN WONDERS what it would be like to take on an ocean. Maybe he's standing kneedeep in a trout stream with a soft current caressing his calves when the thought occurs: a breeze kicks up a chop, spraying his face, and he thinks of waves hurling spume; a stray current nudges his hip and he thinks of the tow of tides and the buffeting of breakers; the tender pressure on his legs, he thinks, would be a cold firm clutch if he were standing in the surf, and wouldn't it be wonderful.

Or maybe he's playing a small perch onto the shore of a pond, and he imagines how it might be just for once to battle a genuinely big fish—10, 15, even 20 pounds—like one of those striped bass he's seen surfmen beaching in books.

Or maybe he just wants to feel what it's like to haul back as hard as he can and heave his lure as far as he can, without bushes or trees or houses to impose their restraints, and to use a rod that's designed to give him all the distance he's able to muster.

What is surf fishing really like? Wo-o-onderful, that's what. Everything you've ever imagined it might be, times ten, a hundred, a thousand. Hot, cold, wet, dry, pulse-pounding hard, and soul-soothing soft—they're all there, every minute of every day of every season along the sea rim. . . .

That magic moment when you uncork the first cast of a new season in the suds.

Spring

On your mark, get set . . .

You're trembling. Yeah, really trembling. Your legs tingle at the thought of the spring surf's first cold kiss. Your stomach clutches at the prospect of uncorking your first cast of another season in the suds. Your juices surge like sap in sugar maples. And your hands, they haven't shaken so much since you said, "I do." Except, of course, for just prior to last season, and the season before, and the season before that.

Summer

A high sun bakes your bare back, spangles a wrinkled sea: siesta time for fish and fisherman alike; a time for basking and bathing and lolling in the shade.

So why the rod on your shoulder as you head out the beach?

There's this rock, see . . . Every surfman seeks one; these Californians found theirs. (Photo: Larry Green)

Why the quick cadence, the resolute look, the optimistic smile?
Well, there's this rock, see . . .

Fall

"It's not a fit night out for man nor beast" is the way W. C. Fields would have described it, but for you it couldn't be better: mist-shrouded dunes looming out of the murk as you trudge into the teeth of a screaming gale that hurls rumbling breakers up a barren beach. Stripers are schooling for their autumn migration. They will be feeding in that foam.

Winter

You thought it was all over. You've resigned yourself to dismal months of feeding on the fat of last season's delights and next season's dreams. Then your phone rings.

Despite the heavy clothes and snow-laden wind hissing across the harbor, it seems an awful lot like summer. (Photo: Terry McDonnell)

"Yeah, bluefish, honestagawd. In the warm-water outlet of this power plant. They think it's still August. Whattaya say?"

And, of course, you say, "YES!" And, of course, despite the heavy clothes and gray skies and snow-laden wind hissing across the harbor, it seems an awful lot like summer.

Spring Again

You've checked off every milestone: the new year's calendar, the sportsmen's shows, the sudden blooming of fishing annuals on magazine racks, the freshly stocked fishing departments that only a few days before had been displaying ice skates and basketballs and hockey sticks, the vernal equinox.

Then the announcement: "They're in!" Cod are chasing smelt across the bar that parallels the beach you haven't seen since last October. On tonight's moon tide they should be swarming through the trough between bar and beach.

Clamnecks are traditional fare. Most of the gang will be using them. But you know this creek, right on the way. You caught smelt there night before last, and tonight you take two dozen in a half-hour. Fresh bait. Cod will clobber them.

Early yet, you think, as you lob your sinker into the trough; half,

With the first spring cod, the glorious golden cycle starts again.

maybe three-quarters of an hour before the water will be deep
enough for cod to cruise comfortably over the bar. But the bar has
cuts, and cod have come through them, and one gobbles your smelt.
As line peels from your spool, you lean forward, crank your bail
closed, reel in slack, and haul up the curtain for another ride on
that merriest of merry-go-rounds where the music never stops and
every ring is made of brass.

There are dawns that seep slowly across a calm sea, spreading
their pastel promise of a new day; mornings when fog clings so
close that you wade utterly alone through a gloriously gauzy world;
soft afternoon hours that surge suddenly into a flamboyant sunset,
then subside like a sigh into calm, cool, quiet dark; star-spangled
nights when an orange moon inches over the earth's edge and a
great gilded fish leaps to greet it.

And there are wild times, too: the sea raging, the surf slamming,
the wind screaming, the sand stinging. You are humbled by their
power, ennobled by your participation.

Even in a clamorous and congested world, the surf still offers
solitude. Yet though a man be blissfully by himself in the surf, he
never need be lonely. Egos make good friends, eager conversa-
tionalists. I never met a sincere surf fisherman who didn't like himself. Along the edge of an eternal ocean, under the canopy of an

Even in this crowded world, salt water can give a man all the solitude he craves.

infinite sky, questions always come easy, answers always are candid. A psychiatrist's couch is much too cramped for a devoted surf fisherman; besides, it's too hard to cast from.

But the surf also is for sharing. The special fish, the witty remark, the awed observation, the incandescent dawn all make mellower memories when they can be recalled with someone you like. Take wives, for instance. The boudoir hasn't been built that can bring wives and husbands as close as the surf can. Mutual memories work wonders for mates who have forgotten how to be friends. "Remember-whens" are ready reservoirs of laughter for lubricating the gears of earning a living, running a household, raising a family.

Like that weekend on Cuttyhunk when Mrs. Fallon slipped on a rock and got the biggest black eye since Louis demolished Galento, and for two interminable weeks I endured the accusing stares of neighbors, merchants, and clergy who were convinced that her purple orb was the product of domestic discord; like my penchant for going over my waders to reach that special rock while Peg plucks out fish right behind me; like her falling four times flat on her pretty Irish puss and still landing her striper; like my slothing back from a dark clamflat, reaching into my waders, and pulling out four fat fish; like hot coffee on cold mornings, warm fires on

Seaside pleasures can also be shared with compatible companions, and this adds a new dimension to your enjoyment.

Even the dunkings make marvelous memories. Mrs. Fallon took four flat-on-her-face nosedives before landing this bass.

cold nights; like the unexpected elegance of cream sherry from crystal glasses in the lee of a looming boulder while the leading edge of a hurricane lashes a saner world.

A 50-pound striper is the only thing I can think of that could brighten up a long dark night on the beach better than the right kind of female companionship. Sure, when Peggy's along I have to put the brakes on my peculiarly masculine fish-till-I-drop determination to do battle with the biggest bass in the ocean; certainly the interruptions are more frequent, the pauses more prolonged; but, ah, the compensations: close quiet moments under an infinity of stars at the edge of an eternal sea—the ultimate intimacy of the Outdoors. Tax bills, food prices, fuel shortages? Never heard of them. Souls seasoned with a little salt manage to keep priorities pretty much in their proper perspective.

It's little wonder, though, that ladies have shied away from surf fishing. Traditionally the sea rim has been depicted as man's domain, an environment of Valkyrian violence where winds scream, waves crash, and skies are laced with lightning, raked with thunder, while hard-muscled males, hip-deep in boiling breakers, struggle titanically with unseen marine monsters. It's enough to scare the skivvies off any sensible lassie, and I suspect that that's what it's intended to do.

Pity. The surf has so much to offer besides wild wind-whipped beaches; so many quiet coves and gentle creeks where fish are plentiful and recklessness is not a requirement. The most timorous can fish these places relaxed and unafraid.

Even beachfronts are manageable most of the time. Their rages are rare and short-lived. When the ocean is on the warpath, smart surf casters, regardless of their sex, head for home to oil their reels and monitor their barometers. When skies clear and atmospheric pressures rise, they return to lay clams in the paths of fish that cruise in close to dine on delectables that the storm has turned up.

But the surf needn't be bathtub-smooth for ladies to take it on. The tug of tides, the buffeting of breakers, an occasional wave over the waders—one soon gets used to these. Anticipation, timing, and a temporary tolerance for soggy underwear can enable the most feminine of females to feel at home in the foam.

Yeah, feminine. Curls, curves, cuteness—the works. It's not necessary to be musclebound and manly to fish the surf. Some of the anglerettes along the Jersey shore could climb the boardwalk at Atlantic City and, even with their waders on, give those Miss America contestants a run for their money. On the Outer Cape in recent years, Joyce Daignault has made more than one passerby believe in mermaids. My own Peg—sleek, slender, and 100 percent feminine gender—is as at home in the surf as she is in our kitchen or at the head of the classroom full of special children she teaches.

These gals, by the way, also are ladies. No concessions to coarseness or lusty language just to join the club. Each exhibits that hallmark of gracious Womanhood, the ability to roll her sleeves up without letting her hair down.

For sons, what better place than the surf to learn that the Old Man isn't all rules and bills and business trips? What better place than the surf for a father to learn that maybe there's a plea behind his boy's misbehavior, that maybe there's a good reason for the long hair and old clothes and short temper?

Daughters, too. Especially when they're little-girl young. Despite the constant hazard of inaccurately aimed hooks, few sights are more delightful than three feet of incipient female winding up like a hairy-chested casting champ and laying a lure right out there where a hungry fish is waiting.

Waders soon give way to pretty dresses, swains soon become

What little girls might lack in finesse, they more than make up in enthusiasm.

more desirable than daddies, but if you're lucky, your sweet sophisticated nineteen-year-old might one day pay you and her mother the ultimate compliment of inviting you to double-date in the surf. . . .

"Daddy, do you think that you and Mother would like to go surf fishing with Bill and me? Bill would just lo-o-ve to try it, and I know you'd just lo-o-ve him."

When your nineteen-year-old daughter invites you and the Mrs. to double-date, you're flattered. A lot of nineteen-year-olds these days aren't even interested in *talking* with their parents. But when the invitation is extended by an extra-special daughter like my Lizzie, you're pleased for another reason: what better place than the surf for sizing up a swain under deliciously one-sided circumstances . . . and for deep-sixing him if he doesn't measure up?

"Sure," I told Liz, "but under one condition: I write the script, I direct the operation. Where, when, how, and how long—you leave all of these to me."

"Uhhh, sure, okay." (Overtones of apprehension. Lize had fished with her daddy before.)

Lizzie's sudden rekindling of interest in surf fishing after half a dozen years out of waders didn't delude me into thinking that she finally had seen the error of her ways. No, her pre-teen sessions in the surf were just pleasant interludes, one phase in the funhouse ritual of growing up in the Fallon family. Mainly she enjoyed them because they afforded her an opportunity for showing those big brothers of hers that she could do anything they could do. But they also were intimations of respect and affection, however tentative, for an ocean that she knew intuitively would have something important to offer her when she was ready. Maybe having a Bill to share it with made her ready.

Bill is what is known as a Ten. Not a mere Nine or Nine-and-a-half, but that rarest of contemporary rarities, a real live Ten. In other days he would have been an Adonis, Handsome Hunk, or simply "Wow!" Today he's a Ten.

All the attributes of excellence were in evidence—trim mustache, full mane, stylish garb, sporty car—but mostly it was that Bill Choquette is supposed to be the World's Champion Nice Guy: trustworthy, loyal, helpful, friendly, courteous, kind . . . the works.

"Everybody just lo-o-ves him," said Lizzie, with an "especially me" flutter of her Maybellined lashes.

Two evenings later we headed for the Massachusetts coast north of Gloucester, and as we disembarked alongside a Plum Island marsh, I pointed to a small rock-rimmed promontory that poked like a knobby finger into a sound that had been softened and silvered by the afterglow and announced, "There." A lovely spot, even to the layman; to the angler, a place of promise, with creeks and bars and boulders in abundance. Trouble was, more than a mile of hills, dunes, meadows, and marshes separated us from "There."

I glanced at Bill. He was smiling. Score one for him.

Bill bore up well under the sweltering heat and swarming bugs during our trek, thereby earning himself another point. He acquired still a third by carrying more than his share of rods, reels, waders, bait, tackle, food, and photo equipment. I almost took this point back when he behaved a little less than heroically during a sudden encounter with a skunk, but, being a confirmed skunkophobe myself, I understood.

"Lions, tigers, gorillas," he said, "I can handle. Even eels I don't mind. But there's something about skunks . . ."

What there was about skunks this particular night was numbers. Our second encounter made us detour toward a dirt road which I was hoping I'd be able to keep Bill away from. Oh, sure, there's a road all the way in to our destination. Yes, we could have driven in, but, hey, how are you going to test a young man's mettle when he's riding in the back seat of your VW?

Bill's grin when he saw the road earned him point #4; #5 he got for the "I'm wise to you, Fallon" twinkle in his eye.

We made headquarters on a low flat boulder at the base of a tall clay cliff, an ideal spot, it seemed, for stowing gear and food while we fished. Donning waders, we threaded our way through rocks still wet from the ebbing tide and commenced casting. Bill cast competently. Not well enough for another point, but his efforts were reasonably smooth and trouble-free for a first-timer. Lizzie was bloody well brilliant! Rump-deep in a dark, cold, fast current with nothing but slippery stones underfoot, she performed as though she'd never been away. From her first cast, her plug sailed a smooth trajectory to maximum range, landing with right-on-the-button accuracy at the head of a hissing little tidal turbulence.

Anyone who can cast that well, I thought, surely must be very discriminating in her selection of a boy friend. Point #6.

When no one had had so much as a hit after an hour and a half of continuous plugging, I suggested that we retire to headquarters.

"Time for a snack and some new strategy."

We could tell that there was something wrong long before we reached the rock. Even in the dim glow of a quarter-moon, we could discern the disarray: shuffling shadows, the rustle of paper, a small alien shape silhouetted against the stars. What confirmed my apprehension was Peggy's laughter. My wife laughs when other people cry. Skinned shins, broken windows, collapsed cakes: "Ho, ho, ho."

"Over there," she pointed. "Hee, hee, hee. Alongside the rock, ha, ha, ha. Another skunk."

I flashed my light on not one but two waddling little wood pussies. Their erect white tails made it very clear that we were to keep our distance while they put the finishing touches on our lunch. Eventually we dispersed them with stones, but not in time to salvage more than a couple of peach pits.

Fortunately they were teetotalers. The port wine I had hidden in my camera case was intact. Love, laughter, beauty, joy. We raised our glasses to a star-studded sky and toasted the author of it all.

By now the tide had ebbed enough to provide the low-water conditions for which I had picked this promontory in the first place. While Bill and Liz resumed their casting, Peg, shining her light from atop a tall shoreside boulder, kept tabs on the skunks: "Look, three now, hee, hee, hee; no, four, ha, ha, ha; one's right inside the bag." Quietly I waded off into the darkness. Once across the creek bed, I was able to ascend along the edge of a shallow clamflat where I knew stripers would be scouring the bottom for grass shrimp, green crabs, and mudworms. So how come all I was toting when I returned ten minutes later was a long slithering eel dangling from my hook? To set the stage for unveiling the pair of stripers in my waders, that's why. The eel brought "Yeeechs" from the girls, "Yuks" from Bill, but the bass brought "Ooooos" of appreciation from both.

The eagerness with which Bill responded to my "Let's go" added point #7 to his total.

"One rod," I whispered when we stopped. "We've got only a few minutes before the tide turns and fills that creek bed behind us. I'll bait and cast, then you're on your own."

No better place than a nighttime surf for sizing up your daughter's swain. Bill Choquette passed his test.

His own was quite enough: a just-right tension for running fish, a just-right timing for setting his hook. In ten minutes he had beaten three fat bass that blasted the night apart with their splashing. By now my waders were full of fish and the tide was flooding. "Time to go."

"But I've still got one more worm."

Point #8.

Yes, I went over my waders on the way back, but if the water was up to my chin, it must have reached Bill's nose. His smile through chattering teeth as he emptied his waders surely was worth #9.

Two hours later a soggy groggy Bill Choquette mumbled good-night to Mrs. Fallon and me at the door of our Chelmsford home. I was prepared for anything—a punch in the nose, a "My seconds will call in the morning"—but when, between yawns, he said with obvious sincerity, "Y'know, Mr. Fallon, this was one of the most enjoyable nights I've ever had," I turned to Lizzie and smiled. She knew what I meant.

Friendships flourish in the surf. Getting along is as important as getting fish, and the two are conveniently complementary: a sympathetic ear enables a man to purge his mind of nonangling distractions; a gentle joshing eases the disappointment of a lost fish. Many a winter evening has been warmed for Mrs. Fallon and me when we have reminisced with our dear friends, Don and Roseanne Sommers, about their first sortie in the surf. . . .

Early in September, Roseanne phoned from the Sommers homestead in Brookline, New Hampshire, to remind me that if I failed to fulfill my promise to guide her to her first striped bass she would cut off my Old Fashioned supply next time we dined at her home. Since it was Old Fashioneds that influenced me to make so presumptuous a promise in the first place, I felt an obligation to produce. However, since my recent experiences with North Shore stripers had indicated that they might be starting to school up for their southward migration, my reply was intentionally discouraging.

"Well, OK, but first let me tell you what you're going to have to put up with. You'll probably be cold. The fish might have left. You're sure to get wet, because even if you wear my waders, they leak. And finally, you'll have to be at my house no later than three a.m."

"Great!" replied the indomitable Roseanne.

"Gawd!" replied the incredulous Don. Don, it should be noted, is not a fisherman. He is a skier. To Don there are two seasons, the ski season and the off season. During the off season he likes to visit his ski lodge in the White Mountains and think about skiing.

Roseanne also skis, but for years she has had this thing about striped bass. "I read about them, I hear you talk about them, I see boats bringing them in when we vacation at Cape Cod, but I can't catch one. Forty dollars for a new rod and reel and I still have to buy my bass at the Brewster fish market."

"At a dollar and a half a pound," adds Don.

"A dollar thirty-five," counters Roseanne.

"I'm factoring in the cost of those buck-and-a-quarter-a-dozen seaworms," says Don.

At three a.m. when the Sommerses arrived at my house, the only thing Don was factoring in was the insanity of the whole enterprise. While he headed for the couch, Roseanne effervesced with the enthusiasm of a kid on Christmas Eve.

"How are they biting? What tide will we be fishing? Is this the right lure? Ooooh, I just can't wait to get there!"

"Honey," Peg reminded me as we stumbled through the darkness toward the car, "you'd better produce."

Conversation enroute started conventionally, with talk of home and school and children, but it quickly turned to fishing.

"How are the kids? Job? House? School? School! Speaking of school, you should have seen the school of feeding bass that Peg and I were casting into last time we were out."

Dawn was just starting to dispel the darkness as we pulled up alongside the dune where we were to disembark. A ten-minute walk along a deserted beach brought us to the bluff from whose base we were to fish. Looking down through the lingering darkness, we could barely discern the apron of rocks clinging to clay cliffs, but by the time we were rigged up and ready for action we could see it all: the jumble of gigantic boulders along the shore; a sprawl of smaller stones and mussel clusters; a pair of currents colliding to form a rollicking little rip along the edge of a small reef. With the tide about two-thirds out, conditions should have been ideal, yet my optimism, dulled by the inactivity of the preceding week, needed igniting.

It soon got it. My Beloved had discerningly cast her plug into a pocket inside the rip, where bass were herding a pod of bait. Before I had finished making a few demonstration casts for Roseanne, Peg was announcing her first catch with all the dignity and restraint of a woman who has just discovered that she is cohabiting her waders with a hornets' nest.

Roseanne, on the other hand, a couple of casts to her right, showed remarkable restraint by staying put. But only until Peg took a second fish a few minutes later. Then all of us converged on her like kids running to recess. Don, sneaker-shod, crossing kelp-covered rocks, resembled Jean Claude Killy more than Frank Woolner, and might—just might—be the only man ever to execute a stem christy on seaweed.

Roseanne soon was launching what promised to be an illustrious career as a surf fisherman. She didn't start very illustriously, reacting to her first strike by jumping, screaming, reeling, yanking, then doing an about-face, hanging her rod over her shoulder, and running like a kid after a Good Humor truck until her fish lay halfway up the seaweeded slope, gasping and no doubt thoroughly bewildered. But after that she performed with increasing poise and polish. Her casts became longer and surer, aimed accurately and retrieved with timing and rhythm that took best advantage of the tricky currents. Before our two hours had ended, she even managed a measure of style and assurance, no small feat in leaky waders three sizes too large.

What ended our fishing after two hours was the arrival by boat of a generous and hospitable friend who, from his houseboat across the bay, happened to glance in our direction about breakfast time. His reaction, voiced in his greeting—"Be danged if I'm going to cook my own breakfast when there are two perfectly healthy housewives handy!"—was an invitation to an hour of crisp bacon, buttery eggs, hot hearty coffee, and delightful conversation, a fitting finale for so memorable a morning.

New friends are made along the sea rim as easily as old ones are

Share a day with friends along the sea rim and your reminiscing will brighten many an off-season evening.

"Call me Worcester," the stranger said. Then he shared a lifetime of experience with two men he'd never met.

enjoyed. Pretense, prejudice, suspicion—these have no place in a seaside world where a man has no need for being more than he is, where all that an angler could ask for is his for the enjoying.

Oh, there are cliques and curmudgeons; we are, after all, a little less than the angels. But most of the people you meet along the edge of an ocean are as generous, open, and sociable as the tall lean stranger who was seated on a worn aluminum lawn chair, a pair of 11-foot rods secured along his flanks and pointing into the darkness like drawn pistols. "Call me Worcester," he said when Bill Stone and I introduced ourselves and asked if he'd mind our sharing the area with him. A narrow terrace worn by fishermen's feet into the steep bank sloping to the Cape Cod Canal provided a platform for casting; the street light on the roadway behind us let us see what we were doing.

Worcester's response was genuinely hospitable. You could tell from his tone, his smile, his enthusiasm: "Glad to have you. Rig up and cast to your right. About over there, toward that light on the far shore. Tide hasn't settled down yet."

Bill and I had decided to try the canal after dropping in at our favorite tackle shop. We had asked if the blues were still around, and had been directed to the freezer at the far end of the store.

"Take a look at the one in there," said the counterman.

We looked and touched and lifted and marveled, as was appropriate for a 23-pounder which at the time nudged the world rod-and-reel record.

"Fellow took him day before yesterday behind Tiny Jim's Restaurant; cut mackerel on the bottom. Get on over there now and you'll probably find Worcester. Best bait fisherman on the canal. Tell him I sent you; he'll show you the ropes."

And he did. From rigging to casting, from playing to landing, he performed with poise and polish that had been honed on the wheel of experience. And every step of the way he shared his hard-earned wisdom with Bill and me.

Rigging: "Cut a piece of this frozen mackerel. Head, tail, or in between doesn't seem to make much difference, although lately they've been a little slower in hitting the head. Number 9 hook through the back, then halfway through again. But first offset the point of your hook with a pair of pliers. A snap swivel above your stainless-steel leader will let the fish take your bait without feeling your sinker. A fish-finder rig will do it too, but swivels are cheaper. With my 11-foot rod I use a 5-ounce weight, but 4 ounces is probably about the best you can heave with that 8-footer of yours. Pyramid sinkers will hang you up every cast. Bells are better, but best is this one here I poured myself with a tablespoon. Here, try it."

Casting: "Get up here on the road. You're a few feet farther back from the water, but you'll more than make it up with the added height. More room up here, too. Bottom runs out kind of flat to center channel. Best if you can lay your bait on the lip of the channel, but plenty of fish in closer, too. Once this tide starts moving, your sinker will drag with it. Get hung up a lot, so expect it. Longest fishing you can expect is about an hour on either side of slack, but usually it's less than that."

Playing: "I set my reels on free-spool, one rod on either side of me in my chair. Like this, see? With your spinning reel you can either light-drag it with closed bail or free-spool it with your bail open. Once that line starts moving out, be ready to sock your hook home. Especially if it's a big fish. One the other night got up too much steam and I couldn't stop him. Cleaned me out, even on tight drag with my rod bent almost double."

Landing: "Use my gaff. Better still, I'll gaff for you if you land a fish. These rocks are slippery and wobbly. With a bull blue on, you're likely to wind up in the drink. Rap him with this billy soon as you get him ashore. Rap him till he stops thrashing, and even then, keep your hands away from his mouth. Those teeth can shred a finger like a stalk of celery."

I didn't need Worcester's gaff that evening, and neither did Bill. We both had a couple of runs, but the fish dropped our mackerel before we felt confident enough to set our hooks.

Worcester, on the other hand, was almost continuously in motion throughout the hour and a half we fished. Blues were sucking up his baits like vacuum cleaners. Yanking, heaving, hauling, reeling, releasing the fish, then baiting and casting again, he scampered up and down that hillside like a general directing a battle.

I think Worcester took five fish that tide between eight and ten pounds, and it was while he was releasing one of them that I got my first glimpse of the character that complements his competence.

"Used to sell my fish," he said, "all of 'em, but no more. Too many blues around. Price is too low. When you consider how much miracle goes into making up one of these beautiful beasts, I'd rather release him. Now I just keep one occasionally for food. Or," he added, beaming, "if I think I've got me a new record."

Later I learned from a friend why Worcester used to sell his fish: "Gave everything he earned to the Jimmy Fund."

During the following week, fishing three additional tides with Worcester, I learned a lot more about this remarkable man: how he popularized frozen mackerel as bait for canal bluefish; how he often helps strangers, so long as they respect their quarry and their environment; how an appreciative stranger, given a 15-pounder by Worcester, asked, "How much do I owe you?" and was told, "I don't take money for my fish, but next time you're near a Jimmy Fund box, drop a couple of dollars in."

But mostly I learned about him the last time we fished together, on a late October dawn when he could do no right and I could do no wrong. With no fish to show for his dozen or so runs, he sat there watching me play and land my third blue in a row, and as he did, he beamed. No envy. No ire. He just sat there in his battered chair, leaning on his weathered rod, sharing in my fulfillment and glowing in the knowledge that his pupil had performed well in recital.

"You did fine," he said, "real fine."

There are fish along the ocean's edges to match every type of tackle. (Photo: Terry McDonnell)

2
Basic Tackle

OKAY, SO YOU'RE SOLD ON SURF FISHING. Nothing you'd like better. You're all set to invest in an outfit, when suddenly you remember the guy in the cigarette ad. Leaning tall and tanned against his Taj-Mahal-with-tires beach buggy and outfitted as if he owns Abercrombie & Fitch, this terrestrial Ahab scares you clear back to your crappie creek.

"Hell," you say, "I can't afford that kind of equipment. And even if I could, I wouldn't know the first thing about using it on big fish in unfamiliar waters."

Make no mistake about it, surf fishing *can* be expensive. A long custom-made rod with reel and line to match plus terminal tackle and a few lures can demolish a hundred-dollar bill faster than bucking a straight flush with a full house. Peripherals such as waders, slicker, sandspike, lights, plug bag, stringer, knife, and gaff can almost double the tab. In short order you'll be wanting to add to your basic arsenal: deep- as well as shallow-swimming plugs, yellow as well as white bucktail jigs, bank as well as pyramid sinkers of 2-ounce and 6-ounce weights as well as 4-ounce. Popping will require a shorter snappier rod, jigging a lighter limper line, and when the fly-rodding bug bites you, you'll develop an irresistible craving for fifty-dollar graphite-fibered wands and twenty-dollar sinking-tip lines. Surf fishing doesn't have to be impoverishing, but the potential certainly is there.

But you don't have to buy everything at once. Until you're sold on fishing the surf, there's no point in spending money that a couple of cold, wet, fishless nights might make you wish you had invested in a nice warm golf cart. In fact, you don't *have* to buy anything. Not in the beginning. Good freshwater gear works fine in salt water as long as it's rinsed promptly and thoroughly after each using. You can learn all you need to know about whether you and surf fishing are going to live happily ever after by using your freshwater tackle on modest-size fish in manageable waters. Not all of the ocean's inhabitants are jumbos. Not all of its edges are constantly charged by towering waves.

My conversion to surf fishing occurred when a stranger let me use his freshwater fly rod to catch tinker mackerel from alongside a jetty in the mouth of a tidal river. At the time I was eight years old and convinced that the suckers in my neighborhood pond back home were the world's greatest sporting species.

More recently I enjoyed one of my pleasantest interludes in the surf after I had broken my 9-foot rod during the first part of a double-header that a friend and I had conjured up as a way of making the most of a rare evening together. We started off casting flies for two hours to school stripers in a Gloucester creek. When rising water wiped out the muddy ridge from which we were fishing, we sloshed ashore to grab a sandwich and then head a few miles up the coast where we could plug the open ocean till the tide bottomed out about midnight. A great idea; strategically sound and logistically feasible. The only flaw was in my failure to bring along a

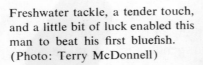
Freshwater tackle, a tender touch, and a little bit of luck enabled this man to beat his first bluefish. (Photo: Terry McDonnell)

backup surf rod. When my rod's tip got pinched in the car door, I had to challenge the ocean with a wispy 5-foot freshwater rod and a reel not much bigger than a thread thimble that was filled with 4-pound monofilament line. Standing on the crest of a dune surveying the sea, I felt foolish, like Don Quixote trying to topple windmills with a pin.

But it was a soft night, bright and calm and still, and there were small pollock and school stripers all over a sandy tongue at the mouth of a small river. My 4-inch swimming plug was a perfect counterfeit of the sandeels these fish were feeding on. Fish, tackle, and environment were in perfect harmony.

Had the fish been appreciably bigger, of course, my Mickey Mouse equipment would not have held up. One run by a raging 20-pound bass would have emptied my spool against all the drag I dared apply. But even against a big fish, a good sweetwater angler often can hold his own with the same rod, reel, line, and lure he uses on that pickerel pond back home. A young man I fished alongside a few years ago was using only 10-pound monofilament on a freshwater outfit the night he tamed a 46-pound striper, the biggest, to my knowledge, ever caught along that stretch of the Ipswich, Mass., shore. More recently I watched another fellow beat a bruiser bluefish on largemouth bass tackle while standing barefoot in a thoroughly inhospitable Bay State surf. Both men were lucky. With the bluefisherman, it was a case of ignorance being bliss, a fact I discovered when he ambled up to me, held out his prize, and said, "Excuse me, but could you tell me if this is a striped bass?" Unaware of the bluefish's reputation for brutality, he simply had waded right in where angels fear to tread and done enough things right freshwater style to defeat one of salt water's toughest adversaries.

The bass-catcher was lucky in that his fish ran parallel to the beach (as stripers often do), giving his companion an opportunity to gaff it when it paused briefly in the shallows. But I've watched this fellow fish a few times since then. The following night, in fact, I saw him subdue several respectable stripers on the same gear without once losing control. For both men, minor-league tackle had been complemented by a major-league touch.

To play it safe, though, start out small. Do your auditioning against lightweights in territory you can handle. Pollock, mackerel, weakfish, tautog, surfperch, kelp bass, rockfish, school stripers, snapper blues, croakers, flounder—all can give your freshwater tackle a good workout while providing a preview of surf fishing's endless variety and excitement. Tidal creeks and sheltered bays are enough like the gentle streams and quiet ponds you're used to so you can make your tidewater debut in comfortable familiar surroundings.

When you're ready to invest in your first surf outfit, how much should it cost you? For rod, reel, and line, no more than fifty dollars. There, you didn't expect that kind of directness, did you? Lots of "Well, first we must define our terms" hedging; "I shall limit my answer to spinning with lures in medium to high surf" qualifying; "This won't buy you the best, of course, but it won't be cheap either" equivocating—that's what you expected, right?

I set a fifty-dollar limit for two reasons. First, I am convinced that in today's well-stocked and highly competitive marketplace, fifty carefully disbursed dollars can buy a lot of outfit. Second, I believe that in the beginning it's better to oversimplify and get on with your fishing than to overcomplicate and risk giving up surf fishing in disgust. Matching a man with his equipment is tricky enough without consciously compounding the complexity.

How would I go about prescribing your ideal first surf rod? Well, to begin with, I would want to know if it will be used with a spinning or rotating-spool reel. Unless you're one of the waning few freshwater anglers who have been brought up on conventional bait and plug casting, you'll probably pick an open-face spinning reel, and your rod will have a reel seat and large-diameter line guides to match. Simple.

Then I'd ask the conditions under which you'll be employing it. What percent of time plugging into rocky tidal rips? Jigging shallow flats? Drifting seaworms through medium-to-fast tideways? Still-fishing cut bait in a mild-to-medium surf? What kind of plugs? (Poppers work best on a rod with a little whip in its tip.) What kind of cut bait? (Half a hefty mackerel weighs more than half an average mullet.) What species of fish? (Three-pound weakfish and 30-pound stripers sometimes occupy the same waters.)

Not so simple any more, is it? In fact, it's impossible. And not just because of the almost infinite combination of conditions I would have to consider. It's impossible because at so early a stage in your surf-fishing career, you have no basis for answering these questions. Until you catch both weakfish and stripers, you can't be sure which species, if either, you'll want to stick with. Until you've compared the topwater thrill of watching bluefish blast the ocean apart attacking your popping plug, with the satisfaction of coaxing a cautious snook out of a snarl of mangrove roots with your shallow swimmer, you'll have no way of knowing which type of plugging, if either, you'll want to concentrate on.

It's impossible also because there are other factors whose influence only you can assess. What waters will you be fishing? What species will you be seeking? What lures will you be using? Answers to these questions will help you define your rod's length, width, taper, and construction, but in the final analysis, the answer that will carry the most weight will be a response to "How does it feel?"

This "feel" is a purely personal input. It involves ruggedness, resilience, responsiveness; how your rod balances with your reel; how its handle fits your hand. It is influenced by your size, your strength, your coordination. "Feel" is intuitive as well as intellectual. As in most major fishing decisions, your brain should be backed up by the seat of your pants.

Your ideal surf outfit is no more likely to be found first time around than an enduring marriage is likely to develop from a first date. Before you're ready to make a long-term commitment to an arsenal that's tailored to your preferences, you'll first have to find out what these preferences are. Will fly-fishing tidal creeks fascinate you so much that you'll want to do nothing else? Will you find the high surf so punishing that you'll want to concentrate on light-tackling tranquil backwaters? Or will you be one of the lucky ones, able to fish on all fronts with equal ardor?

Until you've fished enough of the sea rim to come up with answers, you'll need an outfit that feels good and does the job, nothing more; but, I hasten to add, nothing less. For fifty dollars, that's all you'll get; but that's also all you'll need.

My first surf outfit cost around thirty dollars, the uninflated early-fifties equivalent of today's fifty dollars. I bought it in a small town on California's Russian River, where I had driven following a business conference in suburban San Francisco. Armed with a provincial cockiness plus a silly-looking fluorescent lure with

which I had caught a few New England trout, I was intent on revo-
lutionizing West Coast steelhead fishing. Sure I had read that roe is
the best steelhead bait, but I wasn't after an easy score. Sure I had
heard that steelhead are tough customers, but, hey, I wasn't any
pushover. And just to show what a sport I was, I planned to take
on these big river-run roughnecks with my featherweight 5-foot
spinning rod.

It's just as well that the rod broke on my first cast. At least I
was able to tote it home and have it repaired. If a steelhead had
been foolish enough to fall for my orange absurdity, it probably
would have sucked out my 4-pound mono like a strand of spaghetti
and picked its teeth with my tip top.

My new rod, therefore, had to be a compromise between the
possibility of a brief bout with Russian River steelhead and the
certainty of a long-term love affair with the striped bass I had been
chasing the previous summer along back-home beaches. A season
in the north-of-Boston surf had convinced me that I wanted to take
up surf fishing in earnest. It was time for a buy.

Fortunately, the fellow in the tackle shop on the Russian River
understood stripers. He had caught many descendants of the successful transcontinental transplants made back in 1879 and 1882.
When I told him that I mostly popped on calm bays and plugged in
mild to medium surfs for 5-to-10-pound fish, he understood.

"Any bait-on-the-bottom fishing?"

"No."

"Any extra-long casting?"

"Rarely."

"How likely are you to tie into a cow bass?"

"Possible, always possible."

"Many hangups?"

"Enough. We have weeds and rocks back East, too."

When I said I could afford about twenty dollars, he brought out
three rods that he felt might fill the bill.

"Take these outside," he said, "see how they feel. And," handing
me an appropriate-size reel, "put this on. You can't really get the
feel without it."

I emphasized that I had only twenty dollars to spend, that I
couldn't afford the reel right now, but he waved me off. "You'll

be living with your rod for a long time. Let's make sure it's right."

My choice was a 7½-footer in two sections with a heavy butt that tapered quickly to a whippy tip. The butt could restrain those big fish that dreams are made of, while the tip was limber enough to toss and animate my favorite 1¼-ounce popper. I'd have preferred a one-piece rod, but I didn't dare risk not being able to carry it on the plane.

All things considered, it was a good purchase. Its merits enabled me to handle all forms of fishing that my limited experience suggested I might want to pursue, while its deficiencies did not prevent me from trying new techniques. For almost two full seasons it was the only rod I needed. For two years after that it continued to reign as my Number One popping rod. Finally, it just plain wore out, tip top grooving, finish flaking, wrappings unraveling, and ferrules becoming so ill-fitting that there was no longer any semblance of integrity in its action. I retired it, mislaid it, and eventually lost it.

Today this rod would be about as appropriate for the kind of surf fishing I concentrate on as a dropline. Even as a popping rod, its tip would be too limp for setting a hook in the leathery jaws of fish that so often throw off counterfeits a split second after they strike. But at the time I didn't know this. Nor did I know the thousand and one other things that time on the beach has taught me. What I needed in my first surf rod were versatility, strengths that were suited to my experience, and a compatible "feel." I figure that for $18.75 I got a bargain, even at 1950 prices.

The more you know about equipment, of course, the better buy you can make. Reflecting on all the wrong turns I have taken over the past quarter-century, I find countless occasions where a little knowledge would have saved me a lot of time and enough money to pay for a few of the accessories I currently crave but can't afford. My observations in the paragraphs that follow will enable you to avoid a few of the pitfalls—and pratfalls—that have slowed my progress.

In a way, I suppose, I do you an injustice. Making your own discoveries is much more fun than following in someone else's wake. Lessons underlined by leaky waders, broken bail springs, snarled monofilament, and lost fish will be more deeply etched, more lastingly learned. Yet there's the matter of time: so much surf to be fished, so few and fleeting the hours for fishing it. The sooner you can suit up and get out there, the better.

Rods

First and foremost, surf rods are built for heaving heavy weights long distances and for battling big strong fish in tide-torn and wind-tossed waters. Lightness, comfort, and delicacy of response are considerations, but priority understandably is given to power. That today's surf rods also are light, comfortable, and responsive is a tribute to twentieth-century technology.

Fiberglass made this possible. Before World War II, most surf fishermen were inland transplants. Eager to find out what an ocean might have to offer to men who had beaten fresh water's best, they headed seaward. Like Lancelots with hatpin lances, they took on a hostile ocean with Tinkertoy techniques and Mickey Mouse equipment, and they were converted.

At first the inadequacies in their tackle had to be corrected by

Surf rods are built primarily for heaving heavy weights long distances and for fighting powerful fish. (Photo: Terry McDonnell)

improvising. When metal lures, designed to attract fish by reflecting sunlight, became dull, they restored their sheen by the ingeniously simple expedient of rubbing them with beach sand. When split-cane rods developed the sets they are prone to, they countered these sets (and inadvertently hastened fractures) by turning their rods over and running their lines through a set of guides installed opposite the originals.

All that was needed for converting individual ingenuity into industrial enterprise was a buying public. World War II veterans provided it. Young men conditioned to the elemental existence of combat found the surf an ideal halfway house: action, excitement, barracks-type bonhomie, and a chance to amble back at their own pace to a life that now seemed alien, remote, and a little bit frightening. At the same time plastics manufacturers were seeking new uses for their war-born wares. Fishing rods were a natural. Supply met demand.

The first fiberglass rods were sorry affairs. They were hastily conceived and carelessly produced, for impatient buyers who had little notion of what they needed and plenty of mustering-out pay to make up for manufacturers' mistakes. Ultimately buyers became more demanding, builders more quality-conscious, and today's superior, reasonably priced rods evolved.

Glass rods are either tubular or solid. The heavier weight of solid rods is compensated for by greater strength, but in the surf this rarely is an advantage. Modern construction methods blend light weight with a strength far in excess of any you're likely to need. Today, solid rods are used mostly in trolling.

One-piece rods have an integrated action that rods of two or more sections simply cannot duplicate: motion is sent from muscle to lure with less lag; strikes are transmitted from fisherman to fish with less delay. But did you ever try toting 9 (or 10 or 11 or 12 or 13) feet of rod in 5 feet of Volkswagen Bug? Or on a subway? Or on a plane whose designer neglected to consider the possibility that his craft might one day be expected to transport the two 9-foot rods from Boston's bustling Logan Airport (crowds, congestion, doors that swing shut after you and the butt end gets through but the tip top doesn't quite make it) to Martha's Vineyard, where they're used to such things? A rack on the roof solved my Bug problem, and I've never had occasion to go fishing via subway, but that plane really taxed my ingenuity, not to mention my wife's, pilot's, co-pilot's, steward's, and fellow-passengers' nerves. My solution was to slide the rods along the floor under the three seats in front of me and implore their occupants to be careful where they put their feet. I crossed my fingers and held my breath throughout the whole hour-long trip, but as Peg pointed out, it was better than hanging from the wing.

Fortunately a rod doesn't suffer nearly so much these days if it's sectioned. This is because of glass-to-glass ferrules, which enable facing sections to be slipped together and twisted firmly in place, then untwisted and slipped apart after use. A few years back when all ferrules were metal, fit rarely was right. Even when male and female components came micrometer snug from the manufacturer, they expanded with heat, contracted with cold, and were vulnerable to dents and scratches. Too loose, you'd cast your tip section along with your lure; too tight, you'd have the devil's own time jamming facing parts together, an even worse time pulling them apart. Sometimes they'd be wedded so tight they'd stay together even when sections were separated, leaving one section of your rod ferruleless. Exasperated, you'd grab a pair of pliers, squeeze, crush, struggle, swear, and write a nasty letter to the manufacturer.

Two-piece yet sensitive, lightweight yet strong and responsive—what more could you ask of a surf rod? How about lighter, stronger,

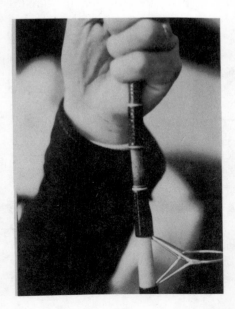

Glass-to-glass connections give two-section rods a one-piece feel.

more sensitive, and more responsive? Recently this quantum leap
in rod quality was made possible by imbedding graphite filaments
along the length of hollow plastic rod bodies. Because these fine
fibers have an exceptionally high ratio of stiffness to weight and
also can stand severe bending, they enable manufacturers to offer
high performance at lower weight. Your present rod's performance,
for example, could be achieved with a much lighter rod; conversely,
a rod of the same weight as the one you're presently using would
perform far better.

Here's how it works. The shaft containing graphite fibers resists
bending. This means that its tip recovers more quickly and vibrates
less than its fiberglass counterpart. The tip's increased speed accelerates your lure (or line if you're fly-casting) at a faster rate,
which in turn increases your casting distance; its decreased vibra-

Rod handles come in many forms and contours. Be sure yours is
comfortable.

tion improves your accuracy. The combination of the shaft's lighter weight and responsive fibers enables you to feel jolting strikes more quickly, to detect tender tugs more readily.

Even the best rod blank can be botched by cheap or hastily installed hardware. Strength, lightness, sensitivity, and responsiveness mean little when handles are uncomfortable; when reels slip out of their seats or rattle every time you crank their handle; when guides rust, fraying lines and allowing fish to break free. Handles come in many contours and configurations. A poor fit can tire your wrist and cramp your fingers; a good fit can guarantee added hours of fatigue-free fishing. Take the time to find one that you can squeeze and cast with comfort.

Most reel seats are roomy enough to accommodate a variety of reels in a suitable size range, but don't take any chances. When evaluating a rod, always try to install the reel you expect to be using with it. Normally the reel will slide snugly under the stationary forward securing ring and the after ring will screw it firmly in place. If the fit is too tight, though, don't assume that you'll just pry or jam the reel into position; if it's too loose, don't assume that you'll just put up with a little play. These might seem like minor inconveniences in a tackle shop, but in the surf anything short of perfection is a major irritation. With today's technology turning out equipment to match almost any build and any budget, the prudent, patient shopper doesn't have to settle for inferior equipment. He can come as close to perfection as his pocketbook will permit.

Be sure, by the way, that your reel seat has a second screw-on securing ring to lock the first one in place. A single ring works loose as quickly as a busy nut without a lockwasher.

Guides must be hard if they are to resist grooving. Your tip-top guide in particular tends to develop ruts as line runs through it under tension. If the rod you're considering purchasing does not have a Carbaloy tip top, put one on. The process is simple. Just heat the neck of this guide where it fits over the tip of your rod until you can pull it off gently with a pair of pliers. A match flame should do the trick. Then with another match, melt ferrule cement onto the rod tip and slip the new guide in place. A paper-wrapped cylinder of cement about the size of a lipstick costs less than a dollar and should be in every surfman's tackle bag. Despite the current phasing out of metal ferrules by glass-to-glass connections, there seems to be no lack of ferrule cement in tackle stores.

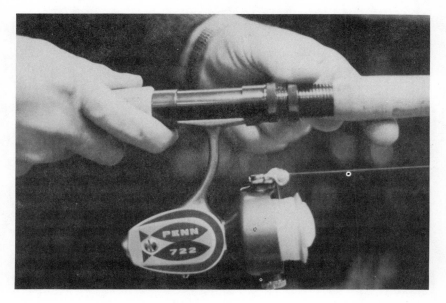

A second securing ring makes it harder for your reel to work loose.

Some guides are lined with ceramic for smoother line flow. No question that friction is reduced, but the resulting increase in casting range is likely to make a difference only to men who consistently cast close to the limit of their equipment. Tournament performers might get a leg up on their competition by using ceramic-lined guides, but on a beach they're just one more thing that can go wrong.

My distrust of lined guides is influenced by an experience I once had with a guide lined with agate, the fracture-prone predecessor of ceramic. After two hours of nonstop plugging, I spotted a school of feeding stripers moving toward me across a bar and into a shallow pocket where I had found bait congregated. Crouching low, I lifted my rod carefully to cast and felt a piece of agate bounce off my knuckle and into the water. Apparently the lining had cracked in a previous bump and was just waiting for the insidiously ideal instant to crumble. The guide's sharp inside edge severed my line first time I tossed my lure, and I never did get into those fish.

Line guides should be secure as well as strong, smooth, and rust-resistant. Too often rod-wrappers are overly concerned with making their products pretty. Colorful patterns and intricate designs are nice, but they don't do a diddly damn for your fishing. Having a loose thread catch your line as it's being pulled off your reel by a running fish is the hard way of learning the value of good wrapping.

Wrappings should be at least two layers of strong thread laid tight and even and protected with three or four coats of varnish that can stand up to sun and salt. Custom-made rods always are well wrapped and coated, usually decorated attractively, sometimes decorated excessively, and understandably are more expensive than their mass-produced counterparts. Medium-to-high-priced rods of reputable manufacturers also are well made and usually attractive. If an inexpensive rod should seem ideal for you in every respect except wrapping, you're in luck. Buy it and have it rewrapped with the highest-quality guides you can buy at a tackle shop that offers this service. You'll wind up with the best of both worlds: custom wrapping, guides that resist ruts and rust, and a price you can afford.

Reels

Your reel is the most sensitive element in your fishing system. A screw loosens, a gear wears, a spring relaxes, and you're out of business. Surf reels are workhorses. When used with lures, they're turning constantly. Even with bait, they receive little rest: weeds must be removed, losses to crabs and cunners checked, sinkers swapped as tides accelerate or slacken. Precision-machined parts of corrosion-resistant metal are the only kind that can stand up for long to salt, sand, and constant cranking.

There are two sure ways to get maximum mileage out of a reel: buy a good one; take care of it. Good reels, of course, are expensive, but they more than justify their high prices by their dependability and long life. With the late humorist Robert Benchley, I share the conviction that all things mechanical have conspired to make my life miserable. Benchley also was convinced that pigeons were out to get him, but my paranoia extends only to striped bass, channel bass, bluefish, etc., that prowl our shores waiting for a chance to swipe my lures.) I thwart most of my reels' mischief by buying the best that I can afford in the first place.

Remember that what you're investing in when you buy a reel— or any other item of equipment—is hours of trouble-free fishing. A good reel reduces your per-hour cost.

Spinning reels

This is the age of spinning. Novices making their first buys, whether for fresh water or salt, almost invariably choose open-face spinning outfits. Rotating-spool reels, once the standard, have been eclipsed in popularity, though not in performance. Closed-face spinning reels, popular with sweetwater tyros, are shunned in the surf, where salt and sand collecting under their hoods are a constant annoyance.

Simplicity is the main appeal of open-face spinning. Line flows smoothly when a spool has been wound under reasonable tension with enough light limber monofilament to bring line-level to within ⅛ to ¼ inch of the spool's rim. No delicately applied and critically timed thumb pressure is needed for braking the spool, as with a rotating-spool reel. Backlashes are a thing of the past.

The open-face spinning reel's popularity adds another dividend: you get to share those clever solutions to common problems that always seem to be brought up during between-tide coffee-klatches; you enjoy the reassurance that when a part breaks on a remote beach, the guy alongside you might have a spare.

If you should have a few extra dollars to invest in your surf outfit, put them into a superior reel that balances well in weight, fit, and operation with your rod. Check its drag, that adjustable arrangement that determines how hard a running fish will have to pull to take out line while your reel handle remains stationary. Is it easy to adjust? Convenient to reach? Is your line likely to catch on or under its adjustment screw? What is your reel's retrieve ratio? How many times, in other words, will its spool turn every time you rotate its handle one revolution? Too few and you'll tire yourself cranking; too many and you'll have trouble controlling lures. A ratio of 3-1 or 3½-1 is popular in the surf.

Your reel also should have an anti-reverse lock. This is a simple on-off ratchet-type switch. Unlocked, it enables the reel's handle to turn backward as well as forward, but when it's locked, the handle can turn only forward. A running fish then has to pull out line against your reel's drag.

It's always desirable to have a spare reel spool filled with fresh line. Once when bluefish started busting just beyond the breakers, I got a snarl in my line that would have made me miss the fast-

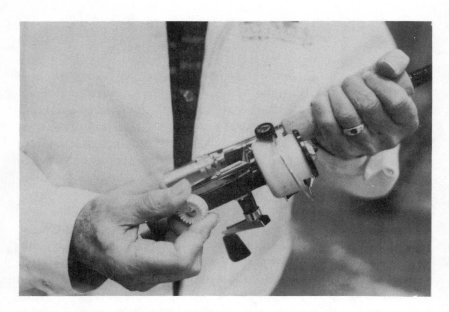

Not all open-face spinning reels have their drag adjustments on their faces.

moving school if I hadn't been able to unscrew one spool and screw on another in less than a minute. On other occasions when I have been fishing bait with line too heavy for casting 1½-ounce plugs, I have been able to reach schools that suddenly started breaking at near-maximum range simply by reeling in and slipping on a spool of lighter line.

Instead of the normal spring-activated bail for your open-face spinning reel, you may want to consider a manually operated pickup arm. With this design, no hoop-type bail springs closed automatically when you start your retrieve. Instead, a roller is mounted on the reel's revolving cup; before retrieving, you just slip your line over the roller with your index finger. The manual pickup is championed by anglers who prefer its fewer moving parts and don't mind the added finger-flicking inconvenience.

Rotating-spool reels

Simplicity, popularity, dependability, and a variety of sizes, models, and prices—a sound set of reasons for beginners to buy open-face spinning outfits. Yet even this remarkable set of attributes has not obsoleted the rotating-spool rigs that ruled the roost before being dethroned by spinning after World War II. Traditionalists still prefer conventional reels for the intimacy of their thumb-braking control and for the prodigious casts that accomplished practitioners always seem to be capable of making. Yet those who employ rotating-spool reels are not just salty old seadogs too hobbled by habit to be taught the new tricks of spinning. Many freshwater converts accustomed to bait-casting have stayed with their rotating spools, and seasoned spinners seeking new worlds to conquer have either converted entirely or added conventional casting to their repertoire.

For most surf fishermen, though, spinning is enough. Braking by thumb pressure requires practice and patience, and both seem to be in short supply when there's fishing to be done.

"Look," they reason, "I get only so much time for fishing, and it's never enough. Why should I invest a large part of it in educating my thumb and unsnarling backlashes? Okay, so I might not be able to cast quite so far with my spinning outfit, but from the first time I used it, I've been able to do reasonably well with very few problems. What's the percentage in my changing?"

For these people, none. Not yet, anyway. But if in time they should start approaching the limits of their equipment, they might

A lot of old-timers swear by the conventional reel. But rotating spool has to be decelerated by thumb pressure if backlashes are to be avoided; it takes practice.

seek ways of achieving closer control, longer and more accurate casts. Then the rotating-spool reel will have meaning for them.

As for this reel's ability to guarantee adding yards to a man's casting range, I'm not sure it would work for just anyone. With all of the subtle variables involved, it would be difficult to make an accurate comparison between before and after. How light and friction-free are the lines being used? How weighted and whippy are the rods? Are line guides smooth? How tightly do the reels' gears mesh? How well are they lubricated? Theoretically, one reel should work as well as the other: spinning line starts from its spool more easily because the stationary spool doesn't need to be put in motion, but friction against the spool's edge increases as line gets lower on the spool; inertia must be overcome to start a rotating spool in motion, but once underway, there is no increase in friction as line continues to leave its spool. The two should balance. Maybe there's more mystique than mathematics to the Herculean heaves of conventional surf casters, but whatever the reason, it's worth looking into when you're ready.

Like the open-face spinning reel, the rotating-spool reel should feature an anti-reverse lock, an easily adjusted braking device, and a replaceable spool. The brake in this case is a star-drag type, so named because of its star-shaped adjusting arm. Be sure also that your conventional reel has a wide enough spool to accommodate the line you will be using (200 yards of 30-pound monofilament for heavyweight fishing, for example), and that it is made with lightweight corrosion-resistant alloys. You may want to consider an automatic line-leveling device, but its friction will reduce casting distance. Most conventional casters prefer to lay their line with their noncranking hand while retrieving.

Lines

The old bromide about every cloud having a silver lining applies even to wars. Although an improved fishing line is a paltry dividend from the devastation of WW II, that's where it all started. DuPont research into high-molecular-weight compounds produced nylon, the substance from which most of today's monofilament spinning lines are made.

It took almost a decade for scientists to refine early nylon filaments to a point where fishermen could use them effectively. De-
terioration had to be stemmed, elasticity reduced, and manufacturing consistency improved before linen, silk, and cotton could confidently be discarded. Within a year of the war's end, though, most
traditionalists had replaced braided linen with braided nylon, persuaded as much, I suspect, by the promise of being able to cast
without scorching their thumbs as by the new material's superior
casting qualities and resistance to rot and mildew.

About this time the rapid improvement in spinning reels provided a hungry market for a smooth, light, limp, transparent line of
fine diameter, and extruded nylon monofilament filled the bill. It
had bugs: instability, inconsistent quality, excessive stretch, and a
diabolical tendency to return to its former dimensions. This last
quality, called "memory," has caused many a reel spool literally
to disintegrate when crushed by nylon trying to resume its original
shape. Rugged reel spools and reduced elasticity in modern nylon
monofilament have lessened this hazard, but even today, mono's
stretching can make it difficult to hook a fish firmly at long range.
The main deterrent to a soundly set hook, however, continues to be
too much slack line.

Any shortcomings in a modern premium monofilament are part
of a calculated compromise between many often conflicting qualities. Stretch, memory, limpness, and visibility are carefully balanced
against tensile strength, knot strength, and resistance to impact and
abrasion. The blend varies between manufacturers, but these in-
gredients are there.

Note that I emphasized *premium* mono. Those "mile and a quarter for a buck and a quarter" bargains are attractive to the novice
with limited funds, but if you're going to skimp, line is not the place
to do it. Postpone the purchase of a lure or two if you must, but
get good line. For under three dollars you can buy several years'
supply of monofilament, but you'll also be buying several hours of
untangling. For a dollar or two more you'll get less line but more
fishing.

Even good mono will keep you untangling if it's wound wrong.
Most packaged lines provide printed illustrations showing how line
should come off the packaged spool in the same direction in which
it goes onto the spool of the reel. Common sense tells you that with

the wrong face of the packaged spool toward the reel, you're winding a twist onto your reel.

Since line twists are one of spinning's major irritations, let's
pause for a few paragraphs and consider some ways in which they
might be avoided. One of the best is to have your line wrapped by
machine instead of by hand. Most tackle shops use simple rotating
shafts on which they mount your reel spool and in a matter of seconds wind on just the right amount of the line you select. The lay
is smooth, the tension uniform, and the distribution on your spool
perfectly even; no bunching at one edge and skimping at the other.
Cost per foot is a little higher than when you buy from the counter
of a discount chain, but you might wind up paying out even less
cash because you buy only what you need. First time I made such
an investment, my five dollars bought me an entire season with
only a small fraction of the tangles I had experienced the year
before. Furthermore, in the previous year I had gone through not
one but four three-dollar spools.

A first winding, however, no matter how smooth, firm, and uniform, is only a start. If you cast and retrieve carelessly, twists and
tangles soon will plague you. Always be aware, therefore, of how
line is being laid onto your reel. Glance down occasionally while
you're cranking; after dark, run your fingers around the spool to
feel for loops. Make it a habit to lift your rod as you flip your bail,
to run limp line through your fingers so it will wind onto your spool
under tension, to reel during jerky jigging and popping retrieves
only when your line is taut. Above all, don't reel in when a fish
that's making headway against your drag prevents your reel from
taking in line. Every crank of your handle will just lay on a twist.

Even with these precautions, you'll get twists: baits spin, swivels
jam, fish can thrash up some unholy messes in their attempts
to fight free. Line twists are as inevitable as death, taxes, and the
occasional skunkings that the fishing gods program into our schedules to keep us from getting cocky. One of the sagest of angling
aphorisms still is: "In order to angle, you have to untangle."

Removing these twists is best done from the fantail of a moving
boat: just trail your bare line astern for a few minutes, then reel it
in, running it through thumb and forefinger of the hand with which
you're holding the rod. For those times when no boat is handy,
always carry a spare spool of line. Then next time you're boating,

untwist your line on the way to the fishing grounds and also on the way back.

A high bridge also can come in handy. When I know that my line is troublesomely twisted from a previous surf session, I drive to the shore via a high bridge that spans a wide river. By paying out line well beyond the yardage I expect to be casting, I can depend on gravity and a good breeze to pull out twists as dependably as the water behind an underway boat.

In an emergency you can at least partially straighten an unmanageably twisted line by letting it out in a fast tideway. Current will have to be fast, with no eddies or backwaters to pull your line off course, and water will have to be weed-free. This is a tall order, usually requiring a high perch in midcurrent. A bridge is satisfactory in those rare instances where you can combine a fast flow of water with a slow flow of boat traffic, but it still lacks the positive pull of a moving vessel. Better to minimize twists by careful winding and reeling, and save what twists you can't avoid for next time you're underway.

So much for twists. As for color, I am ambivalent about its highly touted blessings. Given a choice between the more common colorless translucents and one of the recently introduced fluorescents, I would choose the former. Fluorescents, of course, are supposed to combine camouflage for fish with visibility for fishermen, a blend which is of immense benefit to shore fishermen, who normally must position lines and play fish according to where they *think* their line is leading. (Photographers also appreciate being able to predict where a hooked fish is going to head topside.) The ideal fluorescent monofilament line should be as invisible to fish as it is visible to fishermen, and herein seems to lie a contradiction: what you gain in one direction, you reasonably should expect to have to concede in the other.

Compromises again. Nothing wrong with them, except that in this case you might wind up with line that looks to a fish like seaweed on the front of a lure which looks to this fish like something to eat. It's hard enough to fake out one of these wary critters without adding handicaps. Too often, after watching a fish charge my lure and then veer away at the last second, I have reeled in to find a hook adorned with a single filament of grass or weed that was a dead ringer for fluorescent line. Maybe it sounded the alarm, maybe it didn't, but until my fluorescents produce at least as consistently as their translucent counterparts—and they will; count on it—I'll continue to rely on reel and faith to forecast where fighting fish and working lures are heading.

Nylon monofilament is not limited to spinning. On revolving-spool reels it performs as well as on fixed-spool types. In both cases line test is selected according to where, when, and how you'll be fishing, and what size and species of fish you'll be after.

Regardless of which method you use—fixed-spool or revolving-spool—you probably will back up your business line with 100 yards or more of stronger heavier line wound directly onto your spool. Dacron braid is a good choice. Length of this backing line depends on reel size and how far you'll be casting. Your lead-off line, tied to your backing, is the only one airborne during your cast.

Backing leaves your spool only when a fish pulls it off. Casting qualities, therefore, are unimportant. Strength, limited elasticity, and resistance to rot and abrasion are features to look for when buying backing. Economy used to be a consideration—more backing means less mono—but monofilament extrusions are inexpensive enough these days to allow a full spool of monofilament for anyone who insists on consistent diameter or objects to a connecting knot. Me, I appreciate knowing that when a big battler is giving my line a workout from 150 yards or so offshore, the toughest part of my line is closest to the rocky beach I'm standing on.

Hooks

Siwash, Viking, O'Shaughnessy . . .
Treble, barbless, weedless . . .
Stainless steel, japanned, cadmium-plated . . .
#1, 2, 3; #1/0, 2/0, 3/0; 1X long, 2X short; 3X fine, 5X stout . . .

Choosing a hook can be as bewildering as choosing a lure. If my small sampling of styles, finishes, and sizes doesn't convince you of this, consider that O. Mustad & Son of Oslo, world leader in fishhook production, sells more than 60,000 separate items.

Ironically, hooks rarely receive attention in proportion to the importance of the part they play. Most anglers regard a hook as little more than a length of wire bent and barbed on one end with an eye on the other. Subtle differences in curvature, point shape, and shank length seldom are noticed, almost never evaluated. When, for example, did you last hear an angler lamenting the loss of a fish because he used the wrong hook? Yet the costliest custom-made outfit won't catch fish if its hook is too dull to penetrate past its barb, too weak to withstand a fish's pull. Big fish cooperate too seldom to be lost because of the careless selection of the least expensive part of your tackle.

Fortunately you can select a job-rated hook without having to trudge through a jargonized jungle of rigidly codified designations. Only the super-serious angler need be aware of such esoterica as the fact that a kirbed hook is offset to the right when viewed from the top with the eye toward you, and a reversed hook is offset to the left; that a humped shank is used to prevent the cork body of a bass bug from turning on its shank; that size-to-size variations of small hooks are 1/16 inch until they reach #3, then ⅛ inch through #2 and #1. (You should, however, know that saltwater hooks are sized by the Ocean system from #1/0 through #0/0, with length, weight, and gap generally increasing with number.)

For almost every assignment there are several hooks that will work. Species and size of fish you're seeking and the method you plan to employ in catching them will narrow materials and parts down to a few styles and sizes. Beyond that, you take your pick.

Strong durable materials and finishes are essential in the salt. Corrosion soon takes its toll of the japanned, blued, or lacquered carbon steel that does the job in fresh water; big fish in ripping currents straighten out the fine wire that was strong enough to tame the toughest of trout.

Effective saltwater hooks are made from tinned steel, amply tempered and plated with rust-inhibiting coats of cadmium, nickel, tin, or gold. Nickel-based alloys are popular despite a limited strength that requires a large-diameter wire and a softness that causes points to dull easily. Even plastics have been tried, one of which was touted enthusiastically until a pair of responsible editors decided to test this revolutionary new weapon whose manufacturer wanted to advertise in their magazine. One grabbed the point and yanked while the other held the head of the shank. The resulting "Snap!" confirmed that the age of plastic had not yet dawned in the fishhook industry.

Until the mid-sixties, stainless steel also was unable to make the

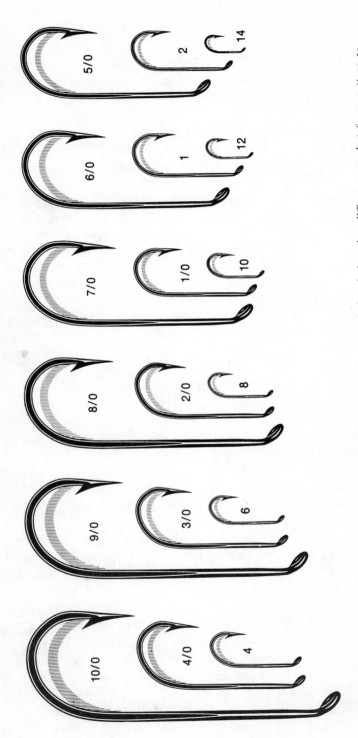

The Mustad Viking pattern, actual size. The relationship of actual size and size designation differs somewhat from pattern to pattern.

grade. Despite an almost total resistance to corrosion, it was disqualified by brittleness and softness. Today's stainless-steel hooks compare favorably with those of tempered carbon steel, and their popularity unquestionably is on the upswing.

There is some criticism because of stainless steel's noncorrosive qualities. When a fish breaks off or is released, claim the metal's critics, it's stuck with the hook for life. I have seen too many fish caught with hooks already in their mouths to believe that a hook in the mouth can seriously interfere with a fish's feeding. A hook in the throat, now, that might be a different story. Still, I doubt that a stainless-steel hook in a fish's gullet would be any greater threat to its survival than one with a good rust-inhibiting coat.

Fishhooks are one of mankind's earliest tools. Cavemen caught fish with gorges—straight, double-pointed pieces of bone, stone, antler, or shell that were tethered to grooves in their middles and buried in pieces of bait. When the bait was swallowed, the line was yanked, jamming the gorge sideways in the fish's gullet. Curved hooks first were made of bone, then copper, bronze, and ultimately steel. More than thirty centuries before Christ, bronze hooks with barbed points and holes in flattened shank ends were being used in Crete. Modern manufacturing methods were introduced in London during the mid-1600s by needle manufacturer Charles Kirby, for whom the still-popular Kirby pattern was named, but until comparatively recently, individual operations were done almost entirely by hand. Bending the wire, turning the eye, cutting the barb, filing the point, applying the finish, and hardening the metal—all were mostly manual operations. Today's hooks, however, more than make up in uniformity and economy for what they have had to sacrifice in craftsmanship.

Even the best hooks normally need sharpening. Even right out of the package, most hooks can be improved by a few brushes with a fine file or a cutting stone. Here's how. Holding your hook by its bend, with its point up and facing away from you, file the point's inside edge a few times on both sides until it has a pronounced cutting edge. Then brush the tip till it's pricking sharp, yet not so thin that it might break when trying to penetrate a fish's bony mouth.

What happens after the hook has penetrated is between you and the fish. And don't delude yourself into thinking that your line always will part before your hook gives way. When daylight finally rang down the curtain on a recent all-night bluefish brannigan, *Massachusetts Out-of-Doors* editor Gene Gallagher and I were stunned as we surveyed in the first light of day the number of our hooks that had been bent, straightened, and in one case even broken. The three dozen blues we tangled with were played carefully—no horsing, no jammed drags—and the hooks were flaw-free and tailored to the task.

Lady Luck plays no favorites. Even the big-leaguers need her smile now and then, and aces like Gallagher are the first to admit it.

"But," they add, "the more you know about your equipment—how it's made, why it's designed the way it is, what it's capable of, what it should be limited to—the more luck you can manufacture for yourself."

Amen.

Knots

There's no excuse for losing a fish because of a poorly tied knot. A reel jams, a line breaks, a hook straightens, and you can conveniently palm off the blame on an irresponsible manufacturer. Usually, of course, it's your own fault—*you* neglected to lubricate your reel, *you* ignored a few frayed feet of line, *you* saved a few pennies on hooks made of weak wire—but it's nice to have a scape-goat.

When a knot becomes untied, however, you've nowhere else to turn. You're at the end of the line. *You* tied it; *you're* to blame.

Recently an entire book was devoted to knots. Hardcover, full-length, handsome illustrations, a pair of world-renowned authors—the works. While much of its exposition is too advanced for anglers who are just getting started in the surf, one of its main themes applies to all fishermen in all waters at all levels of experience: *Make sure.*

Before you cast that lure or bait, make sure your line is tied on tight. Before you reel in those two lines you've just tied together, make sure their knot is solidly secure. Test your connections by yanking several times a little harder than a fighting fish might yank. Pull them gradually until you have exceeded the stress that you feel

IMPROVED CLINCH KNOT

The basic clinch knot with variations is an excellent knot for tying flies, lures and bait hooks to spinning lines or leaders. As shown in the accompanying chart the Improved Clinch Knot retains almost all of the unknotted line strength. Using a double strand or double loop through the eye merely complicates tying without contributing to improved line strength. It is important to tie the Improved Clinch Knot to prevent slippage.

To tie this knot, stick the end of the piece of "Stren" through the eye of the hook or swivel and make five or more twists around the standing part of the line. Then thrust the end between the eye and the first loop, and then back through the big loop as shown in the sketch. Hold on to it and pull tight. Be sure to always cut "Stren." Don't ever try to break it with your hands.

Continued research in our laboratories has proved that greater knot strength is achieved when several twists are made around the standing part of the line. So be sure you make at least five or more twists when tying the Improved Clinch Knot; and tie it up slowly and tie it up tight.

BLOOD KNOT

This is the best knot we know of for tying Du Pont "Stren" to "Stren" when the diameters of the two strands are approximately the same. Here is the easy step-by-step way of tying it.

1. Lap the ends of the strands to be joined and twist one around the other, making at least five turns. Count the turns made. Place the end between the strands, following the arrow.

2. Hold the end against the turns already made, between the thumb and forefinger at point marked "X," to keep from unwinding. Now wind the other short end around the other strand for the same number of turns, but in the opposite direction.

HOLD HERE

3. This shows how the knot would look if held firmly in place. Actually, as soon as released, the turns equalize.

4. And the turns look like this. Now pull on both ends of the monofilaments.

5. As pulling on the ends is continued, the turns gather and draw closer together (at this point the short ends may be worked backward, if desired, to avoid cutting off too much of the material).

6. Appearance of the finished knot. All that remains to be done is to cut off the short ends close to the knot.

a fighting fish might exert. Notice how often your knot comes apart. Amazing.

Fishermen have a natural tendency to hurry their knots, and an even stronger one to take for granted that their knots are tied dependably. As the last, or nearly last, step in a tedious pre-casting ritual, knot-tying is the only act left between fisherman and what he came here for in the first place. The sooner it's over, he figures, the sooner he can get down to the business of catching fish. In the midst of feeding fish, it's even worse. Then a caster's normal carelessness is compounded by eyes that won't focus and fingers that vibrate like tuning forks.

But nowhere in fishing does haste make more waste than in knot-tying. All you'll need for reminding yourself of this is to feel a sudden sickening slack in your line that announces that a good fish has broken free, then reel in a bitter end bearing a telltale pigtail. Yet it won't be enough. The compulsive urge to get into action soon will have you half-tying, half-testing again unless you remind yourself consciously, every time you renew a knot, to tie carefully and completely and to test thoroughly.

Your two needs for knots are to secure line to hooks, lures, leaders, swivels, and occasionally sinkers such as the dipsey; and to join two lengths of line. For the first, the improved clinch knot is quick, simple, and with five or more turns, a means of retaining up to 100 percent of unknotted line strength. For joining lines of approximately the same diameter, as when repairing a line break, use the blood knot. For joining lines of different diameters, as when tying a heavy shock tippet to light monofilament, use the surgeon's knot.

After tying, always trim off excess line, preferably with nail clippers. Even a tiny tail often catches weeds and almost always snags line as it flows from your spool.

Sinkers

Sinkers hold stationary baits on the bottom and maintain drifted baits at desired levels. Occasionally sinkers are employed by wild-eyed improvisors to impart special actions to lures or bait. One surfman of my acquaintance places lead shot in holes strategically located in the bodies of swimming plugs to retrieve them at a special depth through a special rip at a special stage of high moon tides. His successes are legendary, but he drew a lot of blanks before zeroing in on the proper number, location, and depth of holes and the right-weight shot to put in them. More common is the shore fisherman who swings seaworms through a current with a split shot crimped a foot or so forward of his worm's head. By raising and lowering his rod tip while retrieving, he imparts an underwater porpoising action to his worm that in my experience has consistently outscored a straight steady retrieve.

Commonest sinkers in the surf are the pyramid and the bank. The pyramid's sharp edges dig quickly and hold fast in sand or mud bottoms. The bank's rounder contours are more practical for fishing over rocks, where the pyramids would hang up.

Dipseys generally are used the same way as banks but in smaller sizes. Eggs are ideal for swinging bait slowly just off the bottom when tidal flow is light, and then letting a fish run with your bait without feeling your sinker's weight. To keep an egg sinker from

Each type of saltwater sinker is available in a range of weights.

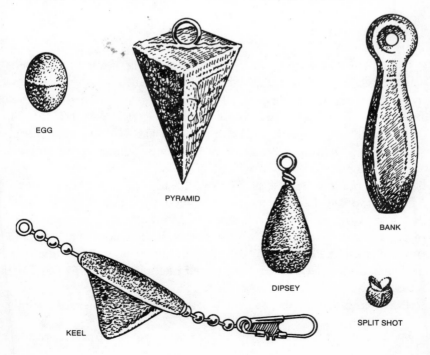

EGG

PYRAMID

BANK

DIPSEY

SPLIT SHOT

KEEL

running all the way down your line to the eye of your hook, run your line through the sinker and tie it to one ring of a barrel swivel. Then tie your leader to the swivel's other ring. Split shot are too light in strong ocean currents, but in slower-flowing backwaters, they can enable you to make deadly-delicate adjustments in the height of baits and lures.

Reusable split shot gets my vote for the cleverest design improvement in recent years. Formerly a split shot was simply a small lead sphere containing a lengthwise slot in which you slipped your line. Pliers or teeth would crimp the shot onto the line, but once the shot's jaws were closed, they stayed that way. To remove a shot, you had to untie your hook, slide the shot off the end of your line, then retie your hook. Now by squeezing a pair of tabs on opposite sides of the shot's slot, you can reopen the shot's jaws and return it to a pocket-size plastic container until next time you want to use it. Brilliant! The container is even compartmented so you can keep all shots of a given size together.

Lead, by the way, still reigns as the number-one sinker material because it has an unusually high ratio of weight to volume and because its dull color does not distract fish.

Swivels

It happens all the time: your light plug picks up a weed and spins; your slowly retrieved eel pulls and shakes and spins; the worm you're working along the edge of a sandbar gets snatched into the current and spins. Each revolution is transmitted to your line, twisting it tighter and tighter until the slightest slack produces a snarl. Soon you can't even cast any more. Without a spare spool, you're out of business.

Swivels prevent line twist. The two basic types, snap and barrel, are essentially a pair of metal eyes joined by a pin in such a way that a rotating lure or bait cannot transmit its twist to your line. Instead, the eye to which lure or leader is tied does the twisting. Both of the barrel swivel's eyes are permanently closed, while one of the snap swivel's eyes can be opened like a safety pin to slip on a lure.

Black and brown finishes are best in salt water because small

FRESH WATER SERIES

General usage: nos. 1 and 2, light spin fishing; no. 2, casting also; no. 3, spinning, casting and trolling; no. 4, casting and trolling; no. 5, heavy casting and trolling; no. 6, extra heavy trolling.

The pound designation figure below each number indicates swivel test.

6R	5R	4R	3R	2R
70 lbs.	50 lbs.	30 lbs.	15 lbs.	12 lbs.

6S	5S	4S	3S	2S	1S
70 lbs.	50 lbs.	30 lbs.	15 lbs.	12 lbs.	10 lbs.

Safety Snap

6L	5L	4L	3L	2L	1L
70 lbs.	50 lbs.	30 lbs.	15 lbs.	12 lbs.	10 lbs.

Lock Snap

SALT WATER SERIES

Designed for use in all types of salt water fishing. Different riggings are available for local fishing requirements and preferences. **Salt water rings are made of brazed monel.**

The pound designation figure below each number indicates swivel test.

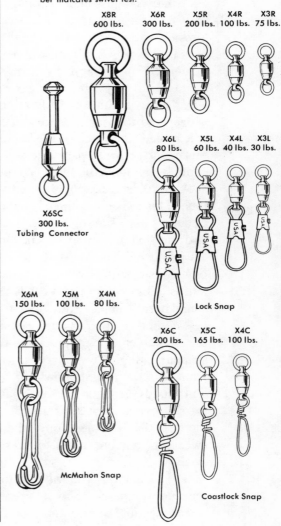

X8R	X6R	X5R	X4R	X3R
600 lbs.	300 lbs.	200 lbs.	100 lbs.	75 lbs.

	X6L	X5L	X4L	X3L
	80 lbs.	60 lbs.	40 lbs.	30 lbs.

X6SC
300 lbs.
Tubing Connector

X6M	X5M	X4M
150 lbs.	100 lbs.	80 lbs.

Lock Snap

X6C	X5C	X4C
200 lbs.	165 lbs.	100 lbs.

McMahon Snap

Coastlock Snap

Swivels and snap-swivels come in all sizes. These are made by Sampo.

schoolfish such as pollock, mackerel, and baby blues often will snap at swivels made of bright steel or brass. Dull finishes also tend to corrode less than brass. Even a thin film of corrosion clogs moving parts, making twist-averting rotation difficult. The same, by the way, applies to salt, so include your swivels in that freshwater rinse you give rods, reels, lures, and hooks.

So how come some surfmen don't always use swivels? Because they feel that a swivel interferes with the natural action of their lures. In fresh water, they might be able to make a case, but big ocean lures in wild ocean water are not going to have their actions influenced appreciably by a tiny assemblage of smoothly moving metal. The only time I advise against plugging with a swivel is when using a lightweight floating lure such as a popper. This lure is designed to float at a prescribed angle to the water so that when it is pulled, the force of the water against its face produces a noise that is attractive to fish. The weight of a swivel can alter the angle enough to impair the lure's action.

A third swivel, popular with bait-fishermen, is the three-way type. This swivel has three rotatable rings around the periphery of a circular band. Line is tied to one ring, hook and leader to another, and the sinker is attached via a metal connecting link to the third. To avoid bait-stealing bottom-scroungers such as skate, a doodle-bug rig is desirable when the quarry is not a bottom-feeder and the bait is light enough to be easily suspended. The doodlebug is just a small barrel-shaped cork float a few inches behind your hook.

Another rig that should be in every bait-fisherman's arsenal is the fishfinder. To appreciate its effectiveness, imagine you're a striped bass. You're hungry, so you cruise in close along the beachfront to scour the shallows for food. It's good worm country, rich and muddy beneath the sandy surface, and the pickings are plentiful. Worms are not swarming, but there are enough solitary swimmers so that you need only single one out, vector yourself with a sweep of your broad tail to intercept it, suck it into your craw, and swallow.

So automatic is your attack, so light and supple is the worm, that you barely are aware of its presence within your jaws, barely note its passage into your gullet. Before the trap of your jaws has sprung, your mind is on your next mouthful.

You sight it sinuating a few yards to your right, a few inches off the bottom. This is a big one, fat and long and appetizing. It will take only a few more like this to make a meal, and already you are scanning for your next course.

This worm, making no headway against the current, swims stationary: an easy mark. Less than half a second elapses between sighting and biting. Your swing into your next sweep is made without pause, without interruption. Then you feel it, a tiny tender tug. Something is wrong, something is different. Immediately you expel the worm.

This is not the hook you've felt. It's the line pulling against your lip. In terms of the microsecond-fast reactions that a fish needs to stay alive, it's a long time between the pressure on the lip and the prick of the hook. A fish that hasn't totally abandoned its caution and isn't swimming with all the stops pulled out can apply its brakes long before your hook has penetrated its mouth. Even with a super-honed hook that's poised for instant penetration—a rare combination on the line of any but the most experienced anglers—there will be a lot of telltale tugging before the fish is snared.

And can you imagine how much tugging four or five ounces of lead can do, especially if it's mired in mud? You can bet that when an almost weightless worm suddenly starts pulling at the mouth of a wary fish hard enough to haul it off course, the fish is going to get rid of that worm fast. Fast enough, probably, to avoid even being pricked by the hook.

Not always, of course. Codfish, accustomed to sucking up anything that looks even remotely edible (I've found stones, shells, and seaweed in their stomachs), are easily caught on an anchored hook. Fast-moving bluefish, in competition with their schoolmates for a limited food supply, sometimes will snag themselves despite dragging a sinker. So will stripers and drums, though less often. And in a wildly tempestuous surf, a yank from anything lighter than a sashweight is likely to seem like just another part of the pulverizing.

Most of the time, though, the less weight and tension a fish can feel, the better. And that's where the fishfinder comes in. No, I'm not referring to the electronic device whose pings and blips enable skippers to seek out and follow fish. This fishfinder is just a simple assemblage of line, swivels, sinker, and hook that enables a bottom-fished bait to cover more ground and a running fish to tote your bait without also hauling your sinker.

Rigging a fishfinder is simplicity itself. A few versions require

The fishfinder rig enables a fish to run with your bottom-fished bait without feeling the weight of your sinker.

leather thongs and plastic collars, but for this description, I'm going to stick to the simplest and, incidentally, the cheapest design. Fellow taught it to me one night on the Cape Cod Canal. After watching me break off three expensive store-bought rigs on three successive casts, he laid his rod on the riprapped bank and said, "Here, let me save you some money."

Slipping my line through the eye of a big brass swivel, he continued: "Works just as well as one of those forty-cent jobs with the plastic rings for running your line through."

Then he tied my line to one eye of a barrel swivel and my leader to the other.

"Now snap your sinker on that first swivel and see how it rides down your line when you cast. The barrel swivel stops it so it doesn't run all the way to your hook. When your sinker bites the bottom, your line slides free as you please through the eye of your snap."

Three things can cause your line to take off after your sinker has taken hold. One is when your bait gets pulled away in the current. This is good, because it enables your offering to move about and find the fish. (Fishfinder, get it?) A second is weeds. They're an irritation, but a sensitive touch and an occasional reeling in and checking your bait will all but eliminate the problem. The third, of course, is when a fish runs with your bait.

Almost any bait will do: a chunk of mackerel, a strip of squid, a mudworm, a skimmer clam. Some surfmen stick their rods in sandspikes with reels set to click softly when their bait starts moving, but this defeats the fishfinder's purpose of making a bait seem as naturally light as possible to a running fish. I hold my rod, reel-bail open, and aim my tip top at the ocean. Then a running fish feels neither reel drag nor rod tension until I lean forward, flip my bail shut, and, just as the last inch of slack is about to sizzle out, haul back hard.

When to set your hook? How to tell when you've let a fish run long enough to be sure a yanked hook will pierce flesh, yet not so long that your line's pressure on the fish's lip will cause it to spit out your bait? This is a complex question. Size and shape and hardness of bait enter into it. Also size, design, and sharpness of hook; as well as how your bait is impaled on it. How much line do you have out? How heavy is it? How long is your rod? How turbulent the water? Is your sinker heavy or light, barely beneath the sand or firmly imbedded in the mud? And, most influential of all, that fish out there: What species is it? How big? How fast? How hungry, mad, competitive, alert?

Leaders

Freshwater fishermen who have caught razor-toothed roughnecks such as muskie, pike, pickerel, and walleyes have some small appreciation for the need to use leaders in the surf. Lightweight mono is no match for teeth whose shape, sharpness, number, and location have been refined by evolution into superbly lethal weapons. The real convincer, though, is the savage spectacle of bluefish or sharks or barracuda on the kill. Only after you have watched the wanton carnage of bluefish threshing their victims to bloody shreds or seen the frightening efficiency of sharks grabbing and rending and ripping and gulping and grabbing again, can you really appreciate what you're up against. Unlike the solitary pikes, which snare and hold their victims in a single beartrap bite, blues attack in large schools at lightning speed and chop continuously.

Gill covers as well as teeth are used by some species to sever lines. Tarpon and striped bass sometimes rush toward you to relieve line pressure, then roll on the slack. Underwater obstacles compound the problems of the leaderless surfman. So do currents that so often seem intent on delivering his line to coral and barnacles that can cleave through monofilament like a blowtorch through butter.

And yet a lot of good surfmen refuse to use leaders. Many species and waters, of course, don't demand them, and in some techniques, such as drifting live bait through a tideway, naturalness of presentation takes priority, but some anglers ignore leaders under all circumstances. One Cape Cod plugging specialist I know catches 10- and 15-pound bluefish on leaderless line while others alongside him are having their lines severed, leaders and all.

"Long as you strike fast and keep 'em coming," he says, "you don't have to worry."

Men like this don't omit leaders out of pride or pigheadedness. Presentation and control are their prime considerations. They accept the risk of a severed line as the price of a higher probability of hooking fish. Superior skill reduces their risk.

Like all big-leaguers, these men make the difficult look easy. Until you have beached enough bluefish to learn their tactics and predict their lightning-fast maneuvers, back up your lure with 12 to 18 inches of braided wire. It won't guarantee protection—I've had many wire leaders chopped by battling bluefish—but it will up the odds of your success.

Braided wire leaders can be bought in various lengths and strengths. You can make your own, but it's rarely worth it. The cost of special pliers for crimping metal collars above your snap swivel at one end and your barrel swivel at the other will outweigh several years of savings for most spare-time fishermen. The same applies to the stainless-steel leaders sometimes used on super-hazardous species in high-risk waters.

Leaders need not always be wire. A foot or two of heavy monofilament—say, 40- or 50-pound—is enough for species such as cod and weakfish whose teeth are sharp but not shearing sharp. Mono leaders can be bought with a hook at one end and a snelled loop at the other, or you can tie them yourself.

Without a strong leader, your line might be sheared by sharp-toothed critters such as these bluefish. (Photo: Joel Arrington)

Big stripers may be smart, but a well-designed and well-fished lure can fool them. (Photo: Charles R. Meyer)

3
Lures

STRUNG ACROSS THE 10-FOOT-WIDE WALL of my barn workshop is a strand of wire with nearly a hundred lures dangling from it. With few exceptions, all of them are different. Shapes, sizes, materials, colors, and finishes impress visitors and occasionally embarrass me when I am asked, "Boy, that one looks like a real killer—what's the biggest fish you ever caught on that?" Invariably my inquisitor seems to be pointing to a plug whose designer was more concerned with appearance than performance and I have to acknowledge that either I never have used it or, if I have, without success.

I suppose I should cull my collection, but there are too many old friends there, too many memories. Scars and scuffs and scratches have earned a lot of them an honorable retirement, but every once in a while I tote one along and cast it a few times just for old time's sake. Who knows?

It's interesting to consider how a lure becomes popular. Classically a lot of people use it to catch a lot of fish; word gets around and sales soar. But where does the design originate? How does the word spread?

Many of our most popular surf plugs are direct adoptions of freshwater prototypes. Tarpon and snook were first caught on plugs designed for freshwater bass. Others are adapted. The famous "Blue Plug" that inaugurated plugging for striped bass in the Cape Cod Canal was a muskie lure with its faceplate bent down so it would kick up a topwater commotion. Improvisors introduced the broomstick, a short length of real honestagawd broom handle with its

A variety of lures—jig, tin squid, plastic eel, swimming plug, popping plug, small jigs.

face beveled to plow up a wake during retrieve. Many of today's plugs are variations on today's broomstick theme.

Early experimenters had few secrets. A man might sneak off to test a hot new imitation but eventually he would return to the company of close pals in popular places. New lures would be scrutinized, successes noted. Early grapevines disseminated results with electronic efficiency. Today's touting is done mainly at sportsmen's shows and via ads, columns, and articles relating spectacular success stories.

Every inquiring angler conjures up a few can't-miss creations of his own. Many of these brain-babies have merit, but most die aborning. Design, development, manufacturing, marketing—all these require heavy investment and hard work, commodities which companies are better able than individuals to provide. Besides, they eat into a guy's fishing time. Rare is the angler who can concentrate on performance curves and cost projections when tide and moon and wind and weather are in concert.

And yet it can be done. Despite a minefield of mishaps and disappointments, Al Reinfelder and Lou Palma carried their Alou Eel through to completion. This marvelously sinuous counterfeit of the long-popular rigged eel is now manufactured and marketed by Garcia.

Plastic imitations of many baitfish have been marketed in recent years, but acceptance has been slow. The idea behind a soft plastic make-believe baitfish is sound: because its soft body seems more natural to a striking fish, the fish retains it in its mouth an instant longer before spitting it out, thus giving the angler added time to set his hook. Their time will come, but not until their action is as authentic as their appearance.

Jigs

With few exceptions, the surf lures that hang in my workshop are either jigs, metal squids, or plugs. Jigs, though the simplest, are the most productive. With all the effort and ingenuity expended year after year on designing and developing new fish-enticers, the old reliable bucktail jig continues to reign as the most all-round-effective seducer of saltwater gamefish. Perhaps its greatest testimonial is that when a deadly and versatile lure was sought for inclusion in World War II survivor's kits, the bucktail jig was chosen.

Yet for all of its effectiveness, a jig is no more than a hook, a hunk of lead, a dab of paint, and usually a few bristles; hardly a combination to inspire the confidence of a fisherman looking for a knock-'em-dead lure. It's not thin like a worm, streamlined like a

The durable and deadly bucktail jig comes in many sizes and configurations.

fish, or long and tubular like an eel. You could stretch a point and say that it has a hint of the shrimp or the squid about it, but certainly not enough to deceive a fish whose very survival depends on split-second distinctions between friend and foe, tidbit and trap. Appearance is not one of the jig's strong suits.

Design, though, that's a different matter. Its heavy head enables it to be cast far and accurately, its concentrated weight pulls it quickly into holes and sloughs where big fish hang out, and its always-upward hook snags more fish and fewer weeds than treble-hooked lures. Furthermore, hooked fish usually stay hooked. Jigs offer little opportunity for struggling fish to gain leverage while trying to work a hook loose.

I was first introduced to jigs on a charter. Even in a book about surf fishing, the experience is worth repeating. It was after an all-night session during which I had caught striped bass up to 45 pounds on familiar swimming plugs. Despite the Olympian reputation of skipper Charlie Haag, I couldn't see much sense in swapping my tried-and-true tempters for this ugly unknown. I wasn't even sure Haag was serious when he said, "Here, snap this on and get it over the side." As a first-timer, I thought, maybe I'm having my leg pulled. Navy recruits, I recalled with some embarrassment, traditionally get told to "Go find me a number six skyhook," or "Fetch me a bucket of steam," as their first shipboard assignments.

But Charlie meant business.

"C'mo-o-on, Fallon," he bellowed, "get the lead out and get your lead in."

Haag had a way with words as well as striped bass.

Trolled astern on Monel wire, my jig took an awesome toll of stripers that morning. I kept jerking my 5-foot rod forward, then easing it aft until, so help me, the fingers of my right hand cramped so painfully that they curled inward like claws. To straighten them, I had to press as hard as I could with my left hand, and as soon as I stopped, they were snapped back into their claw position by tendons that must have been taut as bowstrings.

Yet I kept right on jigging. Intimidated by Haag's benevolent blasts ("No, no, no! You're not hitting a golf ball, you're trying to catch fish.") and enchanted by the way I continued to catch 10- and 15-pound stripers, I learned the tricky technique of trolling with bucktail jigs before the morning tide had ended: face forward while standing in the starboard quarter; hold my rod tip about 45 degrees off the water; swing it in a steady relaxed rhythm using my whole upper body instead of just my right arm and hand. From that day forward, bucktail jigs have occupied a prominent place in my tackle box.

The more I have learned about and used the jig, the more I have appreciated it. Familiarity, instead of breeding the customary contempt, has built in me a respect for the bucktail jig that borders on reverence. When, for example, I discovered that jigs made of shell and bone have been tonging fish all over the world for centuries, I had to marvel at its staying power. Every time I watch another highly touted fish-killer flame and fizzle within a few years, I toss off a spiritual salute to ancient Og, whose inspired combination of dinosaur bone and wooly mammoth hair must have started it all.

And when I discovered that the jig can have an oval, ball, bullet, coin, cone-shaped, or slanted head of stainless steel as well as lead, and a skirt of nylon or feather or plastic as well as hair from the tail of a male deer, I came to appreciate the subtle sophistication of its design.

After my experience with Haag, I couldn't wait to find out if jigs would catch stripers from shore. The model I selected was the Dart, a ½-inch-long lead cone with a gold hook and a sprig of yellow bristles projecting from its apex. Two painted bands, one red, one white, added color. With this jig I had caught shad, rainbow trout, and countless freshwater panfish, so why not stripers in the brackish tidal creek I parked alongside? Mid-May was early, I knew, especially a mile inland, especially with the tide at dead low but the Dart delivered: two small fish, sea-bright and sassy, in the vanguard of a new invasion, as welcome as robins and crocuses and the brassy brightness of an almost-summer morning.

Later when an editor asked me to do an article about the swarms of school stripers that were glutting the Northeast, I had the script practically written: tricky currents, slippery rocks, featherweight tackle, and a tide full of romper-room stripers that gobbled my Darts like gumdrops. Since then this Dart-type jig has accounted for yellowtail jacks and banded rudderfish, and I'm sure it would be equally attractive to pollock, mackerel, weakfish, snapper blues, spot, surfperch, scup, and saltwater panfish in general.

But what is it that makes the bucktail jig so effective? Color under certain conditions can make a difference, but once during a bluefish blitz I watched a friend switch sequentially from white to yellow to red to blue without any abatement in the action. To some fish there's an advantage to being able to sweeten the jig's hook with porkrind, although I've known it to be irresistible when unsweetened. Unquestionably its upright hook simplifies snaring as well as controlling fish, yet I've seen a lot of jigs thrown by hard-fighting fish.

Ultimately, I guess, it boils down to how the jig is manipulated. In the wrong hands it becomes just another lure, too high or low or slow or fast, its action too careless or contrived to interest a fish that can't afford to make mistakes. Sometimes, as I learned years ago on a desolate beach, the fish don't even see it.

I was walking the fog-shrouded shore at the time, searching for my peripatetic partner Bill Stone. We had spent a cold sleepless night on the sand, but at daybreak Bill was off for his favorite rip with all the vitality of a man who had just logged eight hours sack time. When I found him he had three bass on the sand behind him, all victims of a simple, white 1½-ounce bucktail jig. For the next 20 minutes I also used this lure, casting the identical distance, waiting the same three-second interval before retrieving, and jigging in precisely the same jerk-and-pause rhythm. While Bill's jig tallied thirteen more fish, mine was ignored. The reason: he was casting far enough upcurrent for his jig to reach bottom, where the bass were congregated, before the current swung it upward again. My jig never reached bottom because I was casting it straight out.

Metal Squids

To the landlubber, the language of surf fishing seems full of contradictions: a popper is not a device for making popcorn, but a plug that makes a popping noise; a bar is not a place for slaking your thirst, but a ridge of ocean bottom; a rip is not a tear in your waders, but a turbulence in the water; a priest is not a person who prays but a wooden billy for klonking frisky fish; nor is a squid one of those slimy octopuslike animals that squirt ink when they're scared.

A squid to the surf caster is a lure, and a whale of a lure it is.

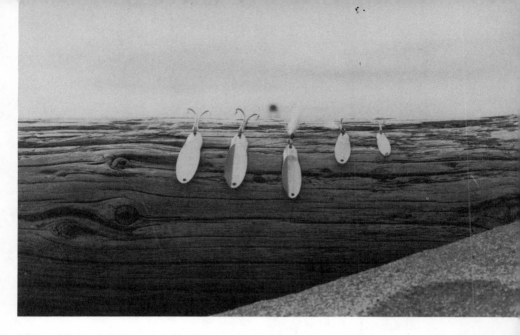

The weight and balance of this Castmaster family of tin squids enables you to cast them long distances with on-the-button accuracy.

In simplest terms it is a piece of shaped metal that wobbles like a spoon yet is heavy enough for long-distance casting. In the early days of surf casting, the squid was the only lure. Plugs had not yet been introduced by inland improvisors. Freshwater spoons were too light to heave any appreciable distance and too easily discombobulated by the fast and often erratic flow from winds and tides. Lead was the most available metal, so pioneer surf casters adapted the heavy drails used in handlining. Modifying and refining their designs, they strove for the best balance of weight for casting, brightness for attracting, softness for shaping, and economy for producing. (Then as now, every experimenter confidently expected that his next model would become the hot fudge sundae of the fishing world and that royalties from its sales would enable him to fish affluently ever after.) Early squids had shaped keels and stationary hooks, but many current designs are keeless and have flexible hooks attached by a split ring and often adorned with a sprig of bucktail.

Lead was far from ideal. Forming it was easy, but a few ricochets off barnacled rocks quickly pounded it out of shape again. Rubbing with mercury or sand brightened its dull sheen, but only temporarily. For a while the more lustrous block tin seemed to offer a solution, but when it came time for quantity production, its price became prohibitive.

Today's squids are bright durable creations that can be propelled with the distance and accuracy of artillery projectiles. Stainless steel is the predominant metal. Most popular on the East Coast are the Hopkins, with its super-reflective hammered surface, and the Kastmaster, whose cleverly beveled fore and aft edges make it flutter enticingly when retrieved. On the West Coast the Sleekee and Spoofer are favorites.

For the life of me, though, I could not imagine why these lures had been dubbed "squids." Even with the rod action of a marionette master making them spurt-pause-spurt-pause squid-fashion, I could not imagine a fish mistaking one for anything more than a cleverly manipulated hunk of metal.

Enigmas like this are easily answered as long as the world has telephones and nice omniscient guys like Hal Lyman, publisher of *Salt Water Sportsman.*

"They're called squids," said Hal, "because that's what they originally were designed to imitate."

Simple. They're not made of block tin and they don't resemble squids, but they continue to be called block tin squids. Tradition dies hard in the surf.

Although metal squids have been dethroned by plugs as the top surf lure, they still command respect by casters who appreciate their advantages. When fish are feeding at maximum range, a heavy squid can get you to them. When weather roughens water and fish might not notice a painted jig or plug, reflections from a squid's shiny surface can catch their attention. For skipping at top speed through a school of blues as they ravage small bright baitfish, a metal squid always is my first choice. Likewise for precision casting, especially at long distances into a wind.

Plugs

Plugs attract fish by their form, color, movement, and commotion. Generally they are shaped like small fish, but size, color, and action play bigger parts than verisimilitude. If this were not so, broomhandles would long ago have been boycotted and soft plastic simulations would reign supreme.

Throw a 5-inch plug at fish that are feeding on 3-inch bait, and it's apt to be spurned. Not always, but often enough to make size a major consideration. Feeders seem sometimes to lock in on the dimensions of the fish they're attacking, to the exclusion of all others. I recall a rainy afternoon of casting with my two teen-age sons across a quiet clamflat when Jack and I caught striper after striper on streamer flies and small swimming plugs while Dan went hitless.

"Here," I said, handing Dan a 3-inch shallow swimmer, "try this."

Within ten minutes of swapping the 5-incher for the 3-incher, he had three bass on his stringer and a sunburst smile on his face.

Yes, color can make a difference, but in my experience intensity of hue and pattern of design have been the keynotes. A plug's color, I have found, is less influential than how dark it is and how its colors are arranged. One popular silver swimmer was sold originally with black or blue backs. Evaluation was easy. Black, my friends and

When jerked across the surface, a popping plug produces a gurgling "blup" that tolled in this hungry fish.

I soon concluded, was better at night, blue during daylight, and we fished accordingly. When the manufacturer started peddling purple-, pink-, and yellow-backed versions without any explanation of why or when or where they might be better, we stuck with our old stand-bys and continued to catch fish. Then I found some purple ones on sale and bought a couple with the intention of blackening their backs. In a hurry to make a tide a few nights later, I grabbed the purple plugs by mistake, used them, and scored. Since then I have had similar experiences with yellow and pink.

So what does this prove? Nothing. Ironclad conclusions are hard to come by in an ocean where subtle and unpredictable factors can throw the most careful of calculations into a cocked hat. A life-time of experimenting is barely enough for coming up with a few semi-confident conjectures. Our conjecture in this case was that darker colors work better after sunset, lighter ones better before. Period. For moonlit nights and overcast days and the thousand and one other variables that must constantly be cranked into our computers, we have made adjustments. When something has worked often enough under similar circumstances, we have ventured another conjecture. Here are a few.

Fluorescent red painted on a plug's belly can make it more appealing.

Red eyes (not necessarily fluorescent) painted on a plug can turn finicky fish on.

When mackerel is the dominant bait, it's a good idea to paint your plug's backs green with black mackerel-like squiggles.

Your plug's movement is intended to convince a gamefish that it is looking at a baitfish that's injured or trying to escape. Injury is simulated partly by the plug's design and partly by the way you retrieve it. No matter how enticingly a well-designed plug might wobble, its appeal can be compounded by clever manipulating. Always keep in mind that what you're hauling in out there is just a hunk of wood or plastic with a peculiar movement. To a wary fish, it *might* be a meal, but unless the fish is extra-hungry or strikes reflexively, it will want more reassurance before it lays its life on the line. The fish will follow your plug, poised to pounce but reluctant to do so until something reassuring happens. The smart plugger varies his retrieve, pausing occasionally to make a stalking fish think it has a setup, or accelerating to make it think its meal is getting away. The most effective retrieve I have used on fish hanging in a tideway waiting for bait to come by was revealed by Bill Nolan, a 150-pound titan who loves to share lessons he's learned in more than a half-century of hard smart fishing.

"Lay a floater out there on the far edge of the rip," Bill advises, "20 to 30 degrees upcurrent. Let it float till it starts swinging into the rip, then sweep your rod horizontally till its tip is almost behind you. Sweep it fast, but reel in slack as soon as you stop. Most of your hits will happen on the pause."

Faceplates of either metal or plastic cause swimming plugs to wobble and to seek various levels. Depth is determined by current, retrieve speed, and the angles at which the faceplate tilts downward and the tie-on eye tilts upward. Depth can be varied by changing the angle of a plug's tie-on eye, but do so at your peril. It's easy to work an eye loose or break it off, difficult to return it to the original angle for which the plug was designed.

Surface swimmers are retrieved on or near the top, subsurface types well below. Other subsurface types employ beveled or grooved faces to impart an erratic darting movement, while still a third type depends on imaginative rod-and-reel action for its enticement. This last class, especially popular in the South, often has a mirror finish.

Topwater plugs other than surface swimmers depend on commotion as well as movement to attract fish. Freshwater trout fishermen, conditioned to tiptoe-and-whisper tactics, will find this hard to get used to. Largemouth fans will have less trouble. All noisemakers are activated by rod-and-reel action plus one of three characteristic designs. Sliders, or stick-baits, have a thin streamlined contour that causes them to swing wildly. Propellor plugs have metal props at one or both ends, or might even tow a metal flap astern. Poppers are hollowed out in their front faces so that a sudden jerk causes a blurping gurgle as well as a loud splash. In a recent innovation, metal balls are rattled around inside a compartment in the plug's body.

A few metal squids and bucktail jigs plus an assortment of surface and subsurface plugs, then, will arm you adequately for any fish you're likely to run into as a newcomer to surf fishing. So many factors influence your choice of size, color, and design that you should seek help from anglers experienced in the waters you'll be wading and with the fish you'll be chasing. If you don't know any, phone the fishing columnist of your local newspaper, call on your regional marine fisheries office, or drop in at your neighborhood fish and game club. If they don't have the answers, they'll tell you where to get them. *Real* fishermen genuinely enjoy helping well-motivated newcomers get launched successfully. Fortunately, the real ones predominate.

As you acquire experience, you will develop preferences. Many of the plugs on my workshop wall, for example, are poppers, because I have found no thrill to match the sight of an angry predator on the attack, no test to compare with how I will react to the sudden swirl of an almost-interested fish. Yet there are swimmers for bright days when fish shun the surface, jigs for when fish must be dredged from the depths, tin squids for when fish are feeding far from shore. Many of my lures bear at least a superficial resemblance to regional baits. A few that neither look nor act like anything in the ocean possess the redeeming attribute of having caught fish when more sensible-looking lures have failed.

For all of my first-team tempters, though, I follow a rule that even beginners can benefit from: always bring a backup. One lure simply is not enough when it is producing. Lose it and you risk losing the interest of fish that might spurn anything else you offer.

Teasers

You also ought to invest in a jar of porkrind. That's right, the same soft wiggly stuff you used to use for enticing largemouth bass. Sinuating from the hook of a bucktail jig, a pork strip can induce strikes when nothing else can, even in bright summer sunlight. Use white to start, but don't hesitate to experiment with other colors as conditions change.

Despite its devastating delectability, porkrind has two big minuses. First is that when it's cast and when it's retrieved in a jerky jigging motion, it tends to double back and foul your hook. Recently introduced plastic strips all but eliminate hook-fouling, and from what I have seen, they're just as appealing as their pigskin counterparts. Second deficiency is that the porkrind's tail is so far from your jig's hook that fish sometimes strike short. Double-layer strips with two hooks in series are used for snaring short-strikers, but I find them too firm to furnish the slinky action that entices fish in the first place.

Real or plastic porkrind can be used to tease fish into striking a plug. So can streamer flies and any number of small lightweight lures. A very effective teaser where sandeels are in abundance is a short length of plastic tubing with a hook in its tail and a barrel swivel in its head. Tie your teaser to a dropper loop with a foot or so of 50-pound mono about two feet upline from your plug, and it will look during your retrieve like a small fish, such as a sandeel or a mullet, being chased by a larger one, such as a mackerel or a pollock. Predators often will hit the teaser in preference to the plug. When several fish are in pursuit, doubleheaders are common.

Another teasing arrangement is the splasher rig. A wooden dowel about two feet ahead of a small spoon, jig, or fly draws the attention of fish to the lure behind it. The dowel's size is determined by the distance you want to cast. Paint it any color you like—or none at all—and tie line and leader to screw eyes in opposite ends.

Closely akin to the dowel splasher is one in which a cork float is positioned ahead of a hooked shrimp, minnow, or strip of fish flesh. It is employed most successfully against southern spotted weakfish and Gulf redfish.

Eel imitators

Imitation eels warrant a few paragraphs of their own. Because live eels have long been appreciated as a favorite food of surf dwellers, luremakers have sought to simulate the real thing. Until the Alou (now manufactured by Garcia) and Burke plastic imitations, efforts were unsuccessful. Where live eels couldn't be acquired, pickled eels or eelskins were substituted.

In the eel bob, an eel's head is cut off and a lead weight sewed under the forward skin. In the traditional eelskin rig, the forward end of an eel's skin is slipped over a lead collar that has a pair of hooks attached to it in series by a wire leader. The skin is tied to a groove in the periphery of the collar and the hooks protrude through the skin. When the rig is retrieved, water flowing through

A second, or teaser, lure often induces more strikes, occasionally produces double-headers. Here Vickie Tallon teases Sea of Cortez fish with a streamer fly and tin squid. (Photo: Jim Tallon)

the collar inflates the skin. Some surf casters are so sold on eelskins that they tie them around metal squids and even slip them over their plugs. With plugs, hooks must be removed before pulling on the skin, then replaced afterward.

Do eelskin-flavored lures work? They certainly have for me. Are they worth the trouble? Why not find out for yourself?

Live bait—your quarry's natural diet.

4

Bait

THE SUN-BLISTERED OLD SURF SERF who advised me many years ago to "Feed 'em what they's eatin' " said it all: offer the fish you're after something that duplicates or simulates the food they're currently accustomed to feeding on, and chances are high that they'll take it in. For an inflexible few who resolutely insist on fishing nothing but artificials, personal prejudice will put the real thing off limits. Even when fish have been sucking up every seaworm in sight and a big juicy wiggler laid in their line of fire practically guaranteed a hookup, I have seen plugging purists stick to their plastic imitations. For them a single fish fooled is worth a dozen caught on bait.

Fair enough. I have no argument with this attitude as long as it's based on a fair and reasonable assessment of alternatives. But too much prejudice—toward race, religion, and sex as well as fishing methods—is based on blind acceptance of tradition, on easy acquiescence to fashion.

Once you have tried bait fishing, chances are you'll add it to your repertoire. It may not occupy the top spot, but you can't ignore its effectiveness any more than you can its enjoyment. Its special blend of challenge and reward ranks high with many capable anglers. How well it works for you will depend largely on how well you select and employ your bait.

And what's so hard about picking the right bait? Just head for the nearest bait shop and order a dozen or two of what's been working best, right?

Right . . . maybe.

Maybe a school of anchovies has moved in and fish won't settle for less.

Maybe fish that were hitting worms on a rising tide will demand shrimp when the tide turns and washes shrimp out of inundated marsh grass.

Maybe the mackerel strips that worked so well during the day will be ignored at night, when fish are seeking eels.

Maybe worms will work on weakfish, but it's bluefish you're after.

Maybe fish that fell for your menhaden before a storm will be foraging in close for clams now that the storm has subsided.

Maybe mudworms will be gobbled up so fast by a sudden influx of sea robins that no gamefish ever will get to see your bait.

Maybe the shopowner is giving you bum dope so he can get rid of bait that he's overstocked on.

Maybe it's the tail end of a weekend and all the bait that's left is too stale and scraggly to interest fish.

Maybe only *live* mullet will work and there's no way to get them but catch them yourself.

Or *maybe* you simply can't afford to buy bait. With food demanding more and more from an income that inflation is making worth less and less, few of us can afford to ignore the economics

Cut herring—an old standby that is durable and easy to hook.

of fishing. Fun still takes priority, but a little less pressure on the pocketbook is a welcome bonus.

An ancient law of economics insists that there are only two ways for an enterprise to become more profitable: put less in; take more out. For the fun-fisherman with low-cost meals on his mind, this pretty much boils down to: pay less for bait; catch more fish. Fish-catching gets constant coverage in the outdoor press. Books and articles break this enormously complicated and eternally fascinating undertaking down into specific and localized elements that you can apply to your own fish, your own waters, your own methods. But the other side of the equation—how to acquire bait at lower cost—has had little attention: you need bait, you buy it; worms cost a dollar and a quarter a dozen, you pay it . . . unless, like thousands of other inflation-plagued fishermen, you have awakened to the fiscally refreshing fact that there are other less expensive ways.

Seaworms

To set the record straight, we are talking under this heading about bloodworms and clamworms, the top baits in the northeastern United States and among the most popular in other sections. Blood-worms (*Glycera dibranchiata*) are smooth, pink, tough, and, except for a retractable snout, essentially cylindrical in shape. Clamworms (*Nereis virens*), also known as sandworms and, on the West Coast, musselworms and pileworms, are green to blue on their backs, orange to red on their bottoms, and are flatter, tenderer, and generally shorter than *Glycera*. Both species are taken principally by raking from mudflats, clamworms a little deeper than blood-worms. Daily deliveries are made from Wiscasset, Me., center of a thriving industry, to West Coast as well as East Coast angling centers.

During daylight, worm holes are easy to spot in mudflats because they usually are filled with sand. On dark moonless nights these worms can be caught out in the open, but a heavy tread or an errant beam from a flashlight will send them back into their burrows with startling speed. Any freshwater fisherman who has tiptoed across damp grass trying to catch basking nightcrawlers will appre-

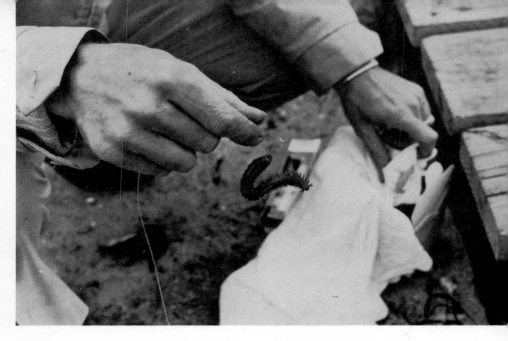

Hooking a seaworm. Even night crawlers will catch saltwater fish, if you can't find these delicacies.

ciate the need for treading softly and striking quickly. And grabbing carefully, too. Worms break easily. They should be grabbed as close to the ground as possible and eased slowly from their holes. They also pinch. Both species have curved pincers which, though built for burrowing, can inflict a nasty nip. A surf fisherman's first worm-inflicted wound along with the "Yeeeow!" that accompanies it is part of his initiation rite.

Heat and sunlight kill worms, so keep yours shaded. Fresh water —and this includes melted ice—also is lethal. Worms will last for days at about 40°F when packed loosely in a covered cardboard box of rockweed.

Inflation seemed to hit the seaworm industry with a vengeance in '74. From their '73 per-dozen price of about 95 cents, multilegged mudworms and smooth-surfaced bloodworms suddenly soared to a dollar and a quarter; even more in places where remoteness reduced competition and raised transportation costs. Those wiggly red things that used to be taken for granted now were costing better than a dime apiece. Anglers sought relief.

It certainly didn't come in the form of declining prices. Along with rods, reels, lures, sixpacks, and life's other vital necessities, seaworms were being sucked skyward in an inflationary spiral. For everyone from the digger on the Maine mudflat to the counterman in your friendly neighborhood bait shop, the cost of living was taking off. Butchers, bakers, candlestick makers, and worm diggers had to earn money just to keep their noses above water.

Do-it-yourself digging seemed an easy solution, but it wasn't as simple as it appeared: wormflats weren't always conveniently close to where a man wanted to do his fishing, tides weren't always cooperative, and digging turned out to be a lot more difficult than it looked. Trapping worms out in the open at night demanded a tiptoe tread that was all but impossible in ankle-deep goo, and a couple of hours of clawing a mucky mudflat with a clamrake while bugs bit and sun scorched was the marine equivalent of migrant farm work. By the time a man collected a couple dozen worms, he might be too pooped to fish.

Biggest deterrent, though, was the license fee. Even if he were willing to endure the mucky muscle-busting preliminaries, a man who lived in one of the many states where diggers must be licensed would have had to make inquiries, fill out forms, await approval, and disburse enough dollars to buy a batch of seaworms in the first place. It simply wasn't worth it. He sought a substitute.

Which is about where I was one April morning when I got that feeling. You know how it is. You're tilling the garden, trying to wrap up all your pre-season chores, when you smell it: FLOUNDER! Makes no difference that you're forty miles from the sea. Makes no difference that the wind isn't even off the water. The tingle in your nose and the tomtom in your chest tell you loud and clear: flatties are scouring the fringes of your favorite Gloucester mudflat; if you hurry you can catch a mess for dinner before the tide turns in.

Somewhere, it seemed to me, I had heard of saltwater species being caught on night crawlers. Or maybe it was just a reflection in reverse of how my sons and I, temporarily out of terrestrial worms, had caught a stringerful of rainbow trout on mudworms in a freshwater Cape Cod pond. Turnabout would be not only fair play, I thought, but, since I had no idea where I could buy mudworms so early in the season, the only play available. With a canful of crawlers from my garden, I dusted off my 6-foot spinning rod and headed for the coast.

An ebbing tide was tailing off as I slogged onto the exposed rocky ridge bordering the mushy mussel bed that sprawled on three sides behind me. I would have less than an hour before a flooding tide would convert my escape route to a quagmire, and I wasn't about to let myself get caught. Once on a black night, preoccupied by trying to interest stripers in flies that they chased but wouldn't hit, I had delayed my departure too long and become so mired in muck that I had to abandon my waders.

An egg sinker above a barrel swivel served the dual purpose of holding my worm on the bottom and letting me feel the characteristically tender tap of nibbling flounder. Except that today their taps were far from tender. Ravenously hungry after their winter in the mud, they hit with authority as soon as my worm came within range. Flounder hit so fast, in fact, that I didn't have to cope with what I later was informed is the biggest bugaboo of using terrestrial worms in sea water: after a brief immersion, they leach and soften.

"Sure," said a skeptic when I told him about my success, "crawlers are great when hungry fish are lined up ready to gobble them on sight, but leave one out there a little while and you're fishing with a pale lifeless blob."

Maybe so, but when I dunked crawlers a week later in Boston Harbor, flounder found them just as appetizing. Fish were less plentiful, less aggressive than they had been in Gloucester, so occasionally our worms were leached and lifeless. Nevertheless, I caught a lot of fish on bait that had been bathing for as much as a quarter-hour.

Crabs

It's poetic justice that bait-stealing bandits such as the blue and calico (lady) crabs can in turn be used for bait. Striped bass, bluefish, black and red drum, snook, and tarpon will take whole crabs in their soft-shell stage and occasionally even when their shells are hard; smaller fish such as tautog, whiting, weakfish, cod, and croakers, as well as little-leaguers of the more sporting species, are par-

Crabs that live under piers can be caught for bait—or food—in a baited wire-mesh trap.

tial to crab parts such as legs, claws, and bits of body.

As crabs' bodies expand, their hard shells become tighter. In order to grow, they must shed these shells. Just before shedding, crabs are known as peelers or shedders; for a short while after shedding, they are known as soft-shells.

Soft-shells are used for bait as is. Shedders should have their shells removed. Hard-shell crabs can be crushed and used for bait, either whole or in parts.

I don't know why it took me so long to consider using crabs for bait. Lord knows I had found enough greens and blues in the stomachs of stripers, cod, and tautog. What made me an instant convert was a young man on a Cape Cod pier, where I had paused for a last lingering look at the Canal before heading home. I had just concluded a successful morning at Woods Hole catching 2- and 3-pound tautog on dime-apiece mudworms.

At first I thought the man had caught the crab by mistake and was preparing to jettison it. Instead, he tore off its claws, dropped them into the water for chum, then cut the body into quarters. He slipped one quarter on his hook and he heaved it 50 or so easy feet, waited for his 4-ounce pyramid to grab the muddy bottom, then sat on a piling and lit a cigarette.

"Those crabs doing you any good?" I asked, still feeling a little smug about the 4 pounds of chowder chunks in the cooler in my car. The bucket he pointed to washed the smirk off my face. Draped over its rim was the broad purplish aftersection of a huge tautog. "Little over 8 pounds," he said. Later along the pier I saw three others of similar size.

These anglers were catching their crabs by dangling bits of fish flesh alongside the pilings. It rarely took long for a crab to grab hold and be hand-over-handed gently to the pier. Traps, of course, are even better. Though they come in many variations, most are just square mesh screens with a depressed center section in which bait—anything from fish scraps to chicken necks—is placed. When the trap is pulled topside by a line with leaders to the trap's four corners, water pressure plus a normal preoccupation with eating tend to keep the crabs in the screen. In shallow water, dip nets work well if you're stealthy and fast enough.

To stock up quickly you can dive with mask, flippers, and snorkel, but be careful. Crabs move surprisingly fast and pinch surprisingly hard. Years ago I tried unsuccessfully to convert a land-lubber neighbor to the joys of seashore recreation. I can see his horrified face now, erupting like a goosed submarine from 8 feet of Atlantic Ocean and staring incredulously at a very mad crab clinging to his index finger.

Crabs are best stored in cool damp seaweed.

Clams and Mussels

After a storm, clams are superb bait from a beach, and with good reason. As the storm subsides, shellfish that have been clawed up

Not only will steamer clams catch flounder, but what you don't use for bait you can take home for your own table.

by pounding breakers and tossed about in the turbulence are easy prey for big, strong-jawed bottom-scourers such as cod, striped bass, and channel bass. Exposed by a receding tide, these shellfish die and open in the sun. On the next flood, dinner is served. Big surf, or skimmer, clams are especially vulnerable, because they dwell just under the surface of close-to-shore sand. Collect them during the first low tide after a storm and fish them on the following flood.

Soft-shell, or steamer, clams are raked from mudflats that have been exposed by receding tides. Because they present the same problems as seaworms—inconvenient locations, uncooperative tides, and usually the need for a license—I prefer to buy mine, but from a small seaside wholesaler rather than a bait shop. Not only is the price lower, but the clams are fresh, not frozen. Furthermore, any surplus—and I always make sure there is one—is brought home for conversion to broth and hors d'oeuvres for introducing a meal of golden-broiled fillets from codfish that can't seem to resist the steamers' rubbery durable necks. Other popular bait clams are the razor and jackknife.

Mussels, too, make good bait, especially for tautog, flounder, and porgies. Rocks, pilings, and mudflats fairly bristle with them, and occasionally you can find 9- and 10-inch giants in the grip of strips of drifting kelp. Like soft-shell clams, mussels are delicious steamed, but check to be sure they haven't been poisoned by pollution or red tides.

Squid

Live squid often are easy to catch, but there's a trick to it. Around piers and bridges, especially at night, they can be attracted by a shiny dangled treble hook. Trouble is, they seem to come up under the hook, avoiding the barbs. Some squid-jiggers improve their catches by weighting their trebles to get them down faster, but an inch or so of plain white plastic tubing above the hook works even better. Squid striking at the tube are snagged on the jerked treble. Live squid are fished most effectively from bridges and piers.

Dead squid can be fished whole or in strips. Fish markets as well as bait shops sell them. When you find yourself with an excess, cut them into bait-size strips and either freeze them or pickle them in brine for future use.

Squid are not dangerous, but they can startle you out of your socks on a dark night. Once while snagging them from an anchored pram, I leaned over the side to inspect what felt like a glob of seaweed and got squirted full in the face.

Squid spoil quickly, so keep yours cool. The reek of a rotting squid will gag a garbage collector.

Shrimp

Shrimp are as popular with fish as they are with people. Snook, bones, weaks, macks, jacks, drums, blues—you'll suffer no lack of customers when fishing sand, grass, ghost, or edible shrimp in their native waters.

Three kinds of shrimp customarily are used for bait. Jumbos are the kind you dunk in sauce and eat before dinner. Just the tail is used. Peeled of its shell, it is one of the surf fisherman's most effective baits in waters where big shrimp are found.

A smaller type, called grass shrimp, is fished whole and live-hooked through the back or tail. These can be caught in a net as a tide washes them from marshes or they can be dipped at night from schools attracted by lantern light.

The saltwater crawfish, popular with West Coast surf anglers, actually is a ghost shrimp. Many bait shops sell them, and they can be dug from their burrows in muddy bay bottoms that are exposed to low tide.

Live shrimp are caught easily with a small cone-shaped trawl, a miniature version of the otter trawl used by commercial boats. On both sides of the cone's mouth are boards angled so that they ride outward when your boat tows the net through the water. This holds the net's mouth open during trawling. Chain and lead, which weight the mouth's bottom, spook shrimp from their daytime burrows. To prevent them from escaping over the top of the opening, the net's upper lip overhangs the lower and is held on the surface by cork floats. Shrimp are swept aft until the trawl has been retrieved. Then a rope that closes the final foot or so of the cone during dragging is untied and the catch is dumped.

If you must depend on dead shrimp—still a very effective bait, by the way—see if you can con an offloading shrimp boat into selling you some of its fresh catch before you resign yourself to buying frozen bait. Most shrimpers will give you a fair shake, some even a bargain.

Sand Bugs

Pompano fishermen are especially partial to these small hard-shelled creatures. Also called sand fleas, sand crabs, and beach bugs, they are sand-colored, smooth on top, rarely exceed 1½ inches in length, and have legs with which they burrow into sand along a tideline. You can catch them by running your fingers through wet sand in the wake of a receding wave or by dragging a long-handled wire-mesh scoop through the wave. As I learned on a recent night every time I baited my hook, they also are attracted by light.

Several sand bugs can be fished on the same hook for bigger

fish. A single sand bug sometimes is used to sweeten the hook of a jig.

Eels

For my money, live eels are the ultimate after-dark striper bait. On so many occasions I have had stripers—usually big ones—suck in my lip-hooked eels as I retrieved them slowly alongside jetties, across rocks, and through grassy shallows that I don't even object to paying the thirty-five-cent tab. I'm sure that if I were paying the buck or better that South Carolina cobia fishermen sometimes have to shell out, I'd feel differently, but three for a dollar isn't bad when you consider all the effort involved in catching, storing, transporting, inventorying, selling, and packaging. Still, a penny saved . . .

Eels are easy to catch in cages designed for the purpose. Entering the cage through an easy-to-find converging opening, they can't locate the tiny exit hole when they decide to leave. After a day anchored on the bottom of a tidal creek, your trap should contain several trips worth of prime bait. By storing your eels in a covered

The popularity of live eels has persuaded many bait shops to invest in tanks and water circulators.

floating carry, you can keep them fresh and frisky. Following a few feedless days, they'll be ready to take on stripers and cobia in hand-to-hand combat.

Eels caught while bait fishing can be a scourge. A 3-footer I hooked a few seasons ago while worm fishing alone at midnight on a desolate clamflat squirmed and slid and slithered, locking my arm and rod and neck in a slimy embrace for ten minutes, until I was able to wrestle it loose from the only hook I had left.

If you should happen to know a place where eels abound, spend some time there hook-and-lining your bait supply before heading out for a night of bass fishing. A friend of mine invariably starts his eel-fishing forays behind a restaurant on a tidal river, where eels always are waiting for a handout.

Nothing is slipperier or slimier than a live eel. Holding one bare-handed when it's trying to get away is impossible. On a jetty, rough cloth gloves or a towel solve the problem; on a beach, a handful of sand does the trick. Hooking is further simplified when eels are immobilized by storing them in a bucket of ice. This literally knocks them cold, but once they hit the water they start wiggling again. The bucket should have holes in its bottom for draining off the melted ice.

A live eel can be drifted beneath a bobber, but when tethered to a sinker, it tends to wrap itself around its leash. Eel, hook, line, and sinker are reeled in resembling a yarn ball that's been dunked in glue.

Bluefish love eels, although with their tendency to hit a bait from behind, they often chop off their stern sections. This doesn't necessarily put you out of business, though. The flow of blood sometimes chums in fish that are perfectly satisfied to eat the remaining half.

Mullet

A favorite bait along the south Atlantic and Gulf coasts, the slender silver mullet is one of the many baitfishes that can be fished alive as well as dead. Keeping them alive for long is difficult, even in bait tanks, so normally they are caught just before being used. They can be encircled with a two-man seine or trapped with a one-man cast net.

The cast net is pulled down quickly over a school by lead weights that line its circumference. Fish are trapped by the pulling of a drawstring that leads through a hole in the net's center and is attached to cords that are tied at intervals along the net's circumference. Always check local laws before netting. Areas, seasons, mesh size, and even net size sometimes are regulated.

Live mullet are fished with bail open (free-spool on a rotating-spool reel) and single-hooked either through the lips or just under the skin aft of the dorsal fin. The free-flowing line enables the fish to run without resistance, unsuspectingly taking the bait into its mouth until the hook is set. From bridges, mullet often are hooked just behind the head and allowed to swim on the surface heading into the current.

When gamefish such as snook, tarpon, and bluefish are feeding on mullet close to shore, anglers often will jig weighted trebles through the mullet school. When one is snagged, it can either be left on the treble, or reeled in, rerigged on a single hook, and cast back into the melee.

Dead mullet are available fresh or frozen from fish markets and bait shops. Size of the fish you're after dictates mullet size. Big sharks or tarpon, for example, should be fished with whole striped mullet, the larger of the two kinds found in the surf. The smaller silver mullet is appropriate for more modest-size fish. Bottom-fished chunks and fillets also are effective.

Menhaden

The oily flesh of this flat, deep-bellied, fork-tailed herring tolls in predators such as bluefish, striped bass, weakfish, and channel bass. Live bait can be bought from commercial fishermen who net them by the thousands in purse seines and weirs, but snagging and fishing one at a time is most practical for the shore fisherman. Although menhaden survive better than mullet in bait wells, it's difficult when fishing from shore to maintain a constant flow of well-oxygenated water. Small portable wire cages containing menhaden can be immersed alongside shore fishermen, but only a few fish can be kept alive for an hour or two this way.

Like the mullet, menhaden are found along the Gulf and Atlan-

Dead menhaden, and even an occasional striped bass, littered this beach when marauding bluefish moved in. (Photo: Terry McDonnell)

tic coasts, although their tightly packed schools move much farther north. Menhaden also are called mossbunker, bunker, and pogies.

Killifish

Small marsh dwellers such as killifish can be caught by the bucketful in cages such as I have described for trapping eels. In fact, I sometimes am frustrated in my attempts to trap eels by killies that throng into my cage, but when there are killie-eating fluke in the vicinity, I'm seldom disappointed.

Alewives

Alewives are caught easily with dip nets when they head up herring runs on their spring spawning sprees. When crowds or "Keep Out" signs make dipping impossible, a weighted treble jigged

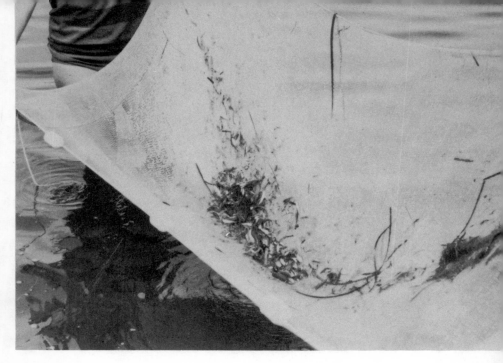

A few minutes with a net in a tidal inlet can supply all the bait you'll need. (Photo: Les Martin)

Hooking a live alewife through the back. If you're careful to miss the spine, this baitfish will really work hard for you.

across the run's entrance often will snag one. Occasionally a striper lurking outboard of the school will dart in and grab a hooked cripple, so stay alert.

When the run is on, even shore fishermen devise ways to deliver live alewives to recently arrived stripers. A few Junes ago while drifting seaworms from an anchored outboard alongside the steep shoreline of a small Cape Cod bay, Bill Stone and I watched three guys haul a plastic bucket through trees, between cottages, down a hill, across a marsh, and onto the beach half a cast in front of us. Opening a weighted mesh cage, they poured in a dozen or so fresh alewives, sank and tethered the cage in shallow water, drifted their baits along the bank, and caught three bruiser bass while Bill and I watched enviously.

"Lots of work," observed Bill, "but you can't argue with success like that. And besides, where are you going to beat the price?"

Waders, slickers, gaffs, lights—all are part of the surfman's arsenal.

5
Accessories

THE RIGHT TACKLE ENABLES YOU to catch fish. The right extras enable you to catch them in comfort and safety, and also add a fine edge to your efficiency.

As every wife knows who's ever bought a bonnet and then had to add a whole new outfit to match it, accessories can be endless. As every husband who's had to write the checks realizes, their cost can be crippling. With the exception of beach buggies, there is little fat in the list that follows. A few changes can be made—substitutions such as chinos for waders in tropical locales; eliminations such as bug spray on an autumn-cool beach—but ultimately most surfmen will want to acquire all of them.

Slicker

After many soggy years in the surf, I finally broke down and invested in an expensive slicker.

"Same kind as they wear on the Grand Banks," said the salesman. "And"—the clincher—"no America's Cup crew would be without one."

That settled it. If it was good enough for Ted Hood, it was good enough for me. I handed him the twenty-four dollars, confident that my garment's moistureproof construction and corrosionproof plastic zipper would guarantee many years of warm dry fishing. Today it's in tatters, two big unrepairable rips reminding me that I should

101

With a good slicker, you can have the best spots all to yourself after the rains arrive.

have been able to predict how easily this material would tear on the thorny thickets that barricade many of my favorite fishing spots. Furthermore, it was too heavy and too hot. On long hauls, its extra ounces slowed me down, sapped my strength; in summer storms I sweltered, often more wet from sweat than I would have been from rain.

An ideal slicker is strong, durable, loose, and light. Its hood and waist can be closed easily with drawstrings, it has elasticized cuffs to prevent water from running up your wrists, and its front is secured by a rustproof zipper that is covered by a flap that either sticks or snaps closed. Recently I found a green nylon garment in a department store that meets all of these specifications, and costs, believe it or not, under five dollars.

Waders

In waders, look for light weight along with rugged construction. Be sure the drawstring around the waist pulls tight and doesn't just bunch up the material. True, you'll probably secure your waist with a belt or a nylon cord onto which you can clip your stringer, but when you forget it, your drawstring is a handy backup. Be sure also that your waders have suspender clips as well as a pocket in front where you can carry a few extra lures.

Try waders on before buying. Proper foot size doesn't ensure proper body fit. A big-butted friend of mine bought waders that were perfect for his feet, but he could barely cram his fanny in; another with extra-long legs couldn't hoist his above his belly button; a stumpy friend had the crotch of his waders snugged before his feet reached their boots.

Check boot bottoms for deep, coarse corrugations that will re-

Hanging waders upside down keeps them dry and ventilated. Few discomforts can match slipping into wet waders on a cold morning.

duce slipping. On wet slimy terrain you may elect to wear chains or cleats or creepers or studded soles, but even on an easy shore, the vagrant weed and the occasional rock always are hazards.

Wool socks over light cotton socks make wearing comfortable and removal easier. Natural-fiber materials absorb moisture and are far more comfortable than synthetics. Wash salt from your waders and hang them feet-up so air can circulate inside. A week in the bottom of a hot closet can make waders smell like King Tut's tomb. While you're fishing, the reek will waft right up into your face. For quick drying after a dunking, attach a vacuum cleaner's hose to its exhaust port and blow the hot air into the waders. Locate leaks by running a flashlight along the inside during total darkness and observing where light peeks through. Holes can be repaired with a rubber patch, the way you would patch a punctured bicycle tire, or with melt-on patching material.

For years I thought there were only three kinds of waders: too big, too small, and leaky. My first set was oversize because I couldn't resist their rock-bottom price. After buying my first surf outfit, there wasn't much left in the treasury, and a little economy was welcome. Looseness, I figured, was small price to pay for a down payment on a couple new plugs I had my eye on. First time I wore them I traipsed all day through a spring sea that was so cold it anesthetized my feet. When the boots rubbed against my heels with every step, I couldn't feel the skin being blistered, then abraded. At day's end, after taking a few waves over my waistline, I poured out quarts of bloodied brine. For a month afterward, I wore slippers to work.

My next set, also a "good deal," were two sizes too small, but I thought I could minimize the pain by walking on tiptoe. Whenever I spotted breaking fish, though, it took me so long to get within casting range that I rarely scored, so I set these waders aside for company. First guest to use them was a wild-eyed Irishman named Joe Heaney with feet like Down East dories. Joe endured the pain for ten minutes, then spent the rest of the night fishing in his underwear.

My third set fit comfortably. They were a gift from my secretary, who, along with being one of New Hampshire's loveliest and most efficient ladies, was wed to a man who worked in a wader factory. Trouble is, his company was experimenting with a new low-cost line and went overboard with their cost-cutting. The material they settled on resembled cheesecloth impregnated with chewing gum. In hot weather it got tacky; in cold I had to put the waders across my knee to bend them. Any time I came within 30 feet of a thornbush or a barnacle, the floodgates opened. After an all-nighter in the suds, my kneecaps were pickled in brine.

My next set fit comfortably, cost under ten dollars, and were impervious to anything short of Mk IV torpedoes. As an added bonus, they were black.

"Great camouflage," I thought. "Black watch cap, a few dabs of lampblack, and no one will be able to see me heading for my favorite holes."

But I headed for no holes in those waders. Talk about heavy! A hernia per mile, guaranteed.

Then a friend showed me a pair he had bought in a discount house for about half the price of the prime pair I currently was trying to con my Beloved into buying for my birthday. Nothing about them was ideal, yet everything was adequate. Even durability has turned out to be good. So far they have survived a season and a half of hard wear with only a slight seepage along one seam.

If there's any lesson to be learned from my experiences, it's that you should know what to look for when shopping for waders. Fit, composition, construction, and weight might have to be compromised to enable you to stay within your budget, but there's a limit below which you never should go in any of these features.

Lights

"Great fishing. Right off the end of the pier. Right under that big light."

"Couldn't catch a fish. Good tide, fast rip, but some donkey kept switching on his light."

"Let's turn on this light and see if we can attract us some fish."

"Turn off that [expletive deleted] light before you spook every fish in the ocean."

"The best light is a miner's lamp."

"The best light is no light at all."

If beaches were bugged after dark, statements like these would be heard often in playbacks of taped conversations between night fishermen. The effects of illumination on after-dark fishing, as well as which light, if any, is best, are argued almost as often as whose turn it is to bring the beer. Dutch Treat solves the beer dilemma, but when partners disagree about illumination, there's little room for compromise. On a narrow stretch of beach, illumination, like it or not, is pretty much a community affair. Opinions about when, how, and whether to employ it had better be shared too.

During half a lifetime of wading beaches, clambering across rocks, sloshing through marshes, and casting from piers, bridges, and jetties, I've seen about every kind of portable light in operation. I've heard them extolled, tolerated, and condemned, and occasionally watched them get jettisoned in disgust. Yet despite the diversity of opinion, I have found that the majority of men who have fished for a variety of nocturnal feeders under a variety of conditions in a variety of environments agree on at least one point: a light can be a help and it can be a hindrance.

Oh, there have been exceptions. Even some of the giants have refused to concede that under the right conditions lights can be beneficial. Charlie Haag, immortal Cuttyhunk guide, was as intolerant of an errant beam on inky Sow and Pigs Reef when he was guiding customers to cow stripers as he was of careless rod handling, and Arnold Clark, one of Massachusetts' super surfmen before he decided to become one of the Bay State's better boatmen, taught himself to tie double improved clinch knots in the dark rather than resort to illumination. But both men fished almost exclusively for striped bass in shallow water, and both men also had colossal cases of piscatorial paranoia—the conviction, shared by all fishermen, that the slightest glow from their favorite grounds will vector in armies of envious interlopers.

Species, conditions, and environment are the key factors in assessing the effects of light on after-dark fishing. Combinations approach the infinite: moon, wind, tide, barometer, bottom, bait, etc. To further complicate matters, there rarely is any way of actually *seeing* how fish react to your light. If fish stopped hitting after you lit a cigarette, *maybe* your match spooked them. If fishing is good along a bridge's light line, *maybe* the light line has something to do with it. Confidence improves every time results are repeated under similar circumstances, but they can't really confirm your conclusions. Without visual reference, you leave the solid ground of certainty and risk sinking occasionally into the soft sand of conjecture.

But, hey, somebody's got to stick his neck out, somebody's got to mine the speculative ore from which Gospel ultimately gets refined, so here goes with a few observations. They're based on some small appreciation of a fish's biology plus a lot of nights up to my keester in ocean, up to eyebrows in spray.

Big solitary fish keep their guards up when prowling close to shore after the sun sets. Yes, I'm aware that these fish have a lot fewer noises to be alert for when bathers have called it a day and boats and fishermen have dwindled to a fraction of their daytime complement. Nevertheless, unlike those anglers who believe that this makes big loners less cautious, I believe it makes them more alert. With all their daytime distractions removed, these fish are able to concentrate on the right-here and the right-now. Alertness, after all, is one of the main reasons they got to be big fish in the first place.

Until big fish are on the attack, they swim slowly, deliberately, as ready to make a quick retreat as they are to pounce on prey. Any abnormality they cannot instantly identify as harmless—the splash of a plug, the flash of a match, the grinding of waders on gravel— is the signal for a fast getaway. In the case of a plug, a spooked fish often will circle back to see if a crippled fish might have caused the commotion, and the caster who lets his plug float for a spell before retrieving usually catches more big fish than the one who starts cranking right away. But a splash, remember, *could* be normal; a bright light can come only from an alien world.

How much light does it take to startle a spooky fish? On a dark night, very little; no more, I suspect, than it takes to jar you out of your pajamas when you're sneaking to the refrigerator for a midnight snack and your daughter, returning from a date, flicks on the kitchen switch.

To appreciate the intensity of the jolt a fish experiences from a sudden brightness, get up in the middle of the night and switch on a light. Hurts like blazes, doesn't it? This is because your eyes, like the fish's, are wide open, your lenses enlarged to let in what little illumination the stars and moon and street lamps can provide. A sudden brightness lances into your brain like a bomb.

And yet one ebony August night, striped bass in a shallow cove seemed to be invalidating all of my ideas when they kept right on cooperating despite the continual flashing of photographer Terry McDonnell's electronic strobe. Terry and I had inched along a narrow underwater ridge that marked where mushy mud merged with solid sand so we could get some photos for a story about after-dark stripers. Slaps from the direction of a broad creekmouth told me where to aim my 5-inch shallow-swimming plug, and on my third cast I connected.

"Stand by," I told Terry, "this is probably the one and only fish we'll get to photograph tonight."

But it wasn't. Slaps seemed to be suspended for a few minutes following each flash, but they resumed within seconds. During the twenty minutes before the tide turned in and the action turned off, Terry and I took all the fish—*and* all the photos—we could handle.

Is there a contradiction here? I think not, for four reasons. First, these were school fish. I am convinced that when fish are schooled, they share some kind of collective confidence. A few genuinely endangered members might trigger an every-man-for-himself exodus, but unless the danger is real, individual fish will startle but stay put.

Second, most of these fish were facing away from me. With their noses into the current waiting for bait to come out of the creek, they received Terry's flashes from behind.

Third, these fish were aggressively feeding. With much of their attention diverted to herding and attacking sandeels, they were less attentive to abnormalities, especially if these abnormalities lasted only a thousandth of a second.

Which brings me to reason number four: the flashes, despite their suddenness and brightness, were so brief that they barely registered in the bass' brain. As Terry put it later, "Those fish were startled, sure, but it was a 'Hey, what was that?' startle, not a 'Let's get the hell out of here' startle."

Sustained flashes, though, these are different. Somewhere between Terry's thousandth of a second and the two-second flash I once saw send stripers scurrying across a shallow bar, there may be some mathematically computable threshold below which it's safe to stay, but even this would have to be factored for phosphorescence, roily water, moonlight, intensity of illumination, and Lord knows what else. The only safe way is to employ a light as seldom as possible for as briefly as possible, shielding the glow and walking well back from the water. As one of my early mentors pointed out, "Scanning a beach with a flashlight can turn up valuable G-2—turbulence over a submerged boulder, samples of recently slaughtered bait—but no strategy can pay off on fish that already have scooted."

If you feel the need for such reconnoitering, slip a red filter—a snug-fitting disk of dark-red plastic will do—under your light's lens. Charter skippers use such lights when gaffing fish, removing hooks, and unsnarling lines, and they keep right on racking up impressive scores.

Steady lights, on the other hand, can magnetize fish. The glows from oil rigs are notorious hot spots. So are beams from piers and bridges. The attraction here is bait. Reassured, perhaps, by the knowledge that cautious predators eschew light, small baitfish congregate in the cone of a beam or on the illuminated side of the line beneath bridges where light and shadow meet. Occasionally an aggressive gamefish will hit and run. I have experienced many a mini-coronary on the Cape Cod Canal when big bass have blasted into shoals of spearing that congregate in the glow of lights from the Corps of Engineers road above the steep riprapped bank. Normally, though, these fish wait just inside the shadows, satisfied to pick up an occasional careless stray until an accelerating tidal flow abets their deadly game.

Imagine the confusion that must develop—oops, *probably* develops—when a heavy concentration of bait can no longer cope with a current. Fish on the downcurrent edge of an illuminated area feel it first. Struggling to stay put, they are pushed harder and harder by the upcurrent mass until finally they are forced from light to darkness. The sudden change disorients them. Confusion compounds their fear. Panicking to regain the security of the light they have left, they swim along the crowded shadow hoping to break through the barrier back into brightness before they are caught. Those that make it are blinded. Desperate, they lash out in any direction, communicating their fright until in a matter of seconds a smooth responsive school becomes a frenzied milling mass . . . easy pickings for predators that have been waiting in the wings for it to happen.

And what conclusions have I drawn (all right, tentatively drawn) from my after-dark speculations? That the best beach light is, indeed, no light at all: one fewer thing to buy and carry, one fewer source of breakdowns, one fewer way of spooking fish. Nevertheless, you need illumination. In emergencies it's essential for removing hooks from fingers or flashing distress signals, and, if you're a newcomer to night fishing, you'll appreciate the occasional reassurance of being able to see where you are and what you are doing.

With experience, you'll find yourself relying less and less on your light. In time you'll learn to tie knots just as fast by touch, to check for weeds by silhouetting your lure against the glow of moon or stars or lights on a far shore. Once when I forgot my last-resort light, the Aurora Borealis helped me unsnarl my line. No, I couldn't see every strand, but what I couldn't see I felt.

A marvelous machine, the human body. When it's deprived of one sense, all others rush to the rescue by becoming more alert, more responsive. Hearing, for example, is honed to a fine edge, enabling you to isolate and identify the slap of feeding fish from among night's myriad murmurs. As you acquire experience, you wade with confidence, angling your feet accurately into the current, probing as you proceed, alert for rocks, weeds, holes, and fish, and primed like a pistol to react.

The ideal light? One that is portable, compact, lightweight, inexpensive, bright, narrow-beamed, and easily directed. For stay-put beach fishing, a properly employed gasoline lantern continues to lead the pack. But none is perfect. Each has liabilities along with its assets. Here are a few personal observations about some of the more popular types.

Gas lanterns

The steady sustained brilliance of gas lanterns makes them the next best thing to daylight. For tying knots, baiting hooks, and seeing which sandwich is ham and which is baloney, they're an incomparable convenience. For my money, though, they have one glaring deficiency: every time a body passes through their glow, fish can get frightened. To avoid this, locate your lantern well back in the sand, where its light won't reach the water.

On the other hand, you might want to try attracting bait by letting your lantern's light reach the water and taking care that no

A gas lantern, popular with stay-put fishermen, can spook fish as well as attract them. (Photo: Terry McDonnell)

one, including passing strollers, walks between water and lantern. It can work. On bright nights I've seen fish foraging in lantern-lighted shallows. Ironically, most beach fishermen heave their baits as far from shore as they're able, ignoring the possibilities of a short cast into illuminated water. Some night try two baits, one near, one far, and compare.

Miner's light

At first glance, the miner's light appears to be an ideal choice for night fishing. It has an elasticized band around your head, and the silver-dollar-size spot in the middle of your brow shines on your hands when your head is tilted forward and your hands are raised to the right level. But the compromise between tipped head and elevated hands can be an awkward one to make. Head shape and eye location require careful adjustments if you are to minimize the inconvenience of trying to tie knots with your eyeballs two-blocked in their sockets.

Another disadvantage of the miner's light is that its battery has to be located some distance from your head, in a shirt or pants pocket. Not only does this mean taking up precious cargo space with a heavy container about the size of two cigarette packs, but lamp and power source have to be connected by wires. First time I tried using one I almost strangled myself casting.

A third disadvantage is that the headband stretches. When not in use, it's worn around your neck. Raising it to your forehead is merely a matter of grab and lift when it clings close and stays put, but when it's loose and limp, you need two hands to get it in place. Then when you dip your head to work on a knot, your visor keeps getting cut off as the weight of the lamp pulls the headband across your eyes.

Leave it around your neck all the time? Sure, you can do that, although frequent positioning probably will be required, but read on. There are easier and less expensive ways.

Cost of one friend's lamp was less than four dollars. Almost twenty years ago the one I used cost more than ten. But based on how easily the only moving part in my friend's lamp broke, I predict that cheap parts and shoddy workmanship will soon take their toll.

Long before that, though, I think he'll be back to his old pocket flashlight. He's a mover, always on the prowl, preferring to chase fish rather than wait for them to come to him. Swapping a single 6-inch cylinder for a cumbersome three-element illumination system just doesn't make sense.

Disposable lights

A recent innovation in on-the-spot illumination is a disposable light about the size of a bar of bath soap. First one I saw I bought. "Never need to replace batteries or bulbs" read the sign on which the sample was displayed. "Just use till your light is exhausted, then replace." For a dollar and a half, how could I go wrong?

By ignoring the economically obvious fact that a buck and a half doesn't buy much of anything these days, that's how. Especially flashlights that come equipped with built-in bulbs and batteries and convenient clips on their pretty plastic cases. Second time I used it, its light had dimmed by about one-third, and it hadn't been exactly A-bomb bright to begin with.

To be a contender, a throw-away light has to have long-lasting candlepower. This costs money, and throw-aways must, by definition, be inexpensive. Conclusion: a good idea, but an economic contradiction.

Penlight

Years ago a friend gave me a clip-on flashlight about the size of a fat fountain pen. I liked its small spot, light weight, and convenience. By slipping it onto my shirtfront, I could keep it handy and out of the spray. Its only deficiency was that I had to keep my finger on its button while using it: no push, no light. Then I found one that not only stayed on without continuous pressing, but had the additional advantage of having its bulb at the end of a 3-inch flexible cable; just press its button, twist its gooseneck in whatever direction I desired, and have two hands free. But the gooseneck drove me ding-dong. The slightest shift in my body made its spot veer off target.

Furthermore, I've never been able to get used to a clip-on's awkwardness. I like a clip-on's carrying convenience, all right, but for positive control in operation, I prefer to hold my penlight in my mouth. And that's exactly what I do today with my new push-once-for-ON, twice-for-OFF penlight.

Stringer

First requirement for a stringer is that it be rustproof. I have found only two that fill the bill. One is a nylon cord whose lightness is appealing but whose clips are too weak to hold heavy fish. The other is a brass chain. Though heavy and expensive, it seems to last forever and it contains two or three more clips than normal. The extra clips mean extra length, but I keep the chain from snagging bottom or entangling my legs by snapping both ends to my belt.

Plug Bag

How to tote a variety of lures, get at them quickly when you need them, make sure they won't hook up with one another while in storage, and keep them out of your way while casting? Pockets in slickers tear too easily, offer little protection for flesh against hooks, and usually are crammed with other gear. Knapsacks are hard to get at and usually produce a jumble of intertwined lures and leaders. Compartmented plug bags worn over the shoulder, although a bother, are your best bet. These come in either fabric or hard plastic shells with removable dividers.

Gaff

Portable gaffs are perilous. Their points, which must be needle-sharp to penetrate the armored hides of tarpon, channel bass, and striped bass, puncture clothing and skin at a touch. Cork and rubber caps offer only brief protection. A short walk, a few waves, and invariably they fall off. Gaffs with retractable heads have been marketed, but apparently the demand has been light. I haven't seen one on a tackle counter in at least five years.

Fortunately a surf angler doesn't need a gaff when he has waves to help him work fish ashore, and in waveless backwaters he can fight a fish to the finish before beaching it. But on jetties a long-handled gaff is a must. Shafts should be painted white, and handles

A gaff, though inconvenient to carry, can be invaluable when you need it.

should have a leather wrist loop and be shaped for firm gripping.

Pliers

Wrestle a fresh fish with a pair of treble hooks firmly embedded in its jaws, and maybe for good measure a third treble hanging from its brow, and you'll understand why hands need help in extracting hooks. Pliers don't have to be heavy to be strong, but a long beak is helpful when a hook is hung deep in a fish's throat. Storage in a plastic sandwich bag keeps off-duty pliers dry and rust-free.

Priest

The surfman's priest is a small billy club, preferably with a little lead in its head, for killing freshly caught fish. For most fish, one or two well placed raps between the eyes is all it takes. Bluefish, however, require a couple of extra clouts, and even then they should be handled with the same care you'd give a vial of nitro.

Tape Measure and Scales

Tape measures and pocket scales that I have used near salt water have rusted so quickly that I've had to jettison them after only a few trips. But I don't miss them. The only need I have for a tape is to see if a fish exceeds minimum length, and this I can do by scribing two marks a foot apart on my rod. The only weights that interest me are of fish far bigger than a pocket scale can handle. Most seaside bait shops have heavyweight scales. When they're closed, my bathroom scale suffices. No, I don't plop the fish right on top; my family long ago notified me that they don't appreciate slime on their soles and scales between their toes. What I do is weigh myself with the fish, then without it, and subtract.

Knife

Small, sharp, and sheathed—these are the qualities you want in a knife. Wash yours promptly and dry it thoroughly after each session in the salt, and resharpen its blade frequently. A few minutes of honing can save you many minutes—and pounds—when filleting.

Scaler

Probably the best investment I ever made in fishing equipment is the fifteen cents I paid for a fork-size piece of aluminum that scales any fish in seconds. One pass from aft forward, and its stiff sharp points pry off every scale in its path, providing the fish has not been allowed to dry out. Scaling a dried-out fish can be a terribly tedious task, but anyone improvident enough to allow a fish's scales to harden and seal deserves all the drudgery he gets.

Insect Repellent

Nothing beats a ripe raunchy stogie for keeping bugs at bay, but after three or four of them your mouth feels like Vesuvius. Repellents are your only alternative. With collar tight and long sleeves buttoned, spray generously around neck and wrist. If you're not wearing waders, tuck your trousers inside your socks and spray your ankles as well. Also blast your hat inside and out. For subsequent applications, carry a finger-size stick of repellent; leave the can in your car. Immediately after spraying, rub your palms in wet mud or sand so the repellent won't contaminate your bait or lures.

Hat

I hate hats. So much so that for years I resolutely refused to wear one. Even when rain soaked my mane and sun scorched my scalp, I insisted on meeting the elements head-on and helmetless. Something in my subconscious, I suppose: too much military headgear, too much time at left tackle. Who knows? Then on Father's Day I received a long-visored cap, wore it once so I wouldn't hurt my daughter's feelings, and have worn it faithfully ever since. With its light weight and snug fit, I hardly know it's there, yet it protects my pate from sun, rain, and wind. It's truly amazing how much longer I can endure even subfreezing cold simply because my head is covered. My cap's biggest by-product, though, is my improved vision. With its extra-long visor shading my eyes and polarized lenses covering them, I can spot fish in water that blinded me before.

Beach Buggy

Except for a chunk of waterfront real estate, about the biggest surf-fishing accessory you can buy is a beach buggy. It may be a motorized motel, complete with toilet, shower, and color TV, but on the beach it's a buggy. Chrome, refrigeration, and clean sheets are okay, but first and foremost, any vehicle that insinuates itself into an alien world of sand and salt is supposed to help a man catch more fish. At the very least it cuts down on home-to-foam travel time and extends an angler's operating range. In its highest application—coordinated round-the-clock patrols, driver-to-driver communications—it lets a lot of friendly folk enjoy more action per hour during the few free moments that a busy life leaves for fishing the oceanfront.

Beach buggies provide mobility, comfort, and a base for swapping experiences and plotting strategy. (Photo: Terry McDonnell)

The days of do-it-yourself buggies have long since ended. The clanking contraptions that ground and wheezed their ways across the dunes of Nauset and Montauk, the Jersey beaches, and North Carolina's Outer Banks during the late '40s and on into the '50s have evolved into slick efficient machines with ample storage space and all the creature comforts. Spurred on by America's post-WWII motor-mania and a burgeoning interest in the newly discovered fishing frontier along the sea rim, Detroit accelerated the evolution. Today everything you could want in the way of transportation and accommodations is off-the-shelf and priced accordingly.

Before you buy a buggy, be sure not only of your commitment to surf fishing, but also that you will enjoy a reasonable return on your very substantial investment. Here's how to figure it. Divide a buggy's useful life into its purchase price, subtract probable trade-in value, then factor in taxes and operating expenses to come up with an approximation of what your buggy will cost per year. Divide that figure by the number of days you're likely to be using it, then ask yourself, "Is the price per day reasonable?"

If your answer is "Yes," great. Welcome aboard. If not, factor in the fringe benefits of better fishing, new country, and nice people, and see if that doesn't tip the scales. One final consideration: Will you be renting a vacation cottage at the seashore? Couldn't a buggy serve as well?

Better-built buggies have not necessarily meant better fishing conditions. Predictably, the considerate majority has had to bear the burden of the callused few. While most of the buggy brigade conscientiously policed their sites, toted their trash, and avoided the destruction of grasses around which sands collected, a minority of shortsighted slobs projected an image of to-hell-with-everyone-but-me irresponsibility. Buggy jockeys have had to buck a tide of prejudice and restrictions—access, deportment, length of stay, etc.—ever since.

Fortunately the more prophetic and practical of the pioneers could see the confrontation coming. In September 1949, the Massachusetts Beach Buggy Association was formed on Cape Cod's Nauset Beach, its sixty-two charter members agreeing to police themselves and to confer with authorities to ensure that the surf would remain open to all anglers on wheels. Today the 2,500-member MBBA, as well as similar organizations along America's seaboard for which it was the prototype, continues to work for equitable solutions to the complex problems of overcrowding, littering, and pollution.

You should know not just the fish you're after, but the fish the fish you're after is after. Examine a fish's stomach to see what's on the menu, then duplicate or simulate it.

6

Surf Species

THE BEST FISH? *Best* is a tricky term in the surf, where records topple with the tides and each new species comes garlanded with its own special assortment of superlatives. Best what? Size, speed, beauty, strength, stamina, performance? Even an unspectacular encounter can be made memorable by a beautiful setting, compatible company, an appreciative frame of mind, or because it culminates a long drought or a hard stalk. That striper I played from a quiet beach one long-gone summer dawn was not exceptional in any way by striper standards, yet I recall every tug of its tussle, every scale of its body, because I shared this victory with a big buck deer as it leaped and stomped in the wavelets only a couple of casts away. Those tinker mackerel were no big deal, even on a flyrod, but, hey, I was only eight years old at the time. That Cuban barracuda wouldn't even give me a tumble; it just lay there ignoring my offerings, spurning my challenges, yet even today, more than twenty years later, I can still close my eyes and see clearly the cold elemental menace of that face.

But, of course, there is a *best* fish. It's *that* one. Right out there. Eyeing my bait, stalking my lure. See it? No, maybe you can't see it. Not yet. But you will, you will.

A surf fisherman soon cultivates the conviction that his every cast is going to interest a fish. No maybes, no reservations. If he positions his lure where he wants it to go and retrieves it the way he means it to move, then That Fish should strike. If he doesn't, the fault is his: his cast was off-target, his retrieve was off-course.

There are no rehearsals for the serious surf fisherman. Every cast runs up the curtain on a shoot-out between him and That Fish out There. He has learned its habits, studied its strengths, discerned its weaknesses. This is the carefully calculated time, this is the precisely plotted place. The right offering presented in the right way *has* to work.

Which, of course, is absurd. For any one of a hundred easily overlooked reasons, for any one of a thousand imperceptible ones, fish just might not be interested. A recent meal might have put them off their feed, a recent scare might have put them on their guard. They might, in fact, not even be there.

But these possibilities have no place in the strategy of a surfman who has done his homework. Probabilities, these are his currency. By learning all he can about his quarry, he can predict with a high degree of dependability where it will be and how it will act under any given set of conditions. Certainty sets in. He plays for keeps. Even the bait-Fisherman tending his rod, sipping a beer, counting the stars, is coiled to react to the ratcheting summons of a running fish that he knew all along was about to strike.

Confidence in surf fishing is an amalgam of awareness, computation, and experience. First, you have to know your fish and how they are affected by time, tide, weather, topography, and the myriad other elements that influence their behavior. Next you must continuously calculate the consequences of any changes in these elements that might dictate a different lure, technique, or location. Finally, you have to put your theories into practice.

This chapter is about Those Fish out There. Observations about fish in general and surf fish in particular are complemented by profiles of species popular along the Atlantic, Gulf, and Pacific coasts.

Fish can see, hear, smell, and taste, but with limitations and peculiarities that are products of long evolutionary adaptation to their environment. Their eyesight, for example, is good only at short range. Because their pupils cannot contract, they see best in dim light. Unquestionably this is one reason why fish normally feed most actively at dawn and dusk and why overcast days often are more productive than bright sunny ones.

A fish's limited vision is offset by an acute sense of hearing. Though sensitive only to low-frequency sounds, it quickly alerts a fish to the plop of your plug, the crunch of your waders. Vibrations are detected by an ear inside the head and a lateral-line canal along head and body. These also aid in maintaining balance.

Sharks and salmon are the ocean's most dramatic demonstrators of a fish's ability to smell. Sharks home in unerringly on bleeding prey, and salmon are summoned back to the rivers of their birth by the distinctive smell of their natal waters.

Remember how you used to catch freshwater catfish with stink-baits that reeked so badly they almost rotted your hooks? One salt-water fly-fisherman I know advocates the same practice. He ties his streamers with moisture-absorbent hair and soaks them overnight in the juices of dead fish before putting them to work. A canny Yankee bait-fisherman pounds pieces of mackerel or menhaden into a beach at low tide, then returns at high tide to harvest the fish that have homed in on the oily aroma. A more conventional method of chumming the surf is to anchor a chumpot in front of you while casting, but I have had success standing in a tideway with a perforated can of fish-based catfood clipped to my stringer.

If you have caught largemouth bass on plastic worms, you can appreciate how little taste must mean to a fish. The technique calls for allowing a largemouth to run with your worm until you are confident that the worm's hook is inside the fish's mouth. Sometimes you have to delay more than a minute. All this time the bass is mouthing a piece of plastic that it thinks is a nightcrawler or a leech. Obviously softness and texture mean much more than taste.

The same is true of saltwater species, although the parallel is not perfect. Surf fish rarely feed casually or run leisurely. Normally there is keen competition for every meal from other members of a school. Food is grabbed and gulped before it is snatched away.

To get an idea of how competitive eating must be among schooling surf fish, watch the gulls next time you toss out a scrap from a fish you're cleaning. Note how, with all their jabbering and harassing, the first bird to get the meat in its mouth seldom is the one that winds up eating it. Competition in a school of frenzied bluefish must be this multiplied by a million.

By grabbing your soft plastic lure quickly, a fish enables you to avoid the nerve-numbing ordeal of watching line peel from your spool while you wait for the right moment to set your hook. You can, and in fact should, set almost immediately. Saltwater hooks are bigger, heavier, more easily detected than the fine wire ones in your largemouth lure.

There is a controversy here worth considering. One group maintains that surf fish are not nearly so sensitive to the presence of hooks as is commonly thought.

"These fish," they insist, "dine regularly on clams, crabs, mussels. They're conditioned to accept hard sharp shells. Why not hard sharp hooks?"

Unbelievers counter with, "What's hard and sharp about a nice soft mullet or menhaden or sandeel or squid? With bottom-feeders, sure, you can bury a hook in a clam or a crab or even a chunk of cut bait without worry of detection, but when fish are feeding on live bait . . ."

Which side is right? Both, but not completely. I have had many fish run 40, 50, 100 yards with my mackerel, menhaden, and alewives despite #4/0 treble hooks in these baits' lips or backs; I have had hot bottom-fishing suddenly go cold for no other discernible reason than that my hook was not camouflaged by my bait.

Solutions to surf-fishing problems seldom are clear-cut. Remember, we are mere humans trying to fathom the irrational behavior of animals that inhabit an unseen world whose complexities we cannot begin to comprehend. Until a result occurs many times in precisely the same way under unvaryingly identical conditions, we are just speculators stumbling through the shifting sands of conjecture. And things seldom are exactly the same in the delightfully dynamic domain of the surfman. What effect does a half-degree difference in water temperature have on fish that are primed to migrate? On fish with no air bladders? On fish with full bellies? Empty bellies? Half-full bellies? Which particular half-degree are we talking about? Can we consider water temperature separately from salinity, turbulence, weeds, sand, suspended chemicals (which chemicals?), barometric pressure, wind direction and velocity, and countless other factors, including how good you feel and how well you're fishing? In any argument, listen carefully to both sides, then seek your solution somewhere in between. Meanwhile, fish often play the odds, and when you're not sure, give the fish the benefit of your doubts.

Do not, however, give fish credit for being brighter than they are. Fish are not smart. Smart means brainy, able to analyze, reason, conclude, execute. A fish's minuscule mentality does not function this way. Its reactions are instinctive, reflexive. Walt-Disney them all you want; during your sentimental moments, anthropomorphize them with dignity, sportsmanship, sex appeal, a sense of humor. But when you're concerned with the cold hard business of killing, keep in mind that fish are beautiful dumb brutes, nothing more. To expect them to react rationally is to sabotage your strategy before you start.

Fish respond to three urges: survival, sex, and hunger. All can be exploited to increase your catch. In shallow water, for example, fish feed with their guards up. They are vulnerable and they know it. The comforting cover of a big boulder is a natural lie for a big fish, especially when wind or current is delivering meals right to its doorstep.

Wading and casting on open water must be done with the caution of a cat burglar. Fish feeding on shallow flats are like racehorses in a starting gate. A splash, a shadow, a sudden change in your silhouette, and they're off. Bonefish and permit are notoriously nervous, fish, probably because they do most of their dining along the clear shallow fringes of tropical islands.

Noise is not always detrimental to fishing. Fall off a rock and the splash will empty the area faster than a shark convention, but stir up a fuss with your lure and you're likely to attract customers. Unnatural noises are the ones to avoid. Plops and blups and splashes that *could* be made by baitfish probably will be inspected by any hungry fish within hearing to see if they *are* being made by baitfish.

Nights pose a problem in that illumination often is required for tying knots, baiting hooks, untangling lines, lighting cigars, etc. Controversy again. Some say no lights of any kind under any circumstances, then spend a half-hour of an ideal tide trying to poke a sprig of mono through the almost invisible eye of a plug. Others, contending that light attracts bait and bait attracts fish, lantern their stretch of beach like Luna Park, then spook every fish, bait included, by projecting their silhouettes across the water. In Chapter 5 I devote a lot of space to light—kinds available, pros and cons of each, when and how to use them.

How can a fish's sex habits enable you to outwit it? Boy plugs for girl fish? Girl plugs for boy fish? No, lure manufacturers have not yet reached this level of sophistication. The only successful exploitation of the piscine sex urge that I have heard of outside a marine laboratory was done on shad. During the peak of a spring spawning run, action suddenly ceased along an angler's favorite stretch of stream. He knew there were fish in every pool, 5- and 6-pounders, but for some reason they had interrupted their noisy courtship ritual: roe-laden hens no longer splashed erratically; anxious bucks no longer bumped eggs from the females' vents. So the enterprising angler supplied his own eggs. Squeezing the stomach of a ripe hen he had caught a short time earlier, he soon had the boy shad bumping the girl shad, which forced out more eggs, which amplified the jacks' ardor, which . . . *vive l'amour!* While I have found no suitable application in the surf for this man's ingenuity, I have benefited from knowing when and where a species spawns and the routes it takes to reach its spawning area.

A fish's feeding habits are its Achilles heel. Predict location, time, and composition of its next meal, be there to present a realistic imitation in a lifelike manner, and the fish is as good as in your freezer. (*If* your hook is sharp, *if* your line isn't frayed, *if* you keep a tight line, *if* . . .) Where and when a fish feeds depends on many factors, the most important of which are discussed in the following chapter. What it eats varies with species, location, and, most important, what happens to be on the menu at the moment. Sure, pompano prefer sand bugs, but they're not going to pass up coquina clams when bugs are scarce; cod might be seeking smelt when they're foraging along a shore, but they'll rarely ignore a fresh juicy clamneck; weakfish are pushovers for seaworms, but not when grass shrimp are so plentiful that they can get all they want without working for them. Always check the water's edge for freshly killed bait, keep alert for scurrying schools of baitfish, and examine the stomach contents of the first fish you catch. When you have concluded what's on the bill of fare, duplicate or simulate it—size, shape, brightness, color, movement, *everything*.

Fish, of course, will strike for reasons other than hunger. Curiosity can capture their attention, anger can provoke their wrath. Even fish so full that their bellies bulge will eat a bait that another fish is attacking, and bluefish seem to kill for the sheer joy of killing.

Do fish remember? I think so. At least to the extent that a particularly perilous experience makes them more wary in the future. After a fish has broken free, it usually sulks briefly, recuperates for as long as it takes its injury to heal, and then resumes feeding. Who is to say that it is not more selective thereafter?

Yes, I realize that memory implies a mentality of much higher refinement than fish possess. No, there's no need to remind me that I cautioned a few paragraphs back against giving fish credit for being smart, for being anything more than the beautiful dumb brutes they are. But, you see, I'm an incorrigible talker in the surf. (Singer, dancer, and laugher, too.) I talk to sun, moon, stars, birds, wind, fog, weeds, rocks, and sand, about joy, love, beauty, people, beer, coffee, candy bars, yesterday, today, tomorrow, and forever. But mostly I talk about fish. And mostly I talk about my lure out there and how those fish really ought to notice it, the way it wiggles and wobbles and dives and splashes, just like a real injured baitfish, and how easy it would be for them to catch it and kill it and eat it, and how sorry they'll be if they miss this once-in-a-lifetime opportunity—things like that. And do you know—I think it works.

Striped Bass

Striped bass and surf fishermen were made for each other. Although stripers occasionally are caught up to a mile or two offshore, they are inshore fish by nature, partial to tidewater, where bait abounds and clashing currents give a strong fast predator an advantage in pursuing smaller weaker prey. Serious bassmen study stripers the way handicappers study horses so they can be in the right place ready to cast when bass break into bait within range of their artillery.

Besides baitfish such as menhaden, mackerel, spearing, and anchovies, stripers appreciate the rich supply of worms, shellfish, and crustaceans that dwell casting-close to shore. The man who lobs clams into a surf that's subsiding after a storm knows that stripers are out there scouring the bottom for clams that have been uncovered by the buffeting, just as the man who drifts crabs alongside a jetty is trying to tempt stripers that patrol these sanctuaries in search of rock-dwellers that stray too far from safety.

The striped bass looks and acts the way a surf fish should. Generally about four times as long as it is deep, it has a tapered, jut-jawed prow, a pair of tall triangular dorsal fins for maneuvering,

Striped bass are favorites of fishermen on both coasts and even in inland waters.

and a broad flat tail that propels it at impressive attacking speeds. Above its white belly, seven or eight longitudinal stripes run along scale rows on its silvery sides. The striper's back can be green, blue, black, and occasionally even a reddish brown.

Size is one of the species' main attractions. While most stripers are under-10-pound schoolies, over-20-pound trophies are caught frequently from shore. When fishing for stripers, there's always a chance you'll tie into a mounting-size prize. Bass bigger than boatman Ed Kirker's 72-pound rod-and-reel record cruise close enough to shore to encourage surfmen in the belief that they might someday win all the marbles. Even Kirker's leviathan, though boated rather than beached, was caught in narrow Canapitsit Channel, separating Cuttyhunk and Nashawena islands in the Elizabeth Chain south of

Cape Cod. I have plugged much of this water from shore, caught a lot of modest size fish. Someday, who knows?

Cuttyhunk is a name that all striper devotees soon come to recognize. Anglers who are provincially partial to their own bass waters might dispute its claim to the title of Striper Capital of the World, but statistics are convincing. It was off this tiny island that Charlie Cinto boated his 73-pounder in 1967; only an island to the east where Charles Church, fishing out of Cuttyhunk back in 1913, brought one of equal size aboard. Neither is recognized as an official record by the International Game Fish Association, Church's because his line was not tested, Cinto's because he was using wire line and ganged hooks, but both are impressive catches.

During the final third of the nineteenth century and for a few years into the twentieth, Cuttyhunk also was appreciated for its surf fishing. Affluent Eastern aristocrats formed the famed Cuttyhunk Fishing Association in 1865. Amidst plush accommodations, they paid local guides a dollar for their services plus a day's supply of lobster-tail baits which they chucked from rickety wood-and-metal platforms. Catches were numerous, though rarely big, and all are recorded in the annals of the Association's clubhouse, now a private residence. By 1907, bass had become so scarce that the Association ceased its activities.

Recently while plugging from atop one of the mammoth boulders that stud the Cuttyhunk shore, I discovered that I was standing on a rusted-out hole that once had held a casting platform's leg. The years seemed to telescope and I heard ghosts kibitzing above the wail of the wind.

Modern-day pilgrims have become more appreciative of the Cuttyhunk surf. Main attraction still is, and always will be, charter fishing, where trophy catches are everyday occurrences, but by plugging the beach between boat trips, a man can enjoy the best of both worlds. As a means of getting a last crack at a pair of almost grown-up sons who are soon to sever the final fragile umbilical strands that bind them to home and hearth, I recommend the combination to all fathers.

Jack was twenty-one, Dan twenty, when I led them to a sprawl of wave-walloped rocks at the base of a towering clay cliff at the island's west end. All their lives we had fished together, from suburban Boston to the backwoods of Maine, for everything from suckers to salmon, but this was going to be the big one, the feature attraction. Unlike most such plans, where dreams rarely measure up to deeds, that's exactly how it turned out.

On an earlier trip I had found fish among these rocks during the same bottom half of a coming tide. On a foggy dawn, after probing almost every foot of the island's shore for two days and two nights, I had discovered bass just beyond the breakers, good fish, 5-to-15-pounders, plus one bruiser with enough authority to grab my plug, head for Martha's Vineyard a dozen miles across Vineyard Sound, and scoff over her shoulder at my feeble efforts to restrain her.

After lunch at the Allen House, one of the island's two inns, and an informative chat with proprietors Ken and Mildred Fullerton, the boys and I headed out-island: through flowered fields, past pebbled beaches, up a gentle slope where a doe paused, twitched her antenna-ears, and bounded over a hedgerow into the brushy beginning of the wilderness that still occupies most of the island.

"WELCOME," said a sign, "c'mon into our property. Enjoy it as we do. But please, no beer cans or candy wrappers." These aren't the exact words, but the sentiments and sincerity are accurate. Most visitors had complied, but the discarded film box, the gum wrapper, the cheap wine bottle in the bushes all confirmed the callused disregard of the inevitable few. May their every fish break off.

"Only one way to get these fish," I told Jack and Dan as we rigged our poppers at the crest of the steep stony shore. "Get right out there with them. Water's cold, but it won't kill you. Just be careful of those slippery rocks. You're not wearing nonskid sneakers."

Wading up to their waists in waves that occasionally toppled them feet over fanny, they were fighting fish before I could score my first hit. Fact is, I never did get my first hit. Lobbing a big plug far offshore in hopes of bagging a braggin'-size bass, I watched enviously as Jack hung eight 5-pounders in eight casts into a shallow rock-rimmed bowl less than 50 feet across. When Dan accepted Jack's "C'mon over," he did as well.

Our half-hour walk back to the Allen House was a dad's delight. My smile was broader than the beam the boys laid across their shoulders for carrying their catch. But this episode, as it turned out, was only Act I.

After dinner, as I was filleting the boys' bass by the shore, Jack hustled down the hillside to announce that Bob Bauer was about to leave the dock. "Yeah," he said, "Bob's charter couldn't make it. You and Dan and I are scheduled to take their place if we can be dockside in ten minutes."

We ran all the way. An opportunity like this was too good to pass up. Normally charters must be booked weeks, even months in advance. Finding an opening on the spur of the moment is like walking up to the stadium window on Super Bowl Sunday and buying a pair of 50-yard-line seats.

Bob's 23-foot MacKenzie bass boat was built for the heavy seas that pound Sow and Pigs Reef, and Bob, a young handsome Cuttyhunk native, was born and bred to the task of guiding her with radar accuracy through an inky night. Astride his stern tiller, he faced forward during the ten-minute run to the reef and instructed the boys, seated in the trolling chairs, on how to let out line.

"Keep your thumb on the spool. Otherwise the wire will spring loose. One bad kink and you're out of business. Okay now," he said as he swung his stern into the rip, "can you feel your plugs working?"

Jack barely had time to acknowledge that he did when a yank on his line almost jerked him hard against the transom. No hookup. Just a hit, a reminder that these were bigger, stronger bass than my boys ever had locked horns with; a preview of what was to come: hard jarring hits followed by arm-aching battles culminating in a flashing gaff and an expertly administered *coup de grace*. Eighteen stripers up to 30 pounds were boated during our three hours of rolling, roaring, crashing blackness, and all the while our skipper stood smiling, smoking, chatting; totally in control, imperturbably efficient.

"You like fishing?" Dan asked Bob during a lull in the action. (I suspect that by now, with weariness and fatigue taking their toll, he was marveling, as his dad had done years before, at how any mere mortal can endure so exhausting an occupation day after day.)

"Sure do," answered Bob. "Be doing something else if I didn't."

The simple secret of contentment. A message for young men wondering where in this big bewildering world they belong. More than the bass and the boat and the night, more than the excitement and the adventure, I was indebted to Bob for these words.

Later with the catch offloaded and iced down, my sons and I

strolled up the empty streets to the Allen House, where coffee and doughnuts always are set out in the kitchen. Night was everywhere as we walked, deep night, dark night, dense night, a soft presiding presence unshattered by traffic's blare or neon's glare. The only sound besides our muted steps and whispered words was the distant sighing of the sea.

After coffee, the boys were ready for bed. It had been a long, hard, enjoyable day, and now that they knew Cuttyhunk, they could return at their leisure. When you're twenty, your treasury of time has hardly been tapped. Sleep is not yet an extravagance. Me, I had a date with a father and son from New York to fish the dawn tide at the West End, then I was scheduled to jig for mackerel off the town dock with two little girls, and after that . . .

Spring to fall is striper season. Occasionally they are caught in winter, but low temperatures keep them dormant and out of their in-season haunts. Annual northward migrations start along the East Coast in the spring after spawning occurs in the upper Hudson and Chesapeake's headwaters.

Remaining in residence throughout the summer all the way up into Nova Scotia, they start their return trip in the fall, when storms and cooling waters send them south. A few areas enjoy small year-round populations, but these are rare today. Leslie Thompson in his delightful *Fishing in New England* (D. Van Nostrand Co., New York/Toronto, 1955) tells of dining on a striper netted through the ice of the Parker River in northern Massachusetts during February 1932, and refers to commercial winter fisheries not only in the Parker but in Maine's Sheepscot. I suspect that the striper's vulnerability to being caught in the 4-foot nets that were lowered through the slots in the ice crosswise to the current soon wiped out most wintering-over populations.

Early-season feeding sprees are worth waiting a winter for. Fall's pre-migration blitzes are far more spectacular, but they are marred by the realization that when the smoke clears the bass will be gone. Spring is promise as well as pleasure. One whiff of that thymelike fragrance, signaling that bass are near, and grown men, despite their determination to regard striped bass as nothing more than dumb animals, become lovelorn adolescents.

Since 1879, when 110 striped bass were released in the Carquinez Strait near San Francisco, stripers also have been West

Coast residents. These fish were survivors of a 135-fish cargo transported cross-country in wooden tanks via railroad car by Livingston Stone of the U.S. Fish Commission. The transplant was a logistic triumph. With nothing more than ice to control water temperature, hand-agitation to aerate water, and sea salt to regulate salinity, enough of the fragile youngsters survived the week-long trip to launch what has become a spectacularly successful sport fishery.

Three years later, encouraged by preliminary results of this first transplant, officials shipped another 400 fish up to 9 inches in length from New Jersey's Shrewsbury River to California's Suisun Bay. Better than 75 percent survived to reinforce the first introduction. When a 17-pound fish was caught in 1883, Californians held high hopes for the species. When a 45-pounder was taken in 1889, there was no doubt that the striper had found herself another home.

Commercial interests quickly capitalized on the striper population that burgeoned in the San Francisco Bay area, but sportsmen got their way before damage was irreparable. In the '30s, the species was declared a gamefish in California, with buying and selling strictly prohibited. Daily limit currently is three fish of 16 inches or better. For many years, after-dark fishing was outlawed, but this rule recently was rescinded.

Meanwhile, stripers ranged north to Coos Bay, Oregon, where they found conditions compatibly similar to those of San Francisco Bay—a food-rich delta with plenty of rivers to spawn in—and they took up residence. Unlike their East Coast cousins, Western stripers remain in the same general area, migrating from delta to river and back as seasons change, rather than along the coast. In California, for example, most stripers enter San Francisco Bay about October after a summer of feeding on herring, anchovies, and smelt outside the Golden Gate. In the bay they fatten on worms, crabs, and shrimp until about March, when they head up the San Joaquin and Sacramento rivers to spawn. In May they return to the bay, moving outside as water temperatures rise and bait supply slackens.

The striper's feeding habits are the key to catches throughout this in-and-out migration. During their spawning run, they rarely eat, so strikes normally are in response to anger or irritation. In spring when they return to the bay, their appetites are ravenous and catches are easier to come by. During their midsummer sojourn in deep water, the fish normally are sought from boats, but alert surfmen enjoy wild action during the striper's sporadic hit-and-run attacks along beaches to the south of San Francisco. Local columnists and broadcasters keep anglers advised. When the bass are in, the word gets out.

Best way I know of to learn a lot about stripers in a short time is to read the late Wyn Brooks' brilliant book *The Shining Tides* (William Morrow & Co., New York, 1952). The book's main character is a 100-pound striped bass. Sounds contrived, I know, but the masterful way in which Wyn has woven the fish into the lives of his characters enables readers to enjoy a tight, paced, balanced, entertaining story and at the same time take a cram course in how stripers behave and why. *Tides* is out of print now, but copies can be found. A few years back I acquired two at—I blush —two dollars apiece through a librarian friend who plugged into some mysterious bibliographic network that seems to know where all the volumes in the world are located and how much their owners want for them. Two dollars! For a person who loves striped bass and the seashore and fine writing, it's worth that just to fondle the pages.

One final point about striped bass: yes, the species' name was officially changed a few years ago from *Roccus saxatilis* to *Morone saxatilis;* no, I have never heard a striper referred to by its new name. As one striper lover put it, "You wouldn't ask me to call my wife Arthur, would you?"

Bluefish

Controversy is common among surf fishermen: the best fish, the best method, the best time. In a form of fishing where individuality is encouraged and opinions often are the products of long and thoughtful deliberation, conclusions rarely coincide. Listen in some evening when fishing-club members debate the merits of a new lure or an old technique.

But one subject that saltwater surfmen seldom disagree on is bluefish. They might not appreciate the terrible toll these marauders take of bait, they might object to how mackerel, pollock, weakfish, and school stripers become scarce when the blues move in, but when it comes to judging the most lethal blend of speed, strength,

Bluefish, the perfect killing machine—a lethal blend of speed, strength, and brass-knuckle brutality.

and brass-knuckle brutality, beach anglers generally agree that *Pomatomus saltatrix* is tops.

A few years ago when hordes of these pugnosed jut-jawed savages invaded northern Massachusetts waters for the first time since the mid-1800s, local surf fishermen were stunned. Long accustomed to the comparatively tame performances of pollock, cod, mackerel, flounder, and school stripers, they literally didn't know what had hit them. For weeks, until word got out about wire leaders and tin squids and ways to cope with the blues' erratic hit-and-run tactics, the north-of-Boston shoreline was a shambles. Rotting carcasses of menhaden, victimized by the blues, littered the beaches; two-dollar plugs were being bid up to five; and the sand and rocks around the mouth of the Merrimack River became the bedroom for hundreds of anglers who napped by driftwood fires until the bedlam began anew.

Blues do strange things to otherwise normal people. Take Al, for instance. I met him in a Plum Island parking lot while rigging up for an after-dark crack at blues that had been herding bait against a sandbar toward the bottom of an ebbing tide. When he explained that he was new to the area, I invited him along.

"Terrible year so far," he said as we trudged through sand, "not a fish, any kind, and I've been out plugging every Wednesday night since Memorial Day. My wife's starting to get suspicious."

Later, when "Fish on," and "Comi-i-ing do-w-wn" were heard in the darkness for nearly an hour without interruption as two and three anglers at a time were into 8- and 10-pound bluefish, I heard Al pleading above the din to the Fishing Gods, "Ple-e-ease, I've gotta catch me a bluefish. My wife thinks I'm out chasing broads."

When the action abated a half-hour later as the tide tailed off, Al sloshed up to where I was cleaning my catch. Three fine fish adorned his stringer, and he smiled like a man whose marriage has just been saved.

"Best fishing I ever had," he said. "Can't thank you enough."

The bluefish is built for devastation. From its blunt steel-blue snout to its broad forked tail, it fits the description of Professor Spencer F. Baird, who, in the 1874 report of the United States Commission of Fish and Fisheries, called the bluefish "an animated chopping machine, the business of which is to cut to pieces and otherwise destroy as many fish as possible in a given space of time." Armed with shearing-sharp perpetual-motion teeth, bluefish schools attack almost anything that moves—menhaden, mackerel, spearing, squid—to satisfy their seemingly insatiable appetites. Water is churned to a bloody froth when bait is butchered, and screaming gulls dive for scraps.

No, you don't need to worry about having your waders shredded when blues chase bait close to shore, but big blues have been known to tear into bathers. At Haulover Beach near Miami on April 12, 1974, fingers, legs, and feet were ripped by rampaging bluefish mistaking human flesh for the mullet they were chasing in the wash. Less publicized are the dozens of fingers that are chomped every season when anglers get careless about unhooking blues.

With birds to spot feeding bluefish for you and almost anything you toss at them likely to be grabbed, your chances of action are high as long as we continue to enjoy the abundance of big blues that have been ravaging the East Coast since the early 1970s. Florida to Cape Cod is prime bluefish country, with bigger fish normally occurring from the Carolinas north. Action traditionally starts in inshore Florida waters in April, extending north until about mid-June, when striper fishermen on the underside of Cape Cod start having their rods wrenched from their hands by their first blues of the season. (No matter how many blues a man has beaten, he's never quite prepared for the season's first.) Autumn storms and tumbling temperatures send the blues south.

Bluefish have disappeared for long periods in the past and they probably will do so again. Each year's hatch must survive storms and predators (including their own parents) before they can reach the food-rich estuarine nurseries where they spend their infancy, and these nurseries are being devoured by developers and poisoned by pollution. A given year class has to grow to four-pounds-or-better snapper bluefish before the bulk of its hazards are behind it. Even then disease can devastate a population.

Recently while mackerel fishing, a friend and I were speculating about the sudden dearth of mackerel and glut of blues.

"Couple of years ago," he said, "it was just the opposite: more mackerel than you could count, and not a bluefish north of Cape Cod. Maybe this is Nature's way of keeping things in balance."

Sounds reasonable, and if it should be true, the pendulum must be about ready to reverse its direction. When the blues have gone, I imagine I shall think often of the young attendant in the gas station who saw my rod racked on top of my VW and started talking fishing. It was the first year that blues had invaded his territory, and I was anxious to learn what he thought.

"Oh, those damn things," he scoffed, "I'm sick of catching them."

I can almost hear him reminiscing to his grandchildren: "Great fish, big fish, acres of them, took over the whole river, slaughtered everything in sight. Stronger, faster, tougher than any fish before or since. Wonder what ever became of 'em."

One of the most poignant passages in angling literature occurs in O. H. P. Rodman's *The Saltwater Fisherman's Favorite Four* (William Morrow & Co., New York, 1948), in which Ollie concludes an account of a wonderful all-hands-on-at-once bluefish bonanza of the late thirties with, "Nor did any of us realize that this was our last bluefishing trip (successful, that is) for too many years to come."

Even with an abundance of blues, one characteristic of the species that works against the surf angler is that adult blues by nature are deepwater fish. Boatmen who have seen square miles of ocean alive with feeding blues will find this hard to believe. So will surfmen who have seen beaches littered with catches. Nevertheless, despite all this visible topside and shallow-water action, big blues spend a lot more time in the depths. They are particularly partial to big rumbling rips created alongside steep offshore shoals when wind and tide kick up a fuss.

But there are places within range of shore casters where similar conditions exist. Sandbars and sudden dropoffs are favorite feeding stations. So are the mouths of rivers and bays when a swiftly ebbing tide sets up a chowline. So, in fact, are places and times that a few years ago knowledgeable bluefishermen never would have tried.

"When the surf gets dirty, the blues get scarce," I was told, but

Once considered only daytime quarry, bluefish now provide prime after dark action for savvy anglers. (Photo: Terry McDonnell)

a shiny tin squid that landed by mistake in sandy weedy water only a few feet from a rocky shore was grabbed immediately by a blue-fish.

"Lots of action at dawn and dusk, but little in between," I was warned, but I decided to try the midnight surf anyway and found 8-to-10-pounders eager to take my plugs.

The spray is barely dry on my face from my most recent revelation. At four a.m., a sizzling tide abetted by a rain-swollen river swept and swirled my partner's unweighted eel alongside a jetty through waters thick with weeds and dense with sand, and yet a blue took it.

Why are blues being found more frequently these days in waters where formerly they never were caught? Partially because they never were sought. As surf anglers have become more numerous, they have spread out, trying new territories, revitalizing tradition with innovation. And blues are spreading out too. Populations increase, bait becomes scarcer, and fish must move farther afield to fill their bottomless bellies. Two years ago I was astounded when a 9-pound bluefish yanked me from my solitary perch on a riverbank 10 miles from the ocean. Today the place is standing room only.

So, yes, you can catch bluefish from the beach. An intelligent assessment of tide, topography, weather, and regional reports will sharpen your predictions, and the blues' often erratic behavior will provide a few surprises. But delay licking your chops until you've landed as well as located your bluefish. The frequency with which blues throw plugs is phenomenal. Despite hitting like triphammers, they're able to gain enough leverage from a plug's body to work free of the sharpest of trebles with their frantic head-shaking leaps. The only way to avoid this is by keeping a tight rein on strong line, reeling your fish steadily toward you so it can't blast off.

Sometimes your blue won't need any urging to swim in your direction. A favorite bluefish tactic is to head full-throttle toward the source of all this irritating pulling. Then only a cool head and a rapidly rotating multiplying reel can keep you out of trouble.

On blues, a strong sharp single hook seems to stay put better than a treble. Singles, besides offering less leverage to fighting blues, penetrate their mouths better in the first place.

A lot of blues—not to mention expensive lures—are lost when lines are severed by their sharp teeth. Two or three feet or so of

50-pound monofilament up front might be protection enough against the dental demolition of most species, but one chomp by a blue will sever it like so much spaghetti. Wire is needed, preferably braided steel that's strong enough to protect against severing yet supple enough to allow most lures to work naturally. These come ready-made in various lengths with a barrel swivel on one end for your line and a snap on the other for your lure.

One more point: a beached blue is not necessarily a beaten blue. Fingers have been frayed when excited anglers have ignored the blues' constantly cocked jaws, never-say-die defiance, and acute eyesight that works as well out of the water as in. Give a blue a chance and he'll let you have the last word: "Ouuuuch!"

Channel Bass

"Bulldogs," they call them. An apt name. Big, strong, and built for battle, the channel bass is second only to the striped bass as a surfman's prize. Catches of 30- and 40-pounders are not uncommon, with 50-pounders being beached often enough to keep surf fishermen coming back for more. Persistence paid off for Elvin Hooper in November 1973, when he caught a 90-pound record-breaker from a Rodanthe, North Carolina, pier.

That's right, November. Fall and spring are when big copper-colored channel bass make their inshore runs along Virginia and the Carolinas, and it's only in these waters that mammoth fish are found. Farther south and along the Gulf Coast, fish rarely exceed 25 pounds. Under 10 pounds they are known as puppy drum. Other common names for the species are red drum, drum, or just plain reds.

The red really is a croaker, cousin to weakfish and other drums. Bigger fish have reddish-brown backs, silver sides, and white bellies; smaller fish have pink or pale-brown backs. Dime-size black spots mark both sides of the base of an adult's tail. Black drum, with which smaller red drum sometimes are confused, do not have this spot. They also have barbels (chin whiskers) and are silver-gray in color.

Big reds require big tackle, not only because of their size and strength, but because long heaves into high surf often are neces-

Spring and fall are when big copper-colored channel bass invade the North Carolina surf. (Photo: Joel Arrington)

sary. Deep sloughs inboard of barrier bars are popular feeding spots, but often reds will chase bait beyond these bars. When diving birds or breaking bait or even the shadowy shapes of reds feeding topside pinpoint action at maximum range, you'll want a rod that will enable you to reach it.

With a spinning rod of 10 to 12 feet you can cover plenty of water as long as your spool is rim-high with light limp 20- or 25-pound-test monofilament. Yes, this line can be a pretty flimsy bond between you and your trophy of a lifetime, especially in high seas, but patience and a not-too-tight drag can beat a firmly hooked fish.

The red's long hard offshore runs punctuated by sulking pauses are predictable.

Heavier line is needed more for handling big baits and heavy sinkers than for playing fish. On a rotating-spool reel, monofilament or braided nylon in the 30-to-36-pound class provides added strength without sacrificing distance, but only to anglers experienced in handling it. Unless your freshwater apprenticeship has been largely on plug-casting gear, stick to spinning.

Redfish do most of their feeding on the bottom, subsisting principally on mollusks, crustaceans, and small schoolfish such as mullet and menhaden. Squid, clams, crabs, shrimp, bloodworms, and strips of almost any edible local species are effective. With bait these days often more costly than the fish it entices, a lot of anglers are catching and freezing their own. Suggestion: After you've lobbed your bait way out and secured your rod in a sandspike, jig in close with light tackle for smaller species. Not only will you enjoy double-feature fishing, but you might lower your bait bill by using chunks or strips of the fish you catch as bait for reds.

Hooks for fist-size baits should be about #8/0; for smaller servings, #3/0 is about right. O'Shaughnessy and Eagle Claw patterns are excellent. First time you buy bait, especially if it's frozen, ask how to conceal your hook so it will be inconspicuous yet at the same time effective. It's hard to hide a hook in unthawed bait. There's always the temptation to hurry, sink the point, heave it out, and hope for the best. With most of your hook exposed, a fish can easily detect your deception. Even if it doesn't, you'll yank your bait from the fish's mouth long before your hook's point can penetrate an inch or two of ice.

Fishfinders and three-way swivels are standard rigs for fishing bait. Sinkers normally are pyramids, designed to hold fast in the sand and mud bottoms on which redfish feed. Select your sinker's weight according to how hard the current is pulling. Early in a tide, four ounces might suffice, but as the flow accelerates, increase your sinker's weight accordingly.

You might, however, *want* your sinker to drag. This will enable your bait to cover more ground. In this case use a bank sinker for smoother sliding. Bank sinkers also are better for walking your bait through a trough parallel to a beach or through a narrow slot such as a harbor mouth.

But bait is not the only way to catch redfish. Jigs and big shiny metal squids work well when bounced slowly along the bottom, and topwater plugs will score when wiggled through breaking bait.

The old chestnut "Early and late in the season, early and late in the day" seems to have been coined with redfish in mind, but beyond this basic rule, few others apply. Though traditional daytime diners, redfish occasionally will go on after-dark binges. Though partial to deeper water, they sometimes will forage in water so shallow that their dorsals are exposed. Though they prefer clear water, they sometimes will seek crabs and shellfish in a storm-roiled surf. Normally, however, they will wait until a storm has subsided before moving in to pick up the pieces. Smart surfmen are there waiting.

Big, predictable, cooperative, aggressive—with qualities like these, what more could a surfman ask of a fish? Edibility, that's what. A bull red's strong and stringy flesh is as unappetizing as a pup's is delicious. The flavor and texture of a steak from an adult redfish have been described with only a pinch of hyperbole as resembling a tweed jacket marinated in last week's chum. And thank the Lord. Were the bull's flesh as tasty as the pup's, the species might soon be eaten out of existence. No such narrowly distributed and vulnerably predictable population could long survive the successes of armies of educated anglers using superefficient weapons.

But the occasional releasing of trophy reds is hardly cause for complacency. Since the start of this century, the red's northern range has edged ever southward—Long Island, New Jersey, Delaware, Virginia. Time has long since passed when anglers south of Brownsville, Texas, could report as Jimmie Lingan did in the *Houston Chronicle*, "THESE REDS ACTUALLY DROVE US FROM PLACE TO PLACE IN OUR SEARCH FOR TROUT AND PIKE"—that is, for spotted weakfish and snook.

Ollie Rodman sounded an ominous alarm when he wrote in his *The Saltwater Fisherman's Favorite Four*: "There are too many people who still think that the piscatorial treasures of the ocean are unlimited; that, therefore, if they can get into fish in such a way that they can take them at every cast, they are entitled to all they can kill and lug away. That is false and dangerous thinking: false, because it is not true; dangerous because it can lead to serious depletion of the species of fish involved. All you need for proof is to survey the commercial fisheries' records for the past fifty years and see the alarming decline in catches, remembering that over this period there have been tremendous improvements in fishing gear and general efficiency of the fishing fleets. Man-taking powers are a serious threat, unless controlled, to even the vast abundance of the supposedly limitless supply of ocean fishes.

"The days when it was smart to come back to the dock or from a trip down the beach and have your picture taken with all the fish you and your guide could carry are gone. Sure, you can still do it occasionally, but you'll win few friends and gain plenty of enemies. Nowadays, the respect and honors go to the man who has the good sense to return (unharmed) to the water all but the few fish he needs or wants for food. For three hundred years we Americans have taken greedily of the natural resources with which these United States are unusually blessed. But the time has come—in fact, it has been here for too many years—when we have to put on the brakes and at the same time do all we can not only to maintain but to increase our resources!"

Ollie's book was published more than a quarter-century ago!

Weakfish

First, let's be clear on what we mean by weakfish. The species has more aliases than a post-office wall. Seatrout (one word), southern seatrout, speckled trout, spotted weakfish, and just plain trout refer to the southern weakfish (*Cynoscion nebulosis*). Its northern cousin, the common weakfish (*Cynoscion regalis*), also is known as gray weakfish, gray trout, yellowfish, and that melodious New England appellation, squeteague, abbreviated squet, pronounced "squit," not to be confused with squid. To muddy the waters even more, the family has a couple of close cousins, the sand seatrout (*Cynoscion arenarius*) and the silver seatrout (*Cynoscion nothus*).

The latter types are quite small, of only minor interest to the sport fisherman. Adult silvers seldom exceed 10 inches, and sands average only 12 to 15. Both are found in the Gulf of Mexico, although the silver ranges north to Chesapeake Bay. *Nothus*, unlike *arenarius*, *nebulosis*, and *regalis*, is predominantly a deepwater fish.

The common weakfish and the spotted seatrout are slim, stream-

The name "weakfish" has several possible origins, but none of them refers to the ways this surf favorite fights. (Photo: Frank Daignault)

lined, and handsomely hued. Along with its blues, greens, purples, and lavenders, the common weakfish has dark splotches on its back and a gloriously golden sheen. The spotted seatrout's blue-gray back is decorated with round black spots which extend to its dorsal fin and tail.

The spotted seatrout is found principally from Chesapeake Bay south and through the Gulf of Mexico, where it moves close to shore in early spring and back into bays or along beaches in late fall. Traditional range for the common weakfish is from Chesapeake Bay to the southern side of Cape Cod. Most catches of both types of fish are made close to shore, although rarely in roily or rough water. Because they travel in schools, one catch can trigger prolonged action on 4-to-6-pound fish. Trophy-size "tiderunners" are more commonly caught in the turbulence of tide rips.

My first common weakfish was caught from a boat, but I caught it in a special way that has made me partial ever since to taking them from shore. It was special first of all because squeteague had been strangers to the Northeast for many years. As a youngster, I used to read about Cape Codders taking dozens of those 4- and 5-pound fish with the strange Indian name, but by the time World War II had relinquished its hold on me, squet had disappeared in one of their perplexing periods of decline. Where only a few years before there had been millions, now there were none. When they returned in the early 1970s, therefore, I headed south to Narragansett Bay with all of the ardor of a swain about to keep a long-delayed date.

The second special feature of my first squet was that I caught it on a fly rod. While waiting to rent a skiff one May morning, this method had been recommended to me by a pair of old-timers who only recently had resumed their long-dormant love affair with their favorite fish.

"Never mind those bucktail jigs," they had told me. "Jigs'll hook plenty of fish for you, but if you want to let those babies really strut their stuff, take 'em with a worm on a nice light limber fly rod."

Less than a half-hour later a 4-pounder hauled the tip of my freshwater fly rod clear under my skiff out the other side, dunking my nose in the process, and I was converted to fly-rodding.

What converted me to fly-rodding *from shore* was a man wading in front of a seawall about 50 yards inboard from where I was drifting seaworms. At first I paused to admire his effortlessly smooth casts. They weren't long—40, maybe 50 feet—but they were firm and they were faultless. His fly went where he aimed it and behaved the way he meant it to. When his rod dipped and a squet of about 7 pounds started thrashing furiously less than 4 rod lengths in front of him, my admiration turned to envy. When, after ten toe-to-toe minutes, the man added this fish to a stringer containing four other fish of almost identical size, I vowed to fly-rod squet from shore at every opportunity.

Opportunities have been few. Biggest obstacle, of course, is the species' unpredictable disappearing acts. Already, after only a couple of banner seasons, some Narragansett anglers are predicting another decline.

"Plenty of big fish," they're saying, "10- and 12-pounders, but not many youngsters bringing up the rear."

Yet even while fish are plentiful, they're hard to get to. Accessible shoreline is pretty well built up, and property owners are reluctant to grant passage for fear their guests might be members of that ugly minority who invariably leave their spoor of beer cans and bait boxes. If you're lucky enough to find a stretch of tree-free bayside that isn't studded with NO TRESPASSING signs, get to it as the tide turns and work with the current; fish often follow bait as it moves in and out of estuaries and tidal pockets. Jetties, piers, and bridges bring fish within range, but crowds, winds, currents, and slippery footing make fly-casting difficult. Surf-slammed beaches normally are unproductive because squet steer clear of rough and dirty water, but they can be caught from deep holes and trenches when a surf is moderate.

Light spinning or plug-casting tackle is ideal for fishing squet with either bait or lures. Most fish are in the 4-to-6-pound class, so 6-pound monofilament usually is adequate. Eight-pound is advisable when rocks are a factor, but in no case would I recommend anything over 10-pound-test, and this only when using heavy baits or when deliberately stalking outsize fish.

Favorite food of weakfish and seatrout is shrimp. An effective way of attracting and holding a school's attention is by chumming shrimp in a tideway. Toss out a handful of tidbits every half-minute or so for about five minutes, then float a hooked shrimp through the chowline. Big squid strips or even whole small squid are lethal on big fish when squid are the predominant bait in the area you're fishing. Smaller fish always find 1x3-inch strips appealing. Seaworms, shedder crab, and cut bait also work well.

Always use a long-shanked hook on weakfish and seatrout. Because they tend to gulp bait, you need something to grab hold of when working your barb loose from one's gullet.

Weaks and seatrout are pushovers for a cork tied a few feet above a drifted bait. When the line is yanked, the cork splashes. Fish investigate the commotion and spot the bait.

Almost any bait-simulating lure of appropriate size entices weak-fish and seatrout. Spoons, squids, jigs, and flies all score well as long as you get them down far enough. Jigs are especially effective in fast currents and on jetties and rocks from which you can reach deeper holes. In recent years the lead-head plastic jig has become even more popular than the bucktail.

A light touch is needed for playing weakfish. Horse one and you probably will tear its mouth, enabling it to work free of your hook. In fact, the name "weakfish" is assumed by most anglers to have had its origin in the fragility of the species' mouth. Two other pos-sibilities are proffered by George Reiger in his *Profiles in Saltwater Angling* (Prentice-Hall, Inc., Englewood Cliffs, N.J., 1973). One cites the suggestion of nineteenth-century tackle dealer and outdoor writer John J. Brown that the name is a corruption of "wheatfish," referring to the harvest months when this species is in greatest supply. The other mentions the premise of nineteenth-century author and second U.S. Commissioner George Brown Goode that the word is merely a corruption of *weakvis,* the name applied to the species by the Dutch of New Amsterdam.

Black Drum

From New York south and around into the Gulf of Mexico, the black drum is a favorite of shore-based bait-fishermen. Clams, crabs, shrimp, mussels, and cut bait are readily taken by this strong high-backed bottom-scourer.

Black drum caught from shore usually are puppies of under 10 pounds, so light tackle is adequate. Occasionally, though, as during a spring run of heavyweights along the Virginia and Carolina coasts, fish over 50 pounds move in close, so be prepared. Check first to see what's doing. Although black drum are active on the East Coast only from late spring to early fall, they are caught year-round by Gulf Coast fishermen.

As with its close relative the channel bass, big black drum make poor eating. The black drum, however, is not the strong stubborn fighter the red is; a worthy adversary, yes, especially on light tackle, where restraint and a tender touch are more important than mere muscle, but not in the same major league as its glamorous copper-hued cousin.

The black drum, a close relative of the red drum, or channel bass, ranges from New York south and around into the Gulf of Mexico. (Photo: Claude Rogers)

Blackfish

Long, pugnosed, and plump, this East Coast bottom-feeder has hard strong teeth for crushing the shells of barnacles, snails, mussels, shrimp, lobster, and crabs. First time I examined a blackfish's intestines, it seemed the coiled rubbery tube would never stop coming. Inside the tube was an uninterrupted flow of shell shards, mostly from barnacles, as well as an impressive assortment of stones.

This fish had been caught on a mudworm from a rocky ledge at the edge of a busy boat channel. All rocks within its range are prime blackfish territory, as are beds of mussels and oysters. Nova Scotia and South Carolina bracket the black's normal range, but it is most abundant between Delaware Bay and Cape Cod. Rhode Island and Massachusetts residents call the species tautog.

Coastal migrations are minor, but within a given area the local population of blackfish moves inshore during spring and fall, offshore during summer and winter. May and October are top tautog months.

Although tautog sometimes exceed 3 feet and 20 pounds, most

Strong, hard, crushing teeth characterize the bottom-dwelling blackfish.

are 3-to-5-pounders. Even these lightweights, however, require heavy line, a rugged rod, and rounded sinkers such as the bank type to minimize hangups and breakoffs.

Seaworms and clams are eaten readily by tautog, but nothing beats crabs as bait. Bottom-fish a quarter of a crab body and use its claws to chum in a school of feeding tautog. Keep a tight line and be ready to strike immediately when one starts tugging. Tautog are expert bait stealers.

All the effort of inching across rocks, all the expense of lost bait and terminal tackle will fade into insignificance with your first spoonful of tautog chowder. Deeeelicious!

Whiting

The northern whiting (*Menticirrhus saxatilis*) is better known in New York and New Jersey as kingfish. Most plentiful between New York and Chesapeake Bay, its range extends from Maine to Florida. Its close kin, the southern and Gulf kingfishes, are found in the Gulf of Mexico.

Kingfish are small, seldom exceeding a foot, but they fight well for their size. Set your hook as soon as you feel their staccato series of tugs, then reel in some of the ocean's most delicious dining. Be-

The northern whiting is a winter favorite with New Jersey pier fishermen. (Photo: Milt Rosko)

cause kings are lightweights, freshwater tackle provides the best sport. Because they are so tasty, however, many anglers, especially on piers, prefer to concentrate on quantity instead of quality by using heavier tackle and three or four baited hooks in series. Multiple catches are frequent while the action lasts.

An inch or so of seaworm on a #1/0 hook matches the king's small mouth. Also effective are sandbugs and bits of shrimp, crab, clam, or squid.

Schools of kingfish are most numerous off beaches in midsummer, although they can be caught there any time from May through September. Many anglers score heavily by fishing sloughs and dips at night after bathers have departed. Piers are popular with kingfishermen; so are jetties at the mouths of bays and rivers while a tide is ebbing.

Pollock

This handsome hard-fighting cousin of the cod, though mainly an offshore fish, is caught regularly from shore in northern New England and Canada, occasionally off Cape Cod's Race Point, Rhode Island's Point Judith, and Long Island's Montauk Point, and once in a while as far south as North Carolina. Brief runs of big

Plentiful, pugnacious, and cooperative, the pollock is as delicious as its cousin the cod. (Photo: Terry McDonnell)

fish, some exceeding 20 pounds, occur in spring and fall. One-to-2-pounders, often called harbor pollock, can be caught throughout the summer where water is cool and food is plentiful. Big tackle-busters that sometimes top 30 pounds are deepwater residents.

Small forage fish such as sandeels and smelt are the pollock's principal fare, so shiny metal squids, jigs, and spoons are taken readily, especially at morning and evening twilights and throughout the dark overcast days of autumn. A wooden-dowel splasher about 2 feet ahead of the lure can double its deadliness. Small plugs also work well so long as currents are not so strong that they tumble them. Brightly tinseled streamer flies are snapped up by feeding pollock, so many anglers keep their lightweight fly rods handy in case they should corner a school.

Pollock are excellent eating if cleaned promptly and cooled immediately. No matter how fast the action, pause occasionally to make sure your catch doesn't soften and spoil in the sun.

Atlantic Mackerel

The mighty mac, like the pollock, is an offshore fish which often feeds close in along the Canadian and northern New England coasts. From about Boston to the normal southern limit of its range at Cape Hatteras, it rarely is taken from shore.

Cold water and small baitfish are the keys to success with *Scomber scombrus*. When one of the mackerel's constantly moving schools is seen dimpling the surface, any small shiny lure is likely to work. Most popular is a diamond jig, eyed at one end and hooked at the other. Its well-distributed weight enables it to be cast far and accurately with the light tackle suited to 1- and 2-pound mackerel, and it sinks with an enticingly erratic descent. Cast the jig across a school, let it sink a few feet, then reel in while alternately raising and lowering your rod tip.

Late spring through mid-autumn is prime mackerel time with fastest fishing throughout the summer. Any time of day is mealtime for mackerel, but few are caught at night. Last time I took one from a darkened beach—on a swimming plug, by the way, that wasn't much bigger than the fish—I think I was more surprised than the mackerel.

Anglers who enjoy eating the mack's rich oily flesh often try to catch them several at a time by tying three or more jigs in series to simulate a school of bait.

Scup

Generally about the size and shape of a large crappie, the scup's pronounced pug nose gives it a rough-and-ready appearance which it more than lives up to on the action end of a light spinning or fly rod. Though their hits usually are more tap than tug, they run fast, fight hard, and play a tidal current for all it's worth. Generally, scup are a pale iridescent pink on their backs and white on their stomachs, but I have seen their flopping forms span a shimmering spectrum of blue, green, yellow, silver, and gold. Beautiful!

The East Coast is the scup's home, where it is known in its northern range as porgy, with an R. Pogies—no R—are menhaden, those superabundant oily herring whose vast compact schools are the delight of commercial netters, who take them by the millions for conversion to fertilizer and fish meal, and striped bass and bluefish, which regard pogies as the equivalent of a hot fudge sundae.

Worms and small crustaceans are the bulk of these bottom-feeders' diet, but they can be caught on streamer flies and small jigs such as the shad dart. During their inshore summer sojourn, schools often will congregate along a channel's edge and at the mouths of

The handsomely hued scup, or porgy, is surprisingly strong for its panfish size.

bays and rivers. When scup schools are plentiful, try walking a weighted piece of seaworm along a steep sandy dropoff.

Commonly, shore-caught scup weigh less than a pound; offshore catches occasionally exceed three. Fortunately they are a meaty fish, so, despite their small size, they are much sought after as table fare.

Winter Flounder

An ideal fish for introducing youngsters to the delights of fishing from shore, the "blackback" is plentiful, cooperative, a respectable fighter, and a delicious meal. Muddy bay bottoms are this fish's favorite habitat. Very sensitive to extremes of cold or heat, the majority of winter flounder move inshore in spring, seek cooler depths during summer, return to shallow bays during autumn, and spend their winters offshore. Spring and summer action for the shorefisherman can be spectacular.

Like all flatfish, the winter flounder feeds on the bottom. Sea-worms, clams, and mussels are excellent baits, but only small pieces should be used because of the flounder's tiny mouth. For the same reason, only very small hooks are appropriate, with long shanks to facilitate removal. Flounders are gulpers.

Many a youngster has launched his saltwater career with winter, or blackback, flounder. (Photo: Terry McDonnell)

Inshore flounder rarely exceed a pound or two, although commercial netters sometimes dredge up 6- and 8-pound "snowshoes." This is a light-tackle fish, but when heavy sinkers are needed for holding bait in a strong tideway, line of at least 10-pound-test is recommended; anything less is likely to snap during casting.

Flounder fishing can be feast or famine. Even during spring and fall, when most blackbacks have returned to bays, some patches of bottom can be barren of fish while others only a few feet away can be standing room only. It is important, therefore, that you scour an area, moving from place to place, casting in different directions, until you hit paydirt. To make the most of your discovery, you might want to use two hooks. This can be done by tying your first hook's leader to your line just above your pyramid sinker and your second a few inches above that. Because the hooks tend to foul in this arrangement, tandem hooks are more frequently fished in parallel. This is done with a spreader rig, consisting of a curved piece of strong wire that has a loop on each end and a snap swivel at its center. The line is tied to the swivel's eye, the sinker is hung from the swivel's snap, and baited hooks are suspended by leaders from the loops on either end.

While the winter flounder's active range extends only from Canada to Chesapeake Bay, there are more than 200 species of flatfish in the Atlantic and Pacific oceans. Next time you catch one, observe its eyes. Both are on the same side of its head, the right side. This makes the blackback *dextral*. If its eyes were on the left side, it would be *sinistral*. Try these terms on your ten-year-old next time she starts humiliating you with her Modern Math homework.

Summer Flounder

Another flatfish popular with surf fishermen is the summer flounder, or fluke. The Middle Atlantic states are the center of greatest activity for this species, but they can be caught from Maine to South Carolina.

Summer and winter flounder differ in many ways. The summer flounder is much larger on the average, with rod-and-reel catches generally about 3 to 5 pounds, and bigger "doormats" often topping 10, occasionally even 15. The summer flounder also is aggressive,

Bigger and more aggressive than the winter flounder, the summer flounder, or fluke, will attack lures and live killifish. (Photo: Nick Karas)

with an appetite for small baitfish and a mouth large and toothy enough to accommodate them. Rods, therefore, should be sturdier and lines stronger when fishing for fluke.

Inshore fluke season begins when water warms sufficiently in the spring. The first catches are generally the smaller fish, with size and number increasing as the season progresses. When waters cool in late fall, they move offshore into deeper water.

Mud and sand bottoms are the summer flounder's natural habitat, although they will forage along channel edges and other natural current lanes along which bait is carried. The quickness with which they can bury themselves in sand is startling. Often they will lie motionless, completely camouflaged, with only their eyes showing while they wait to ambush prey. Try swimming close to a sandy bottom while wearing mask and flippers. See if you can spot a pair of eyes peering at you. Be prepared for frequent nerve-shattering eruptions as spooked fluke explode from the sand and wiggle away with amazing speed.

Fluke are especially partial to killifish, but will strike at any small baitfish, dead or alive. Dead baits are most effective if moved occasionally by raising your rod tip and reeling in slack. Squid, clams, crabs, shrimp, and worms also will strike at lures that simulate small fish.

The summer flounder, by the way, is "left-handed," or sinistral.

Tarpon

This armor-plated acrobat surely is the most spectacular performer among inshore saltwater gamefish. The soaring leaps of a hooked tarpon symbolize to many surfmen the ultimate encounter between man and fish.

More often than not with a sizable tarpon, that's as far as the encounter goes. A lot more tarpon are lost than landed. Hooks are thrown during their head-shaking struggles, leaders are chafed against their rough hides, and lines are snapped by fish that frequently exceed 100 pounds.

Brackish bays and estuaries are best tarpon territory, although they will swim several hundred miles upriver and thrive as well in fresh water as in salt. Responding sensitively to seasonal changes in water temperature, these mammoth members of the herring family move inshore in spring, offshore in autumn. Tarpon are most plentiful along east and west Florida and the Gulf of Mexico, but occasionally they are caught as far north as Virginia.

Mullet, squid, shrimp, crabs, and pinfish are popular baits; feather jigs and jointed swimming plugs are tops among the artificials. Enormous tarpon have been caught on streamer flies, but these are heroic feats by expert anglers who generally stalk their tarpon from small boats. Baby tarpon, however, provide superlative sport for fly-casters who can find clearings along the banks of canals. Small or large, most tarpon are released because they make poor table fare.

Hardest part of catching a tarpon is persuading it to strike. Even the unnerving sight of a big fish rolling close to shore does not mean action. More likely these fish are just taking air into their gas bladders, lunglike organs which enable them to survive in waters where oxygen content is low. Even big tarpon, unless they are feeding aggressively, usually will mouth a lure gently, taking it on an upward roll and closing its mouth only after it has started its descent. A premature strike—very difficult to avoid, by the way, after watching a big fish swoop up after your lure—pulls the hook from the fish's mouth before the barb can penetrate flesh.

Best bet for your first few tarpon expeditions is to fish a bridge at night. Imitate the boys who appear to know what they're doing, and keep at it until you score. You'll need all the patience and persistence you can muster. You also might want to bring something along to settle your nerves when the night is ripped apart by a 100-pound showoff leaping aloft to shake hands with the stars.

Snook

In the Florida–Gulf of Mexico cornucopia, where most snook fishing is done, no fish offer a better blend of sporting and eating qualities. Most snook are caught from boats during summer and early fall as they exploit tidal conditions in bays, creeks, and rivers in pursuit of baitfish, but their shallow-water foraging often makes them vulnerable to shore fishermen. When they lurk off inlets and passes waiting for bait, they can be caught from jetties. When mullet

Snook make delicious dinners, but you'll have to earn every mouthful.
(Photo: Mark J. Sosin)

migrate along eastern Florida in late fall, they are taken from beach fronts. Bridge fishermen clever enough to swing a plug against a night tide and work it into holes at the bases of pilings hook a lot of snook, and canals are dependable producers of smaller fish. Snook have been known to reach 50 pounds and almost 5 feet, but a 20-pounder's rollicking thrashing runs will make any angler earn every ounce.

Breakoffs are frequent when battling snook. No, their teeth are not abnormally large or sharp, but their gill covers will slice easily through heavy monofilament. The rocks, pilings, oyster beds, and shell-encrusted mangrove roots around which snook feed also are used to full advantage for severing lines.

Wire leaders, therefore, are essential. These impair a lure's action, but fortunately snook respond to plugs manipulated wildly through turbulent water. Pull, jerk, yank, whip, and swing a surface-disturbing plug when snook are feeding topside; work a wobbler or diver more deliberately when they're deep. Metal squids, jigs, and eel-simulators also are effective, as are shrimp, pinfish, and, of course, mullet.

Bonefish

Schools of 4-to-8-pound foragers are plentiful on shallow flats along the Florida Keys, where they move in on high water, out on low. With a little practice, bones are easy to spot through polarized glasses, and they never seem to get enough shrimp, crabs, and squid. Why, then, are these pig-snouted jet-propelled torpedoes so hard for the wader to catch?

First, because he has to know what to look for. Granted, a school often signals its presence by gray puffs of marl while "mudding" for food, or by its tails when grubbing in very shallow water, but it takes a trained eye to sort out the sponges and urchins and grass patches. Angling author Frank Moss calls the bone "glass fish" and recommends wearing tan-tinted eyeglasses and looking for movement rather than shape.

It also takes practice to stalk and cast without frightening these super-spooky fish. The merest shadow or vibration or splash can trigger an instant exodus. One second you're inching into range, the next you're gawking at a muddy cloud. "Ghost of the flats" is an appropriate nickname.

Because bones are so easily spooked, light tackle and careful casting are essential. A 7-foot rod and 6- or 8-pound mono are about right, but bring several extra prewound spools. A sizzling 25-mph run of up to 100 yards will pop such light line against a drag that's even slightly tighter than it should be.

Best lures are ⅛-to-¼-ounce shrimp-simulators such as a leadhead jig with bucktail or a plastic body. Drop your jig ahead of a school from as far away as you can cast accurately. Feeding schools

Super-spooky and lightning-fast, the bonefish is a favorite of waders on clear shallow Florida flats. The angler is Milt Rosko.

are less likely to spook than moving ones, so closer casts are possible to fish that have their snouts in the marl. How close? Rules are as unreliable as bonefish are fickle. One day they scoot when a lure plops anywhere in their vicinity, next day—same tide, temperature, sunlight, etc.—they might stay put despite a depth-charging. Caution, however, always is the best course. A reasonable practice when casting to tails or muds is to begin by dropping your ⅛-ounce jig no closer than 4 to 5 feet, your ¼-ounce between 5 and 7, then diminish the distance if the fish aren't nervous. A school moving at a steady speed in a straight line is best stalked with a lure dropped 25 or 30 feet ahead of it, then retrieved slowly to intercept the school.

Bonefish are a favorite target of fly-fishermen, but success is enjoyed only by those who consistently can bullseye a lot of line with a minimum of false-casting.

Pompano

How can so small a fish as the pompano command so large a following? Easy. By being year-round available, tauntingly elusive, and just about the most prized table fare in the sea. Freshly caught pompano are so highly prized—and priced—that an informal industry has built up along Florida's east coast. Restaurants and fish markets are ready customers for these slim, oval, snub-nosed bantamweights.

Most pompano are in the 2-to-4-pound class. A fish over 7 pounds is exceptional. Anything exceeding 10 pounds is more likely to be an Atlantic permit (*Trachinotus falcatus*), a fast wary warrior that sometimes tops 50 pounds.

Ironically, despite their small size, pompano are sought with heavy tackle. Rods of 12 and 14 feet and lines of 20-pound-test or better are standard equipment on Florida beaches. Many such rods are custom-built for pompano fishing.

Range and payload are the reason for heavy artillery. Sloughs and bars, where waves churn up the sandbugs, shrimp, clams, and crabs that pompano feed on, are likely to be located well offshore. Heavy sinkers of up to 6 ounces are needed to propel these lightweight baits. Small jigs can be effective, but only on those rare occasions in those few locations where pompano move in close. This sometimes happens toward the top of a tide on a steeply sloping beach when waves suck sandbugs into the wash. Even then it's a good idea to spice your hook with a sandbug or two.

Multiple hooks are used by anglers who want to increase their harvest when the nervous unpredictable pompano finally puts in an appearance. Market fishermen tie as many as a half-dozen #1 or 1/0 hooks behind pyramid sinkers, spacing them far enough apart so their leaders won't tangle, but such a load is hard to cast without a lot of practice.

Best pompano fishing on Florida's east coast is during winter and spring. Here they move north in spring, south in early autumn. Spring and summer are best on the Gulf Coast. Look for them in white water, where tide and wind and waves stir up bait, and cover a beach thoroughly with your casts. Concentrate on dawn and dusk, but don't miss any opportunities in between.

Surfperch

Ranging from Alaska to the Mexican border, the surfperch probably provides more enjoyment for Pacific Coast anglers than any other fish. Among the many species which constitute this family are

Rainbow, black, barred, calico, walleye—these are a few of the many kinds of surfperch that provide more action for West Coast surfmen than any other species. (Photo: Larry Green)

the black, barred, rainbow, calico, spotfin, redtail, silver, and wall-eye varieties. Most surfperch are caught in the white water along rocky or sandy shorelines while they are spawning or feeding. Many also are taken from wharves, docks, and piers, where marine organisms from the pilings keep them well fed.

Best bait along the oceanfront is the sand crab (*Emerita analega*), especially those wearing the soft shells characteristic of molting. The largest of the molters are dug as close to the surf's edge as you can safely get. Shrimp, worms, clams, mussels, smelt, anchovy, and bits of cut fish also work. Even tiny spoons, jigs, and weighted flies can be effective.

Surfperch are small, rarely exceeding a pound or two, so light tackle and small hooks are called for. Long-shanked baitholder hooks should be used with softshell crabs, and gentle casting is necessary to ensure that these baits don't fall off.

Suggestion: fish perch from a pier during a downpour. They go on feeding sprees when the skies open up.

Lingcod

The biggest of Pacific Coast rockfish, the ling often exceeds 50 pounds, but a shore-caught ling over 20 is a noteworthy achievement. This is because they head right for the rocks, wedging themselves in and defying you to haul them out. Their sheer holding power makes an up-and-down tug o' war a losing game on anything less than 20-pound line, and even heavier line is easily abraded on the rocks' rough edges. Wire leaders are one solution, but anglers who have lost a few ling this way soon learn the futility of pulling straight up. Instead they walk along the jetty or rockpile from which they're fishing and apply sideways pressure.

Ling are partial to small fish. Herring, hake, cod, flounder, and squid are favorites. Don't be surprised, when you're reeling in a flounder or even a sea bass, if a lingcod grabs it enroute. Bucktail jigs bounced alongside reefs and jetties also are constant scorers.

California to Alaska is lingcod country, with the Northwest especially productive. Juan de Fuca Strait and the San Juan Islands are renowned hot spots. Areas marked "Rky" (for rocky) on your

tide charts are good bets when the water over them is fairly deep—
say 40 to 50 feet—and a fair tide is running.

Ling are excellent eating, but don't let your taste buds make you
overanxious when that big-mouthed head finally comes topside.
Gaffing or netting a lingcod from rocks requires care and restraint.
So does hook-removal when you have to probe between those facing
pairs of ice-tong teeth.

Getting right out there in the squeteague's dining room paid off with a doubleheader for this Rhode Island pair. (Photo: Frank Daignault)

7
Surf Strategy

ESSENTIALLY THERE ARE TWO WAYS to fish the surf: keep moving in pursuit of fish; stay put and wait for them to come to you. Usually the former involves artificial lures, the latter bait. Each method offers almost limitless permutations of time, tide, weather, and location, and the two can be combined. Many prowl-and-plug anglers, for example, prefer to concentrate on a tightly limited area; many bait-and-wait fishermen move about as conditions change. One lovely little promontory that I fish frequently has a rock-rimmed sound on one side and a mud-bottomed creek on the other. Because the rocks offer superb plugging on a flooding tide and the mud provides excellent jigging on an ebb, I generally can find all the action I want within a 200-yard arc. A gently sloping beachfront from which I sometimes bottom-fish bait toward the top of a tide is too shallow when the tide drops to less than half full. A short distance down the shore, however, is a finger of rocks that becomes exposed as the tide ebbs. When fishing fizzles on the beachfront, I just reel in and head for the rocks.

On any given foray, in fact, I usually will use both lures and bait. Rarely will I prowl and plug a shore without a few worms in my pocket; seldom will I monitor my rod in its sandspike without plugging or jigging occasionally with a second rod.

One of the first lessons the successful surfman learns is to cover as many bases as possible. Sometimes bait will work when nothing else will. A few years back, stripers to 27 pounds were sucking in my live eels every time I wiggled one through a couple feet of moonlit water, yet they ignored my favorite sandeel-simulating plug. On another night I wiggled eels and worms alongside and across a sandbar at a dozen different angles and speeds, yet bass started hitting in earnest only after I had switched to the same plug they had spurned a short time before.

Of course, there was a reason for the fish's apparently contradictory behavior. There always is. In the first instance I was in eel country, a grass-fringed clamflat where eels abounded and bass sought them out under a full moon. In the second, I was in sandeel territory, a fact I should have inferred from the sandy bottom and the schools of shiny skinny baitfish I had seen there previously.

Which is the better method, bottom-fishing bait or combing a shore with artificials? Under the right conditions, either can be as enjoyable as it is effective; when conditions are wrong, both can produce as little fun as they do fish. On almost any given winter night at the bars of seaside fishing clubs you can hear champions of both methods arguing their choices.

"So answer me this, will you? What sport is there to heaving out a hunk of meat and waiting for something to happen? What sport, huh? That's about as sporting as a trip to the fish market. And another thing, that lawn chair. You can't tell me that anybody can fish right when he's leaning back in a lawn chair sucking on a beer and listening to the ball game."

"Yeah? Yeah? And you can't tell me that anybody can fish right either when he's traveling a hundred miles an hour. Couple of casts and zoom, you're off to your next stop. Just like on a bus route. Fish no sooner makes up its mind to go after your plug and presto, it's gone. And hey, that lawn chair: I go fishing to relax, not break my butt, not get a nervous breakdown. You, you nut, you work harder at fishing than you do at your job. You don't even give yourself a chance to enjoy the environment."

"Enjoy it? Hell, I'm part of it! Right out there where the action is, not parked on my can up there in the sand waiting for a reel-click to tell me something that any real fisherman would want to feel— not just hear, *feel*."

"Oh, yeah, well, let me tell you . . ."

No, the question is not which is the better method, but which is the better method for you. Your answer has to be personal as well as strategic.

You might, for example, be convinced that fish are feeding a mile down the beach, yet be prevented by a bad heart (or an over-weight body or a contemplative disposition) from hustling after them. Or your occupation might make so few demands on your mind that you welcome the continuous calculations required by keeping constantly on the move. Or catching fish might be so far secondary to just relaxing and unwinding under the stars that it is quite enough for you just to lean back in your lawn chair and listen leisurely for your reel's click.

Fine. There's a place for every angler in the surf. Every age, every strength, every inclination can be accommodated. Just be sure you don't short change yourself; don't try one variation of one method under one set of conditions, decide that it's for you, then never try any others. There will be times when a nonstop session of wading and plugging will be a perfect way to burn off a backlog of energy; others when sitting and waiting will suffice. Try them all. Broaden your repertoire at every opportunity. Learn to match your method to your mood.

Once you have decided on the species you'll seek and the method you'll employ, it's time to put together your strategy. For all the word's somber War Room connotations, strategy to a surfman means simply deciding how to be at *the right place* at *the right time* using *the right lure* in *the right way.*

The Right Place

Your selection of the right place to fish is limited, first of all, by what you fish for. Bonefish in Boston Harbor? Pollock at Padre Island? Bluefish in San Francisco Bay? Of course not. All species are born, live, and die within a geographically identifiable territory. Storms, stray currents, abnormal temperatures, population explosions, and a declining food supply can extend or contract a species' range, but most catches are made year after year within the same definable area where they have found conditions for feeding, spawning, and surviving to their liking.

Just as strategically important as where a fish lives is where a fisherman lives. No point in being a snook specialist if you reside in Seattle; no percentage in having your heart set on nothing but California surfperch if your home is in Portland, Maine.

Within a species' territory is a variety of terrain, some suitable, some not. You would not seek tautog on a sandy bottom any more than you would seek blackback flounder on a rocky one. Tautog are much more likely to be found among rocks with the crabs and crustaceans they're partial to, flounder on bay bottoms where sea-worms abound.

But how do you cast to a bay bottom whose shores are barri-caded by *No Trespassing* signs? How do you reach rocks that are a four-hour round trip distant when you have to be home in three? Accessibility and available time also must be part of your planning.

The ability to read a beach is critically important to a surf fish-erman's success. Ridges, dips, rocks, troughs—all under the right conditions can attract fish; all under the right conditions give hints of their presence. The observant angler sees beneath the surface of his sea. Study, concentration, and common sense reveal a bottom's contour as clearly as a topographical map.

Years ago on an island south of Cape Cod I learned this lesson the hard way when tide rips, whipped by a sudden wind, forced my

These Plum Island anglers were waiting for bluefish which they knew would be herding bait along the sandbar during a dropping tide.

friend Bill Stone and me to spend an unscheduled night under the stars. Monomoy Island is a long narrow barrier beach of virtually barren sand along whose bait-rich edges some of the world's largest striped bass and bluefish are caught. For a fledgling surf fisherman, it's also a great classroom.

The sudden change in Bill's and my plans was not entirely unexpected or unprepared for. After many years of trolling the shoals between the Cape and its offshore islands, Nantucket and Martha's Vineyard, we had learned how quickly millpond calms can be churned into seas that 16-foot outboards have no business being in. Sleeping bags always are part of our cargo on Monomoy trips.

Bill and I were bedding down in the lee of a dune after completing a few cursory goodnight casts when we discovered that we weren't alone. Four men with rods over their shoulders loomed out of the murk moving from right to left along the beachfront 50 yards away.

"When in Rome," said Bill. We grabbed our rods and followed their footprints for a quarter-mile until we heard them hollering in the dark about 30 yards down the beach: "I'm on . . . Here's another one . . . Hey, look at this baby go . . ."

The Promised Land! Their dialogue suggested that the ebony ocean in front of us must have been teeming with stripers. Yet a half-hour later, after heaving swimming plugs, popping plugs, metal squids, and bucktail jigs without so much as a jostle, we trudged back to our dune harboring the incipient suspicion that maybe there's more to this surf casting than just casting into the surf.

Next morning Bill discovered the answer. Traipsing off through a gauzy fog, he followed a path that had been worn in the sand by fish being dragged right through our bedroom while we slept. It terminated in a well-trampled 20-yard stretch at the water's edge, the battleground where the trio had been hitting their fish the night before, and directly in front of Bill was a boiling tide rip that was tailor-made for hungry stripers seeking an easy meal of tumbling baitfish. The rip was created by currents churning across a submerged sandbar. From within the trampled patch every cast landed among feeding bass; from outside of it you couldn't hit a bass with a bazooka. Although only a few yards up the beach the night before, Bill and I had been casting into an empty ocean.

Since that experience, I have spent more hours fishing from

beaches, fewer from boats. Part of my reason for changing was the awesome success enjoyed by those men who knew what they were doing; nothing succeeds—or inspires—like success. Part of it was the fascinating prospect of discovering the infinite subtleties of tide and topography that can so easily make the difference between blank and bonanza. But the biggest inducement of all has been the incomparable intimacy and challenge of surf fishing: up to my fanny in the fish's own environment, playing the game on the fish's turf, by the fish's rules, with the odds for a change in the fish's favor.

Books taught me a bit about the surf, but most of the saltwater texts I could find had been written to help the good surf angler become better. An occasional article was aimed at the neophyte who would like to take on an ocean but doesn't know how to go about it, but most of these also were slanted at the angler who already knew his way around the ocean's edges. From nonfishing books— *Kingdom of the Tides* by Samuel Carter III (Hawthorn Books, Inc., New York, 1966), *The Sea Around Us* by Rachel Carson (Oxford University Press, New York, 1951), *Life Nature Library*: *The Sea* by Leonard Engel and the Editors of *Life* (Time, Incorporated, New York, 1961)—I came to appreciate the seashore as the locale of man's awesome evolutionary transition from sea to land, as a fragile nursery for young fish, and as a promising source of future food, but the fishing of it I learned mostly from experience. A knowledge of the ocean's edges must be absorbed through the pores as well as assimilated through the mind. The brain of a good surfman always is ably assisted by the seat of his waders.

The traditional way to learn a beach is to study it first through binoculars from the crest of a dune at low tide, noting every edge of its slope, every undulation of its bottom, every rock and mussel bed and weed patch, and then to confirm your findings on foot. Walk, watch, wonder, and questions will come easy. That ripple on the water, why is it there? That sandy ridge, won't it provide an ideal ambush when the tide is about halfway up and bait comes tumbling across its top? That shallow pocket, won't it make a perfect *cul-de-sac* in which predators can corner bait? Every curve, every winkle can mark routes that will be followed by foraging fish when the tide is high.

One surf fisherman I know carries low tide a step further by running his skiff along the edges of beaches when the tide is at its lowest.

Low tide is the best time to learn a beach. Every wrinkle, every rise, every depression is a clue to where fish might be found when the tide floods. (Photo: Joel Arrington)

"This enables me to study the bottom for many feet beyond what is exposed," he points out. "And," he adds, "there are low tides and there are *very* low tides. Twice a month, when moon and sun are at right angles to one another, the lowest water of the month occurs. Neap tides, they're called. There's more to be seen, more to be learned during these extra-low tides."

You also can extend your range by snorkeling. With inexpensive mask, flippers, and plastic breathing tube, I have discovered fish where I never expected them to be: bluefish beneath bathers, stripers right at the feet of fishermen who were casting futilely 50 yards beyond, flounder that blended so perfectly with the bottom that I wasn't aware of their presence until I touched them.

Interpreting your topographical findings is part common sense, part intuition, and part experience. Trial-and-error teaches lasting lessons, but it gobbles hours that are much too few in the first place. You need a good teacher to get you on target quickly. No, I don't mean one of those omniscient oracles who's got all the answers and doles them out at so many dollars per hour. These guys are professional guides, well worth their fees when you've got only a few hours to squeeze all the action you can out of an unfamiliar territory, but too expensive, too mechanized a way to become a surf fisherman. You can pay with dollars to learn how to fish *a* surf, but to learn how to fish *the* surf, you have to invest yourself.

The kind of teacher I have in mind is one who's just enough ahead of you in experience to enable you to avoid a lot of unproductive wheel-spinning, yet not so far ahead that he can't pick up an occasional pointer from your observations. Ideally he should be close enough in age and interest to ensure compatibility; of about the same physical condition so you won't slow him down; patient enough to help you unsnarl your line even when the fish you've been seeking all night suddenly start busting right in front of you; and wise enough to realize that for a lesson to be lastingly learned, his explanation must be reinforced by your experience.

And how do you go about finding such a blend of pedagogue and pal? Try the direct route: join a club, present your case to a savvy member with whom you think you'll get along, and he'll probably invite you to accompany him next time he has an opening. A desire to share is a quality common to most surfmen I know. But be prepared to pay with punctuality, patience, and persistence for every lesson learned, every secret revealed, every locale disclosed. These men have worked too hard acquiring their knowledge to dispense it casually to the undeserving.

Arnold Clark was my mentor. This long, lean, redheaded resident of Massachusetts' Cape Ann knows the wrinkles on many north-of-Boston beaches better than most people know the furrows in their faces. Arn and I were introduced by a mutual friend who gave up surf fishing halfway through his third consecutive all-night session with Arn and me because, after a combined total of almost sixty man-hours of prowling and plugging, we hadn't scored so much as a swirl between us. When I kept right on casting as our friend disappeared over the dunes to log a few hours' sleep in his car before going to work, Arn figured that I showed promise. A half-hour later, when fish suddenly started hitting everything we threw at them and I handed my rod to a man who had broken his, Arn smiled approvingly and allowed as how I might want to join him a few nights later in "this little out-of-the-way backwater I know."

Since then Arn and I have prowled a lot of shore together. Day and night, through rocks and weeds and sand and marsh, in the mildest as well as the wildest of weather, we've made thousands of casts, caught hundreds of fish, and come to a few conclusions.

"Differences," Arn told me early in our association, "that's what to look for. A long flat stretch of beach rarely is worth your attention, but when you see the flatness interrupted, that's when to start casting."

Pockets, dips, and ridges constantly are being formed by the pounding and clawing of the surf. Some of these stay to become long-term features of the shore's conformation, others soon are flattened and filled by storms. Knowledge deteriorates when it isn't updated regularly.

The sloughs inboard of barrier bars are favorite feeding grounds. Beach-wise anglers often concentrate at cuts in these bars, knowing that gamefish will be cruising through when the tide is right. Subtle creases in the current are all that observant anglers need to locate these hot spots, but when stiff breezes obliterate the creases, they find the slots anyway. Bearings pinpoint them, angles they've stored in their data banks to gauge the direction toward prominent and permanent landmarks: a light, a house, a point of land.

Composition is as important as texture when sizing up a beach bottom. Occasionally sand is inexplicably interrupted by a patch of mud. Resident mussels and worms are notorious fish attractors.

Rocks always are worth investigating. Crabs, eels, lobsters, and snack-size fish seeking food and protection among their weedy caves are an attraction to hungry predators; big lazy fish often lie in their lees conserving energy while waiting for the flow to deliver an easy meal.

Food-carrying currents also make river and creek mouths popular with hungry fish. They also give the lie to the belief that beaches should be fished only a couple of hours before and after top tide. One of Arn's most valuable lessons has been that fish will hit at any tide if you can find and entice them. Sure, he acknowledges that

Crabs, eels, lobsters, and small fish that live among rocks are a constant attraction for hungry predators.

moving water is a plus for faster fishing, but, he asks, how often do you get a perfect set of circumstances? There always are better times or better places or better weather: cold slows fish down, heat makes them lazy, a recent meal takes the edge off their appetites. The idea is to brew up the best available blend of all elements. When one is extra-bad—slow flow, high surf, roily water—you make up for it by picking an extra-good place or fishing it in an extra-special way.

The best bluefishing I've ever had occurred in the estuary of the Merrimack River in northern Massachusetts when a bottoming tide exposed a broad sprawl of sand where the river elbows to its right before its final half-mile run to the ocean. Unable any longer to escape across the top of this sandbar, menhaden were easy prey for

The tip of a jetty at the tail end of a dropping tide—fish often congregate here to wait for the tide to deliver their breakfast. (Photo: Terry McDonnell)

the blues that had herded them against its steep curved slope. Only a few miles from there is a small marshy pocket at the confluence of two creeks where I now appreciate low tide as a prime time for striped bass. For two years, dead low had been when I paused for a beer, because there was only six inches or so of water over the mushy clamflat across which I cast. Then I discovered a narrow hard-packed ridge that I could inch along right out into the middle of the mile-square cove. For better than a half-hour on either side of dead low I now jerk jigs or drift worms along the channel's edges, usually scoring better than from shore.

Arn also asks, "How well do you know the fish you're trying to outsmart?" Every species offers the alert surfman evidence of how he can outwit it by exploiting its habits: what it eats, how it feeds, when and where it migrates, what type of water and bottom it prefers. You'll catch few blues in a roily surf, or big redfish on surface lures, or bones on a shallow flat when a tide starts pouring out, or cod close to shore once the water has warmed.

Recently a young woman complained to me that she and her husband had spent an entire Sunday on a northern New England beach and hadn't caught a single striped bass. "I can't understand it," she said. "Last summer we caught them in that some place every time we went. We even used the same bait, big juicy seaworms right on the bottom." The difference was that this was April. Stripers migrating north wouldn't be arriving for a month.

For the alert surfman, beaches abound with signs. Every gull that swoops over the water does so for a reason, and that reason usually has something to do with fish. Casters come a-running when dozens of screaming birds are diving into feeding fish, but the Surfman—capital S—he was casting as soon as the first bird pulled up short and dove to investigate a suggestive shadow. Even sitting gulls have a message for him if they're swimming nervously, craning their necks, waiting for action to erupt.

He also notes boats. Rods bend as fish move through. By observing the path of the bending rods, he plots and predicts the fish's course. When the school comes within casting range, he's there to meet it.

His eyes are down as well as up while he wades, polarized lenses sharpening his vision. Occasionally he'll spot small fish scurrying frantically through the shallows, sometimes clear up onto the sand. Before the predator that's been pursuing them is able even to veer back toward deeper water, his lure is on its way.

His sight, his smell, his hearing—all are honed to a fine edge. A bass attacks, and he hears the smash above the slapping of the surf and the rustle of the current. A school of blues breaks the surface, and his plug is waiting, vectored by the telltale melon smell they exude. Every cell of his body, every fiber of his brain pulses and ticks and tingles, poised to detect, primed to react, and over it all, like an oily slick on a surging sea, is a soft quiet calm of contentment. The ultimate attainment of the human condition: a man doing what he likes and doing it surpassingly well.

The Right Time

The most obvious restriction on *when* you fish is time of year. In any given location within its range, a species can be present one month, one week, one day, and gone the next. The dock from which I catch snapper blues in July produces only smelt and tomcod in January.

Within its season, a species has periods of unusual activity, both fast and slow. Stripers, for instance, when schooled in autumn for their southward migration, go on reckless feeding binges that can give a surfman more action in a week than he has had all summer, yet in August-warm waters these same fish sometimes fast for days.

Time of day is as strategically significant as time of year. Early morning and early evening always are good bets because surf fish, seeing best in the dim light of dawn and dusk, normally are on their feed. For the same reason, overcast days are better than bright ones.

Nights are notoriously good for fishing, and not just because they're the only occasions when most wage-earners can squeeze in

Night—a whole new ballgame for the surf fisherman, with wary fish foraging in close and the best spots available for the asking.

their hours in the surf. Many species—blues, stripers, cod, weakfish, to name a few—often feed as actively after dark as before.

But night fishing is not just the same old thing with the lights turned off. No longer do diving gulls and breaking bait and rods bending in nearby boats help you to locate your quarry. No longer are rocks and weeds and buoys easy to see and avoid. Twists and loops in your line, visible during the day, now can go undetected until—usually about the time fish start cooperating—you find yourself reeling in a monumental tangle. And the bugs! On warm nights when the wind is soft across the marshes, endless swarms of attacking insects—up your ankles, down your neck, into nose and eyes and ears and mouth—can cancel your casting as surely as a school of killer whales.

There are compensations: solitude in an age when getting off by yourself is becoming an increasingly rare luxury; a minimum of traffic, enabling you to fish blissfully undisturbed; the real prospect of tying into a big fish foraging in close. And there are ways to offset the handicaps. Here are six.

First, get there early. By starting an hour or so before dark, you can refresh your memory about details such as rocks and sandbars and you can reconnoiter for recent accumulations of weeds and flotsam and for newly installed mooring buoys and lobster pots. By embarking immediately after work on the hour-and-a-half drive to my favorite plugging point, and by eating a sandwich enroute, I save ten minutes. By rigging my rod and securing it in my roof rack beforehand, I save a few more. By laying out lures, stringers, flashlight, insect repellent, plus a minimum of spare tackle in accordance with a well-memorized checkoff list, I am able to be rigged, dressed, and on my way across the dunes within five minutes of disembarking. By the time darkness descends, I am well adjusted, confident of my casts, sure of my footing, and mentally rehearsed about what I shall do differently as conditions are modified by the tide.

A second way to compensate is to listen attentively. Sounds, unless they are drowned out by winds and waves, are easier to hear at night than during the din of day. With no outboards' drone or bathers' laughter to obscure it, the slap of a fish's tail or the scurrying of a school of baitfish can pinpoint your targets as accurately as diving gulls.

Third, look as well as listen attentively. Phosphorescent flashes frequently will reveal the presence of fish, provided you're alert for them and you know what to look for. One August night in a moonlit surf, stripers were all around me, yet I was unaware of their presence because the moon's reflection obscured their movements. A friend, who can see a striper in a bucket of tar, told me how to spot them. "The shadows," he explained, "look for the shadows."

Feeling more carefully is a fourth way to make up for your decreased vision. Line loops, weeds, and hooks that hang up on one another—impediments you'd quickly see and correct in daylight—can be detected just as quickly by running your fingers along your lure before each cast and around your reel spool before each retrieve. One night in a moonlit marsh I was plugging with a brand-new spinning reel when fish began swirling about 30 feet away on the far side of a creek. It was a made-to-order situation that lasted about 20 minutes, every second of which I wasted trying to figure out why my line kept getting tangled every time I tried to cast. My problem was a bail screw which, because of a manufacturing imperfection, would not screw up flush; my line was snagging behind it. Next time out I simply twisted the body of my reel each time I pulled back the bail prior to casting. Both actions were automatic and made in the same motion.

Despite all of your precautions, you'll still get more tangles at night than during the day, so as your fifth compensation, always bring along at least one extra spool of line. Small tangles you can take the time to untie; larger ones, you're better off cutting off until such time as your shortened line appreciably lessens your casting distance. Then you can slip on your spare spool.

Compensation number six is illumination. Even with a cat's vision, a deer's hearing, and a touch as sensitive as a safecracker's, you'll still at times need a light. Which kind to get, as well as when and how to use it, is discussed in Chapter 5.

Tides more than any other factor affect the timing of inshore fishing, yet few surfmen bother to learn much more than when high and low tides occur. A high tide produces fish for them one week, so they give it another try the next. But next time the moon no longer is full, so the flow is slower and the rise is lower. Bait now can cope with the current and avoid predators; mangrove roots where baitfish tried to hide no longer are flooded. Smart strategists learn the tides' causes as well as their effects.

Say you're fishing a jetty. Same low tide as last time, same far-out rock. Even though weakfish are walloping your jig on almost every cast, you're careful to head back for shore when the tide is about halfway in so you won't get cut off, only today you have to swim across the dip that was dry last time you headed in.

Say you arrive at the bait shop early to make sure you'll have a good selection of the long fat mudworms you like to walk along a channel's edge for striped bass, but today there aren't any big worms; there aren't any worms at all.

Or say the man with the stringerful of jumbo bluefish recommends that you fish the Cape Cod Canal. Straight out from the street light about 40 yards, he says; mackerel chunks on the bottom. So you run across the road and through the field and down the steep riprapped bank, do exactly what the man said, and lose six dollars' worth of terminal tackle on the rocky bottom.

All of these mini-catastrophes occurred to me before I learned how to make tides my ally instead of my adversary. Had I known in those days a little more about tidal dynamics, I would have realized that height as well as time of high tide varies from day to day; that on the Massachusetts coast where I do most of my fishing, mean tidal range between Boston and Martha's Vineyard can be as much as 10 feet and as little as just over 1 foot.

Consider what inconvenience this simple fact could have saved me. On that jetty I would have realized that on my previous visit, the cut had been starting to fill at half tide. Checking the tide table that I had been given gratis at my local tackle shop, I would have found that half-tide on that day had been half of a 6-foot rise, or 3 feet, while today's was half of a 9-foot rise, or 4½ feet. To get across the cut before tidal rise topped my 3-foot threshold of safety, I would have had to head back before the tide got to be one-third in.

In buying mudworms I would have considered that the exposed areas on mudflats diminish as tidal heights increase. When my chart predicted a much-higher-than-average tide, I could have planned my strategy around walking live eels after dark or bottom-bouncing a jig and porkrind instead of depending on mudworms.

And one look at the canal's sizzling tideway would have shown me the futility of fishing bait on its rocky bottom. Obviously a sinker would stay put only during a brief period on either side of high and low water, when the flood is slowest. The man with the blues, of course, had scored during one of these periods.

I learned that bottom-fished bait is deadly on Cape Cod Canal bluefish, but only when sluicing tides slacken.

Despite the influence of tides on marine angling, most saltwater sport fishermen learn little about their mysteries or their mechanics. As far as Joe Angler is concerned, tides just happen. Sometimes when he arrives at the ocean, the water level is high, other times it's low; sometimes its flow is fast, other times it's slow or has ceased entirely. Like gulls and waves and sand and shells, tides are part of the perpetual pageant of the seashore. He observes them, he copes with them, but he rarely capitalizes on them.

First thing to be aware of when cranking tidal action into your strategy is that tides are caused by the gravitational pull on the earth by the moon and sun. In theory, even the remotest star exerts its attraction on the deepest drop of water in the sea, but in practice, we need consider only the effects of moon and sun.

The moon, of course, plays the major role. The sun, though its mass is 27 million times that of our tiny satellite, the moon, is so far from earth that its influence is only about 46 percent that of the moon. The way Newton put it in his law of gravity, two bodies will rotate around a common center of gravity if their centrifugal forces equal their attractive forces. This is the case with moon and earth: overall, their centrifugal and attractive forces balance.

A given point on the earth's surface, however, is affected by the particular combination of forces acting on it at any given instant, and this combination varies continuously as the moon revolves around the earth, and the earth, to a much smaller degree, around the moon. The resultant force tends to pull the earth's surface out of shape.

Yes, even the rigid surface of the earth responds slightly. Even more pronounced is the daily rise and fall of inland waters, an occurrence which the late Richard Alden Knight predicted and published in his *Solunar Tables* because of his conviction that moon and sun play an influential part in determining when wildlife feed.

Greatest movement, however, is in the oceans. Tidal action is maximum when sun and moon are in line, so that their gravitational pulls are combined. This condition occurs twice each month, a few days after full and new moons, and produces the abnormally high water levels of spring (nothing to do with the season) tides. Minimum tidal movement occurs at twice-a-month neap tides, midway between spring tides. At these times moon and sun are at right angles and their pulls work against each other.

Each day normally has almost two complete tidal cycles. Not quite, because the lunar day happens to be fifty minutes longer than the solar day. This means that in most places a given tide will occur a little less than an hour later on each succeeding day. One noteworthy exception to this rule is the island of Tahiti, where, with slight variations, high tides *always* occur at noon and midnight, low at six a.m. and six p.m. This peculiarity occurs because Tahiti happens to be located where the moon's influence is barely felt.

While it's easy to get the impression of the sea surging back and forth twice every twenty-four hours plus fifty minutes, this is not what happens. Tides are waves. In wave action, a given point of water has very little lateral movement. It simply rolls in a circular path as the wave passes through it, just as a beach ball does in a surf before the waves break. As the wave approaches shore, it is slowed and pushed higher and higher by the upward-sloping bottom until, too heavy to support itself any longer, it collapses with a crash.

As the earth rotates, therefore, a sort of wall of water moves along its oceans, with the highest point on the wall being where the moon is closest. When the wall approaches shore, the tide comes in (floods); when the wall recedes, the tide goes out (ebbs).

Perfect tidal motion would occur if a smooth spherical earth were covered by a uniformly thick layer of ocean. The ocean's floor is not smooth, however, and continents have irregular edges, shelves of varying depths, and shorelines that stretch in different directions.

Further complicating the picture are the vast natural basins across which water moves back and forth like waves in a tub. Remember what happens when you test your bath water? Dragging your hand across the surface, you make a wave rise on the side. The wave reverses direction, diminishes to its lowest height at the tub's center, then rises till it hits the other side and again is reflected.

This oscillating phenomenon is called a seiche. Its effect can be seen most dramatically in the basin of the North Atlantic. Here the sloshing back and forth occurs about once every twelve hours, almost the same period as for tidal motion, so seiches reinforce tidal action to produce the world's highest tides. Spring tides in Minas Basin near the head of the Bay of Fundy have a stupendous rise of about 50 feet, yet on Martha's Vineyard, only a few hundred miles away, the tidal range is little more than a foot. This disparity occurs because the Vineyard is near the node of the basin—the middle of the bathtub—where motion almost ceases.

With so many complications, how can you predict what tides will be like when you'll be going fishing? Easy. In the tide tables I mentioned earlier, all computations are done for you. Just look up the date and read high and low tides for that day. The only adjustment you'll have to make is for your specific location. Say, for example, that your tables have been computed for Boston and you'll be fishing at Gloucester during the afternoon of July 20. Alongside this date you read that there will be a high tide of 10.5 feet at 12:34 in Boston. From your "Table of Tidal Differences" you see

Surf fishing can be a waiting game. When conditions are right, regulars snap into action. (Photo: Milt Rosko)

that you must subtract three minutes from Boston (12:34) to get Gloucester (12:31). Normally this time is computed for Standard or Daylight Saving, depending on which will be in effect at the time. The table, by the way, also contains other strategically valuable data such as times of sunrise, sunset, and moonrise, and dates on which phases of the moon will occur.

Tides influence fishing principally because of the way they affect movement and distribution of bait. Despite its traditional topwater tranquillity, the underwater world is the scene of a constant struggle for survival: gamefish stalking baitfish, baitfish trying to elude gamefish. True, there are times when a myriad of factors—fright, full bellies, too-warm or too-cold water—deactivate the appetites of the fish you are trying to catch. Granted, a fish will strike as readily from anger, alarm, or inquisitiveness as from hunger. And, of course, the contour and composition of the bottom must be considered along with height, direction, and velocity of tides. But these are other pieces of the puzzle. Marine anglers must calculate constantly, their cranial computers whirring and beeping and blinking with continuously changing conditions. Gamefish and their supply of food comprise only one of the equations they must keep in balance, but it is an important one, normally the *most* important, and tides are a major factor in this equation.

Consider a school of sandeels as it struggles to make headway against a 4-knot flow. These tiny fish are easy marks for a strong fast predator that has no trouble coping with such a current. When tossed about in turbulence, bait are even more vulnerable. This is why savvy saltwater anglers always are on the lookout for commotions caused by currents clashing, or waters churning over rocks or shoals, or wind whipping a contrary tide.

Distribution of bait is determined to a great extent by how much territory a tide covers. Grass shrimp in an inundated marsh are sucked into deeper water when the tide ebbs, and it's no coincidence that weakfish often are waiting in ambush. Conversely, on a low tide both prey and predator are concentrated in a much smaller volume of water.

Local topography can combine with tides to produce conditions that attract fish. One of my favorite striper spots is a rocky peninsula from which I can plug into a broad pocket between a mudbank on my left and a creekmouth on my right. During the middle half of an ebbing tide, the water's flow and the bottom's slope create a gentle countercurrent across a mussel bed that I can just reach with a streamer fly from atop a cluster of barnacled boulders. Baitfish congregate here and bass make the most of it. For bluefish I am partial to the estuary of a broad river, where a long tongue of sand tails off from a sharp elbow of shoreline. As soon as this sandbar is bared by an ebbing tide, thereby cutting off escape across its top, blues herd bait against the *cul-de-sac* slope of its upcurrent side.

Some species habitually wait for certain tidal conditions. Anadromous fish such as salmon and steelhead sometimes need an assist

from the extra-high waters of spring tides to make it across obstacles such as sandbars and rapids that block the mouths of their
natal streams. Surf feeders such as striped bass and bluefish can get
inboard of a barrier bar only after rising water floods the cut they
must swim through. Bonefish must wait for high water to graze
along the food-rich inside edges of mudflats. Even at the headwaters
of my favorite shad creek, 10 miles inland from the ocean, action
is influenced by the tides. You don't notice the difference in the
height of the water on the aldered banks, you don't feel it in the
pressure against your waders, but action almost invariably is
faster when fish can ascend against the firmer flow of an ebbing
tide.

Which tides are best for fishing? High? Low? Ebb? Flow? Fast?
Slow? There's no simple or universally applicable answer. Even
the "two hours before and two hours after high water" that many
anglers regard as gospel doesn't apply when you can't deliver your
plug to snook that are feeding among mangrove roots after they
have been covered by a flooding tide. In fact, the opposite is true
when fish are waiting off a river's mouth for an ebbing tide to deliver their dinner.

Even slack-water periods, generally regarded as the worst tidal
times of all for filling stringers, can be prime fishing time. Slacks
are those interludes at and on either side of low and high water
when tides slow down and change direction. Because one of the
main functions of a tidal flow from a fisherman's standpoint is to
deliver food to fish, it's reasonable to assume that when the current
peters out, so does a fish's chowline. Logically, then, a fish could be
expected to lie doggo till its catering services resumed rather than
forage far afield for bait that's much harder to corner and catch
when it has no current to contend with. That's how I used to think.

Then one bright night I was catching pollock after pollock on
light spinning tackle until just before the tide topped off. Then
nothing. As suddenly as if a switch had been thrown, action ceased.
The stillness was startling, ominous. I stopped casting and waited
for the start of the something that I knew intuitively was going to
happen. It started with a swirl. Then there were ten, twenty, a
hundred. Stripers had herded the pollock against the beach and the
blitz had begun.

Aha, I concluded, high-water slack is prime fishing time after all.
So the following month I headed a few miles up the coast, where a

friend had run into big bass on the previous tide. Another knockout of a night: bright, calm, cool. This time I was casting live eels along the edge of a marsh and the bass couldn't have been more cooperative. Throughout the entire half-hour before the tide's peaking, stripers struck on nearly every cast. Then that switch got pulled again, only this time it stayed pulled.

The fish were there. Twice in the following ten minutes a boat-man goosed his engine and the water around us erupted with stripers, yet they could not be persuaded to strike.

So what do you conclude? That high-water slack is a good time for fishing? That high-water slack is the time for breaking out your thermos until the tide picks up again? What about low-water slack in a shallow pocket that I plugged for hours without a strike, yet two weeks later on the same low-water conditions I edged my way along a sandbar, plugged along the channel's edge, and couldn't stop catching fish? And what about the Cape Cod Canal, where sluicing currents make its once-every-four-hour slacks the only practical periods for fishing bait on the bottom?

With all these exceptions, is it possible to predict how tides are going to influence fishing? And if it is, can it be done without making fishing seem like an exercise in binary arithmetic? Sure it can. The following four principles have enabled me to fish for many years with a maximum of enjoyment, a minimum of fuss, and a reasonable degree of success.

1.   Know the basics of tidal technology: what causes tides; how, when, and to what degree tides respond to these influences; how their responses affect fishing.

2.   Listen to the old maxims—good fishing at high water, poor fishing at slack, etc.—but always adapt them to your locale.

3.   Appreciate tides for what they are: an important factor in planning your fishing strategy, but only one among many. Continuously crank in other factors—wind, weather, time of year, time of day, condition of water, species you're seeking, etc.—and always leave room in your calculations for a little luck. Surely you too have a smelly old fedora or a patched and tattered parka or a salt-encrusted lure whose influence on fishing far outweighs the gravitational attraction of a mere 79.2-million-million-million-ton celestial body.

4.   Remember these wise words that an old-timer once told me:

"Somewhere fish are waiting to take you on regardless of the tide. Go find 'em."

Winds also affect when you should fish. Sometimes winds complement tidal conditions, as when an onshore blow reinforces a flooding tide, pushing water higher onto a beach, deeper into a marsh; other times they contradict, as when the same onshore wind works against an ebbing tide. For the surfman, wind and tide are intimately intertwined, two elemental forces with a single resultant vector.

The time to consider wind is *before* you leave home. What is its present direction and velocity? How will these affect the shore you plan to fish? What changes are forecast? Fishing a favorite spot just because you have enjoyed good times and good catches there in the past is sentiment, not strategy. Love of a special location certainly should not be ignored when deciding where you are going to fish, but priority should be given to whether fish are likely to be present and feeding.

Some winds bode well for fishing, others poorly. The East Coast angler welcomes the warm gentle southwesterlies that prevail during summer because they stir up bait along his beachfronts. During a stiff southwesterly, he can enjoy furiously fast action, but there are drawbacks: casting is difficult; feeling a bite and setting a hook against the slack of a ballooning line are next to impossible. Two or three days of a southwest wind can dirty the water so badly that his hooks will continuously be clogged with seaweed, straw, and debris. Always there are liabilities along with the assets. Strategy is the art of making sure the pluses always outweigh the minuses.

Classifying winds according to compass direction can be confusing. Instead, look on winds as either onshore or offshore. A blow full in your face will produce the problems and benefits described in the previous paragraph; from behind, it will enable you to cast a country mile but often into a sea so flattened that fishing is slow because baitfish are staying put and marine morsels such as crabs, clams, and worms are not being buffeted from their sanctuaries.

Most winds, though, are from neither directly ahead nor directly astern. Sure, our Atlantic and Pacific coastlines run essentially north and south, our Gulf coastline essentially east and west, but none is a straight line. You have only to round a bend to get a quartering wind behind you; to move into the lee of a dune to cut off a crosswind that's interfering with your cast. Clever strategists fish where wind and tide and topography blend into a battle plan, yet allow for tactical adjustments as these elements change.

The normal brand of bad weather, in my opinion, is a lot less detrimental to surf fishing than is commonly assumed. Surf fish may feed less during storms, but feed they do. The angler who is willing to endure a little discomfort often can have them all to himself. I have caught too many fish during too many storms to cancel out on a surf spree just because of a little thunder and lightning. The postman's "Nor rain, nor snow, nor sleet . . ." belongs on every set of waders.

In fresh water there is sound reasoning behind the "fish bite better when it rains" theory: bugs and worms are washed into streams; fish instinctively capitalize. But the fare of saltwater is not significantly affected by a reasonable rainfall. Prolonged downpours, of course, can lower salinity, especially around river mouths. Then everything from fish kills to red-tide blooms can result. During the normal course of a fish's active season, though, the principal way in which normally unpleasant weather reduces fish catches is by keeping fishermen at home.

Violent storms are a different story. Fish cannot feed along an ocean front that's being assaulted by towering waves and torn by screaming winds. Fortunately, periods like this are signaled by a rapidly dropping barometer. When the weather man warns something like "29.92 and falling fast," you're not likely to catch many fish.

Yet even under these conditions, I hesitate to say stay at home. Sheltered backwaters still might produce. And even if they don't, even with the scales almost straight up against your scoring, the surf has it all over a TV screen.

Just as a dropping barometer can signal slow fishing, a rising one can mean that fish's appetites are starting to improve now that fair weather is on the way. The storm may not even seem to be abating, but if the barometer has bottomed out, head for the shore. A lot of famished fish will be waiting.

The Right Lure

The right lure? Probably there are several. Under most circumstances, surf feeders do not scrutinize a meal before deciding to eat it. They can't afford to. A second's delay, and another fish will have beaten them to it. Competition usually persuades a fish to eat first and ask questions later.

Selectivity is further diminished by dirty water and extremes of light and darkness. The perennial effectiveness of many lures that bear only superficial resemblance to sea creatures—tin squids, for example, and jigs, and many noisemaker plugs—confirms that movement and flash are more important than verisimilitude.

Nevertheless, there are times when only one lure will work. This might occur because there is so much easy-to-kill bait around that fish can feed at their leisure, making the slightest suggestion of phoniness easy to detect. Or it might happen when clear water, unfamiliar territory, or the suspected presence of predators makes fish supercautious, hence superchoosy.

Since trying to forecast a fish's frame of mind is about as chancy as picking three-horse parlays, play it safe by starting with a lure that looks as much like the currently predominant bait as possible.

A bait can be dominant for many reasons. A burgeoning of the menhaden population can increase the effectiveness of bunker spoons designed to resemble them. A sudden glut of squid can make fish infuriatingly singleminded about their diets. Migrations of mullet and seaworms always ignite feeding orgies; so do alewives pouring in seemingly endless procession along the shores of bays and canals toward the mouths of spawning streams. Eels come out of their covers after dark and predators await them. Crabs live in rocks.

Normally a hungry fish will eat anything that's edible; a hard plastic plug will be as appealing as a soft plastic eel. But not all conditions are normal, not all fish are hungry. At these times a lure that bears a no-questions-asked resemblance to what fish currently are conditioned to feed on can give you that extra edge.

As for that silly-looking old standby that for some unfathomable reason always seems to catch fish, and that sexy space-age number you couldn't resist buying because you just *know* fish are going to find it irresistible, use them. Confidence and a good track record still are the best endorsements.

But why bother trying to simulate bait anyway? Why not use the real thing and eliminate all possibility of arousing fish's suspicions? After all, that's what fish eat; not plastic, wood, metal, feather, and fiber imitations. Three reasons. First is personal preference. Some anglers spurn live baits because they consider conning fish with counterfeits to be a far greater challenge.

"A mullet swims by," one said to me once, "a snook grabs it. Big deal. You think a guy should get a gold star just because his hook happens to be sticking out of the mullet's back?"

Oversimplified, of course. His hook happens to be in the mullet's back because he put it there; delicately enough for the mullet to swim naturally, unobtrusively enough for the snook to overlook its presence. Furthermore, the mullet swims by because the angler maneuvered it into position at just the right time in just the right way. This is no small achievement when a bait with a built-in awareness of its vulnerability wants to one-eighty it out of harm's way. Stick to artificial lures if you like, but for rational reasons: because you prefer the constant casting, the opportunity to experiment with new designs and new retrieves, the chance to halt and twitch and wiggle your lure when a stalking fish needs to be teased into striking. A blind prejudice has no place in picking preferences.

A second reason why some surfmen eschew live baits is that they are difficult to present properly from shore. From a small boat, a nose-hooked menhaden can be trolled with precision across the rippling ridge of a submerged sandbar when you suspect that big fish are lurking in its lee, but from shore your menhaden goes pretty much where it wants to. One well-exploited exception is where you can walk a tethered baitfish through a tideway that runs alongside a sharp dropoff; another is where crowds are thin enough to allow you to fish your baits effectively from bridges. When conditions are right for live-lining, enterprising surf anglers lay aside their lures.

A third deterrent to using live baits is the obvious difficulty of acquiring them and keeping them alive. It can be done. Freshly caught—or bought—eels are carried in mesh-bottomed buckets under a layer of seaweed. Ice cubes keep them quiet, and sand, cloth gloves, or a terrycloth towel makes handling easy. Even port-

Live alewives are netted for striper bait when they swarm up herring runs on their spring spawning sprees.

able cages occasionally are anchored in shallow water as bait containers.

For most surf fishermen, however, live baits are targets of opportunity. They employ artificials or easy-to-manage naturals such as worms, clams, shrimp, or cut bait until a school of baitfish comes within range. Then they snag one on a treble hook and let it flop and thrash until a big fish singles it out and strikes. This technique can pay off handsomely when fish are on the attack, but when the school is just passing through, a single bait—even a wounded one—can get lost in the crowd. A live bait is most attractive where competition is at a minimum.

This fact was exploited by a resourceful sailor recently on the tip of a sandy spit at the mouth of a Cape Cod bay. Sighting a school of menhaden along the inside edge of the spit, he ran his sailboat aground, grabbed his rod, and snagged a bait by casting a weighted treble hook across the school and jerking hard. Then he hustled around to the ocean side where an ebbing tide was boiling over a patch of boulders. Just as he figured, big stripers were right behind them waiting for an easy meal. Within minutes he was wrestling a 34-pounder while incredulous pluggers wondered what they were doing wrong.

The Right Way

Presentation begins long before you wind up for your first cast. A loose knot can make a plug respond slowly, react sluggishly; a bulky or untrimmed knot can look suspicious, pick up weeds. The snap swivel that's so convenient for changing lures and so valuable for absorbing the twist of one that misbehaves also can interfere with the lure's action. Line weight, guide corrosion, reel lubrication, and even you yourself—your strength, comfort, coordination—all affect how your lure will look to a fish. Add tidal conditions, wind direction and velocity, how much line you leave loose while casting, whether you cast overhead, sidearm or in between, and a hundred and one other influences, and you can appreciate the complexity of a doing-everything-just-right presentation.

You also can appreciate the soothing simplicity of worm-and-bobber fishing, so before you head inland for your favorite perch pond, let me emphasize that most of these things will happen right automatically, even after very little practice. Every friend I have introduced to surf fishing has been able to make fair to good presentations better than three-fourths of the time after only one hour of casting; good to excellent after two hours. And this includes five- and six-year-old youngsters of both sexes.

Here are a few ways in which you can consciously improve your presentation.

1. Keep in mind that the cast you are making is the final element in your four-part strategy: the right place, time, lure, and presentation. Flub it and all prior work can be for naught. You are stalking a specific fish that behaves in at least a partially predictable way. If the fish is out there, where is it? Behind that rock? In the tail of that turbulence? Alongside that sandbar you discovered yesterday when the tide was low? And what is it doing? Feeding? Migrating? Avoiding its enemies?

2.   Aim every cast. Select where you want your lure to splash down, and keep your eye on that spot. Not only will you catch more fish this way, but you will improve your accuracy for those glorious occasions when breaking fish eliminate the guesswork.

3.   Consider how wind will affect your cast, and compensate accordingly. When a stiff blow billows your line, start reeling in slack before your lure hits the water. You can't sink a hook on a slack line.

4.   Allow also for how current and tide will carry your lure.

5.   Cast overhead rather than sidearm; accuracy and distance are easier to achieve.

6.   Leave enough line between lure and rod tip to inhibit tumbling. An end-over-end cast reduces distance and usually concludes with a lure's splashing like a sashweight. Length of this line varies with your lure's size, weight, and balance, but you'll probably find

Leave enough line between lure and rod tip so your lure won't tumble during the cast.

it to be longer than you expect. If a lure tumbles consistently, replace it. Later on, return it to its manufacturer with an explanation.
He'll appreciate the free field-testing and probably will send you a
couple of replacements.

7.   Cover an area completely. Concentrate first on the most
likely spots—rocks, sandbars, mussel beds, creek mouths, etc.—
but don't ignore any part of your casting sector, including right at
your feet. Fish often will follow a lure suspiciously, delaying their
strikes until it appears to be escaping into the shallows. One accomplished surf fisherman suggests at least three casts across every
promising patch, theorizing that fish, scared by the first and interested by the second, will strike on the third. His "fright—not quite
—bite" theory, he calls it.

8.   Cover an area carefully. Fish sometimes hang in the head of
a rip as well as in its tail. Work your lure first through the forward
edge of the turbulence, then a few feet farther back, then a few
feet more until you have covered the rip thoroughly. If you suspect
that a fish is lying behind a boulder, work your lure alongside it
rather than across its top.

9.   Vary your retrieves. In daylight start fast and erratic, in darkness start slow and steady, but if these don't produce, mix them up.
Follow a fast spurt with a slow recovery, the way a tired frightened
fodder-fish would behave. Use rod tip as well as reel to reinforce
the illusion of an injured bait. Let your floating plug set for a few
seconds after it lands, and be ready when you twitch it for the
pounce of the fish that's eyeing it.

10.   This was going to be a suggestion about what to do immediately following that electrified instant when a fish strikes, but only
tentatively: the swirl, the boil, the stunning slap, but no hookup.
Then it occurred to me that I am the last guy in the world to talk
about restraint and composure while fish are showing. I've sling-
shotted too many lures past the ears of pals, wet the insides of too
many waders. Furthermore, there are some parts of fishing that
don't belong in books, that are too private and unpredictable for
one man to try to prescribe for another. Strategy stops with the
strike and resumes with the hookup. In between is extemporaneous.

Playing and landing a fish in the surf is mostly a matter of keeping common sense in balance with adrenalin. Even when your heart

pounds and your hands shake, you have to remember the location of every submerged rock and coral clump and to make sure your fish doesn't get the chance to grate your line against them. Every stationary object—pier piling, bridge abutment, mooring line, wreck—can be your fish's key to freedom. A tight line and a clear head are essential to keeping them apart.

But not too tight. That's what reel drags are for. Before making your first cast, pull your line with one hand while adjusting your drag with the other. Stop when you feel that a fish of the size that you are likely to tie into will be able to pull freely but with difficulty; easily enough so there will be little danger of its breaking your line, yet against enough tension so it will tire quickly. Then tighten your drag one more notch. Small fish still will be able to strut their stuff, while heavyweights will find the going just a little bit harder.

Recheck your drag occasionally while fishing. Some have a tendency to tighten with use. Some loosen, too, I suppose, but I have

Playing and landing a fish in the surf is mostly a matter of keeping common sense in balance with adrenalin.

been plagued only by increasing tension. It happens so gradually that you don't notice it until a heavy fish strikes, runs, and snaps your line, leaving you standing there with an empty egg-on-your-face feeling while the fish you've been waiting weeks, months, years to tangle with heads for the horizon with your $2.75 lure in tow.

One of the most helpful precepts I know is that a fish under pressure is a fish under control. Sure, the statement should be modified for special situations: a big fish that's about to leap against a taut light leader, for example, should be leaned into, lest one jerk of its head exceed the leader's limit. Yet as an overall rule for playing fish, I can't think of one better than: always keep your fish under pressure. Hold your rod high. Make the fish fight the rugged resilience of fiberglass as well as the tensile strength of nylon monofilament.

There's a corollary to this rule that also is worth remembering: a temporary slack is the best invitation to a permanent one.

Two pointers about that critical period when you finally have your fish coming, when you're he-e-eaving back to haul it toward you, then leaning forward to reel in the line that you've gained. Heave back only to the point where your rod is at right angles to your line; beyond that the effect of your efforts tapers off fast. And maintain tension on your line as you lean forward while reeling; avoid the natural tendency to bow, then reel.

Your fish is visible now, finning only a few rod lengths in front of you. A handsome fish. Not just braggin' big, but broad in its back and full in its chest and wide in its tail, an awesome expanse between stem and stern that has to be at least—at the very minimum— a mile and a quarter. As you lead it tenderly toward the beach behind you, backing and reeling in careful coordination, you imagine it mounted on the wall on your den.

"Great fighter," you'll tell your friends when they pause to admire it. "Battled all the way into the wash. Made me earn every inch. Finally worked it into the last wave, washed it right up to my feet. Just had to lean down and gill it . . ."

And that's where your dream dies. Stooping, you lowered your rod, slackening your line and enabling the fish to use the pull of the receding wave to break free.

Surf fish remind me of Volkswagens: they always seem to have a reserve tank. Once they realize that they're not going to be able to leap or run or sound their way out of a predicament, it's a good bet that they will decide to give ground and size up this thing out there that keeps pulling on them. Sometimes they'll swing off at an angle, making the current work for them, other times they'll rush right at you, but whatever their move, it probably is a tactical gambit to conserve energy until they can find an opening: a slack line, a loose hook, a rock. The farther they get from the security of deep water, the more frightened they become. The feel of foam on their backs and sand on their bellies plus the terrifying sight of your wadered torso looming above them can make them shift suddenly into overdrive. If you're not prepared, you'd better start looking at wallpaper samples for your den.

During these final few feet, when an inordinately high percentage of losses occur, here are a few points to keep in mind.

1. Play your fish a little longer. Make it use up most of its energy in deeper water, where normally you can control it better. In your urgency to catch another fish before that school you've been waiting all these hours for moves on, don't risk losing the fish you have on right now. More important, don't miss out on the most important phase in all of fishing, the hard-earned struggle that culminates strategy, stalk, and strike. Sure, that Hercules-in-a-hurry down the beach from you might winch a lot of still-green fish through the wash, but he's not fishing; he's just catching fish.

2. Keep a carefully regulated pressure on a hooked fish right up

Let a fish play itself out before you work it in among rocks. (Photo: Larry Green)

to the moment when you slip your fingers under its gill plate or gaff it or slide it onto shore.

3.   As soon as you can manage it, try to work a fish between you and the beach. Many a fish has made a last-minute escape by the simple expedient of rolling on a loose hook that has opened a hole in its jaw. If it's tired and toward shore, you have a good chance of heading it off.

4.   In the words of a lifelong Yankee striper fisherman who still admits to an occasional last-act loss, "Don't count y'r basses till they's beached."

Information

No strategy can be effective without information. Accurate up-to-the-minute intelligence is what enables an angler to put theory into practice. A well-timed phone call sometimes can be more valuable than a whole tackle shop full of equipment.

Recently on a moonlit beach, a man with whom I have fished for many years remarked how little we used to know in our early days.

"A lot of times," he recalled, "we were plugging in places where we didn't have a prayer of catching fish. There just weren't any there. When I think of all those casts we wasted . . ."

· No cast ever is wasted, of course. At the very least, it provides exercise and practice. But catching fish is, after all, the ultimate objective of fishing. No, it's not essential to enjoyment; the soul can be full even when the stringer is empty. But the catch *is* a component of completeness. Without a fish or two to reward your efforts, something—big or small, depending on the attitude of the angler, but something—is missing.

Today that man on the beach probably catches ten times more, and bigger, fish than when he started. He gets blanked maybe once every dozen times out, and even then he probably is experimenting with a new method or sizing up a new location. Ironically, his casts are not that much longer or more accurate. He presents his lures and plays his fish well, but he always did; a long freshwater apprenticeship had enabled him to catch on quickly.

The main reason for his spectacular success is that today he *knows* more, not *does* more. Much of his knowledge is cumulative. He has read, listened, observed, argued, experimented, always adding facts, culling fallacies, modifying misconceptions. Today he probably knows more about the species he seeks and the waters he seeks them in than any man alive, but, short of his sharing his knowledge with you, there is no easy-to-tap source of such information. Nor should there be. With canned strategies and guaranteed catches, fishing is little more than calisthenics.

For all his experience, though, this man still depends heavily on G-2. The written records that he keeps of every outing—date, time, weather, tide, what he used, how he made out—have provided him with valuable strategic patterns of how his fish behave, but to make necessary tactical adjustments, he needs to know how they're behaving *right now*.

Except for tide charts, printed information rarely has much tactical value. Writing, editing, typesetting, proofreading, reproduction, collating, binding, and distributing take so long that happenings have become history before they're off the presses. Hot fishing cools off so fast that even a daily newspaper can hope to be only lukewarm in its reports. Weekly and monthly periodicals often must buy their manuscripts as much as a year in advance, books sometimes twice that. Fortunately for fishermen, responsible publishers are fastidiously careful about dating their stories.

Television can be as current as daily newspapers and infinitely more instructive, but high costs prevent most stations from keeping teams in the field and films on the screen. Frank and Jack Woolner used to do a delightful weekly show out of Worcester, Massachusetts, in which they combined films and interviews with on-camera telephone reports from friends in area hot spots. Even from 50 miles inland, I could easily catch the same fish on the same tide that these reporters were describing an hour before.

Radio is the most immediate medium for disseminating local angling information. Not the batch-taped "Here's something swell to do this weekend" fillers, but the daily—even hourly in some places during in-season weekends—"What's new on the fishing front" formats. If the area being covered in a radio report is broad, however, don't delude yourself that there's a guy down on the beach doing precisely what the reporter is describing. Compiling, writing, and editing delay dissemination.

Best sources of on-the-spot information are on-site tackle shops. Successful shops are combat information centers as well as supply depots. The ones that flourish do so not so much because they sell the wiggliest worms or the sharpest hooks, but because they dispense honest current information freely: no need for prying it loose, no fear of being talked down to. The shopowner who convinces his customers that he is as concerned with their catching fish as he is with selling merchandise is assured of a return trade.

Pick a good shop in each area where you fish regularly and do most of your buying there. Get to know the owner and clerks. After a few conversations, they'll understand the kind of fishing you're looking for. When you arrive, your answers will be ready.

To make sure the first answer won't be "Go home, there's nothing doing," phone ahead. A fifty-cent phone call can save a day. Just be sure to have your questions ready and to keep the conversation brief. Begin your call by asking, "Are you busy?"

Tackle shops, of course, don't have all the answers. Even their hottest G-2 is likely to be a few hours old, because anglers seldom stop fishing till a tide expires. By the time they drop by to swap stories, the conditions they describe won't be duplicated for another six to twelve hours. Their reports are valuable, but not necessarily valid.

The surf itself, that's where the answers are. Will bonefish once again be grazing on that flat as they were on the previous two floods? Have those channel bass that were being caught yesterday from boats moved within range of the beach? Will last night's cold snap have sent the weakfish south? Are those menhaden that have been swarming into the estuary being chased by stripers and blues?

As you approach the shore that your study and experience and queries and intuition tell you is *the right place*, at *the right time*, switch on your radar. Scan the water, read the beach, check the birds and boats and bowing rods so you can complete the picture by using *the right lure* in *the right way*.

There are plenty of customers out there for your streamer flies and popping bugs.

8

Fly-Fishing and Other Special Methods

ONCE BACK-COUNTRY BAIT-CASTERS LAUNCHED their invasion of the surf, it was inevitable that fly-fishing soon would make its debut. Reports of 20-pound catches within a few feet of shore whetted the appetites of men to whom a 14-inch trout and a 4-pound bass had been once-in-a-while events, and the prospect of brush-free backcasts sweetened the pie. Flyrods started alternating with heavy artillery.

There were problems. Casts crumpled in the face of onshore winds; even with wind astern a man had trouble reaching fish. Streamer flies designed to imitate finger-size freshwater baits were ignored by ocean inhabitants accustomed to dining on foot-long mullet, mackerel, alewives, and menhaden.

Techniques, too, were inappropriate. The fastest of freshwater retrieves was too slow in the surf. Tide and waves snatched loose line from a caster's hand.

But fly-fishermen welcomed the challenge. If all they needed to get at those 20-pound fish out there was modified equipment and refined techniques, they darn well were going to come up with them. With an assist from enterprising manufacturers and a boost from the intelligence networks of organizations such as the Salt Water Flyrodders of America, they have succeeded in impressively short order.

Weight-forward lines have been a big boon. With a minimum of false-casting, a man can launch a heavy tip that tows the rest of his flyline through his guides. These torpedo heads may not be able to lick a heavy wind from head-on, but they can fight it to a draw. Fly size couldn't be reduced—in fact, flies were burdened further by heavier rust-resistant hooks—but 9- and 10-foot salmon and steelhead rods were adopted to increase range. Distance was further expanded with popping bugs, whose splashy jerky retrieves proved to be appealing to many saltwater species. Leaders tapered from 40 to a sturdy 15 pounds enhanced casting and encouraged the application of muscle when one of those 20-pounders finally took. Delicacy, these trailblazers discovered, is no more necessary with leader size than with fly design.

With practice they learned to exploit current and wind to make their flies move faster; to find those feeding stations where even big fish would be partial to small baits; to fish the more hospitable creeks and bays when weather lashed the beaches; to match their efforts and equipment to smaller fish as well as heavyweights. With loose line coiled in their teeth or in baskets strapped to their waists, they shot their flies across an open ocean; when a high flat rock was handy, they climbed, crouched, and coiled their line at their feet.

Most of the problems of marine fly-fishing had to be solved in a hurry by my photographer friend Terry McDonnell when his son, Terry, Jr., suddenly became interested. Because the boy was only eight, his dad's difficulties were magnified. Their experience bears repeating.

In Terry Senior's favor was the fact that he never had subscribed to the cop-out contention that salt water, a young son, and fly-fishing automatically spell disaster. The potential, he knew, was there, but patience always has been one of Terry's long suits. A careful analysis was called for.

Manipulating a flyrod, he reasoned, is inherently hard for a boy who has been weaned on spinning gear, even without waves and wind and tide adding to the obstacles. Young Terry was expecting to be able to transpose the same easy actions he had employed in dropping dry flies on windless trout waters. A frustrating succession of accordion casts into a stiff blow, or lost fish on surf-slackened lines, could have him calling it quits before he even got off the starting block.

But what do you say to a son who's all revved up about accompanying you to the seashore the following morning when he asks, "Can I bring the flyrod?"

Terry answered, "Sure, bring it along. Keep it handy while we're plugging and jigging. If we find fish breaking in close, you can

Saltwater flies require little sophistication. Simple baitfish-imitating bucktails do the trick.

switch." This encouraged the boy's interest while establishing reasonable parameters for the flyrod's employment. Wisely, he had concluded that the best way to fuel a youngster's interest in saltwater fly-fishing is to make sure he catches fish. Unless chances for success were high, he didn't want to risk having his son's enthusiasm extinguished. Adults, he knew, could be content to keep casting till the cows came home, but for eager action-oriented eight-year-olds, a half-hour of all cast and no catch can be as exciting as beating rugs.

But fish didn't break in close. Not that day or on several trips thereafter. Mackerel and pollock often hit the boy's jigs, school stripers occasionally pounced on his plugs, but always they were too far out from the pier from which they did their casting. Oh, the lad enjoyed his spinning, all right. "Boy," he would say after landing a fish, "that was some scrapper," but always there seemed to be tacked on the end an implied, "bet he would have fought even better on a flyrod."

So Terry Senior planned his next trip around Terry Junior's catching his first saltwater fish on a flyrod. The way he went about it—sensitive, analytical, practical, and in some ways downright clever—merits the consideration of any dad whose fledgling flyrodder wants to take on an ocean, as well as of adults who want to add a few marine species to their list of freshwater conquests.

Site selection was Terry's first concern. Not only was he seeking a place where modest-sized fish probably could be caught within the boy's limited casting range, he also wanted solid footing and plenty of open area for backcasts.

In the seaside neighborhood where Terry and his family were vacationing at the time, he and his son found two almost-eligible locations on a broad canal and a narrow creek: a deep bowl behind the canal's rock-rimmed mouth looked like a natural corral where stripers could herd bait when the tide flowed east, but footing was insecure on the wet weedy boulders; the mouth of the creek, though touted as classic fly water, was barricaded by *Private Property* and *No Trespassing* signs. Safety and respect always have been part of the McDonnell outdoor curriculum. Ultimately the two Terrys agreed on a pair of easy-to-get-to sites: the deep sprawling trough inside the jettied jaws of a second creek, and a rocky elbow where the canal bends west beyond the outlet of a power plant. The creek offered wide-open casting into water well known for its small stripers, blues, and pollock, and the elbow on a west-flowing tide was at the base of a boil in which Terry recently had caught stripers within 20 feet of shore. At the last minute he would make his selection according to how the wind was blowing.

Wind direction was critical, because young Terry would need all the help he could get to deliver a 3-inch streamer fly 20 feet. The freshwater fly that his Dad had chosen was lighter than the bushy heavy-hooked streamers he normally used, but a 4-foot boy wasn't going to lay it out very far with a 7-foot flyrod unless the wind was from his stern.

They fished the canal that August afternoon, and today both of them smile when they remember. Wind and tide were complementing each other in a swirling little close-to-shore turbulence as father and son edged down the riprapped bank. The boy should have no trouble bullseyeing the lightweight Black Ghost salmon streamer that his dad was tying onto his 5-foot leader.

But . . . Terry Senior paused, examining the water. But.

"What's the matter, Dad?"

"Current's too fast, son. Fly won't sink deep enough. What do you think we ought to do?"

"How about a sinker?"

John Fallon Jr. remembers some tense moments when his dad was teaching him to fly-fish, but he retains his sense of humor—and his love for fly-fishing.

Of course. Terry had used the trick often, but better to let a boy think out his own answers.

"But won't that make it harder for you to cast?"

"I can use that loop cast you showed me; you know, where you kind of roll your line out over the water instead of lifting it over your head behind you."

A roll cast. The boy had learned his lessons well. Raising his rod till his hand was alongside his right eye and the belly of his line just behind his right elbow, he slammed the rod forward, releasing line through his left hand while his fly looped up, over, and out.

Oh, there were tangles, and maybe once or twice young Terry wished for the extra range and old-shoe comfort of the spinning rod his dad purposely had had him leave at home. But given the chance, he wouldn't have swapped, because right from the start he knew that all the tangles and awkwardness and inconvenience would be worth it: his dad, demonstrating a cast, had hooked a pollock, handed his son the rod, and enabled him to experience the incomparable intimacy of playing a strong fish in fast water on a flyrod matched to the size and strength of both fish and fisherman.

Featherweight Fishing

One fact of life in the surf that newcomers soon learn is that most of the ocean's residents are small. Not by freshwater standards, to be sure, but few measure up to the dimensions of the leviathans you expected to be locking horns with when you first invaded the foam. Since big fish earn most of the laurels, they are the objects of most of the effort. The big lure, the stout rod, the strong line, the long cast—these are the tools for taming tigers.

But in between tigers, one runs into a lot of long, dry, discouraging stretches. There are plenty of pussycats around to take up the slack—pussycat fish on pussycat tackle. Dimensions are different, but proportions are the same.

No, I'm not equating a 20-pound snook on rugged tackle with one a foot long on lightweight gear. Both require maximum talent, but the muscle, endurance, and composure that are essentials for subduing a heavyweight add a whole new dimension. Mathematics alone cannot account for the differences in size, speed, time, and distance.

Still, there is superb and plentiful action to be enjoyed with small fish on light tackle. Note that I did not say "ultra-light." This term implies a line of less than 3 pounds test and a rod of under 3 ounces. This is a laudable attempt to establish parameters for people interested in catching the biggest fish on the smallest equipment, but in any but the most experienced hands, it can be a discouraging business. Ultra-light is for warriors who have slain their dragons and now want to take on themselves. They expand the limits and we are in their debt. By all means look forward to trying ultra-light, but for now lay it aside in favor of featherweight fishing.

The distinction is that featherweight fishing attempts merely to tailor the tackle to the fish; no new records or expanded horizons. It is the ideal way to make the most of small to medium fish, and it is for Everyman.

And Everywoman, too, as Mrs. Fallon learned when she joined me in capitalizing on the hordes of kindergarten-size stripers that had been driving other anglers to distraction.

"Right out there," I told her, "at the tip of that string of boulders. The farther out, the better. I'll give odds that when you wiggle your plug through the lee of that boil you'll get yourself a bass."

Now, it wasn't so much that I was trying to move Peg out of my favorite cove, from which she'd just plucked her second striper in a row while I stood by cheering halfheartedly (and cussing wholeheartedly); the pleasure of her company always more than offsets the pressure of her competition. Nor was I trying to collect on her life insurance. So okay, she hasn't got the best balance in the world, and, well, maybe those rocks *were* a little slippery and that current *was* a little fast, but hey, she's the mother of my children, the manufacturer of my meals, the ironer of my underwear. What would I do without her?

No, I sincerely wanted Peg to experience the exquisite excitement of battling a bass on modest tackle in the fish's own environment with odds for a change in the fish's favor; no feet anchored firmly on solid bottom, no quiet hazard-free water to play it in. I wanted her to learn that a cast made too soon or too hard could send her skidding off her rock; that every rotation of her reel, every raising and lowering of her rod had to be carefully counterbalanced by a shifting of head and trunk and arms (but not feet); that a strike responded to too suddenly would almost surely guarantee a dunking.

My prediction that the bass were there was accurate. As Peg's

5-inch shallow swimmer swung through the rip's rippled inside edge, its wobbling slackened slightly. This change of pace must have made the fish curious, because when Peg jerked her rod to wiggle her plug, the bass was right behind it primed to pounce.

Unfortunately my prediction about Peg's ability to remain on the rock was not accurate. What I had neglected to consider was that my spouse's customary reaction to a striper's strike is along the lines of a Go-Go doll that's been wound too tight. She jumps, she wiggles, she twists, she turns—all to the accompaniment of screeching the likes of which hasn't been heard since the banshee blares of the London blitz.

"Honnneee!" she hollered, hauling back, straightening up, and, after a slipping, sliding, Frick-and-Frack performance, toppling like a felled tree. She took three more over-the-waders nosedives before I was able to reel in and slosh across the shallows, but when I reached the rock on which she finally had come to rest, she was wearing a "Pretty good, huh?" grin and holding up a 16½-inch striped bass for me to admire.

I know, I know: striper-seekers accustomed to judging the quality of their catches in pounds instead of inches aren't likely to make room over their mantels for the likes of this midget. Nevertheless, I haven't met one yet who doesn't envy Peg her rollicking roller-coaster-ride excitement, and that includes some pretty salty old bass-baggers.

Neither Peg nor I had had a "Don't take your striper for granted" crusade in mind when we started chasing small fish. In fact, we, like most New England striper fishermen, had been lamenting the baby bass that seemed to be everywhere, snapping up everything we cast, trolled, or drifted in our attempts to entice big fish.

"I can't fault them for their courage," I had commented to Peg. "The spunky little squirts are ready to take on all comers. I can't criticize their performance, either. Any cow that put up a scrap like these peewees wouldn't have to worry about being anybody's dinner. But hey, 2-, 3-, 4-pounders on 20-pound line and 8-foot rods?"

"Hmmm," said Peg, cranking her legendary intuition into gear, "hmmm." She and I had a Sunday-morning session coming up two days later and I could see she didn't want to risk having me go into one of my patented "Humph, anyone can catch those midgets!" sulks when she outfished me.

When small stripers like this abound, the smart angler breaks out his featherweight gear.

"Well," she said, "of course I never mind catching small fish, but I know you're used to much bigger ones than I am." (After twenty years of marriage I have come to recognize this as a long, slow curve designed to massage the male ego and lower the male guard as the ball cuts the corner of the plate for a called strike.) "But how about this for an idea . . ."

She went on to suggest that maybe a rocky point in back of the island where I had caught nothing but schoolies on a half-dozen recent tries might eliminate the need for heavy tackle; that by matching light tackle to small fish we might be able to capitalize on the courage and scrappiness of school bass.

"What's that wise old adage I've heard you say so many times?" she concluded: "If you can't fight 'em, join 'em."

Steee-rike!

On Sunday, my hands were trembling so much with anticipation that I had trouble tying a 3-inch silver swimmer to my 4-pound mono. For several minutes, while Peg pulled her 5-inch swimmer across a creek mouth, I tried to slide my line's bitter end into the second loop of an improved clinch knot. I finally poked it through the bullseye, reached to pull it taut, and snapped the line in two as Peg's "Honee! I've got one, I've got one" shattered the Sabbath silence along with her husband's nerves.

She was working her 4-pounder into the grassy fringes of a mussel bed by the time I could retie and start casting. Judging from her bouncing and beaming, the 8-pound line and 6½-foot rod I had rigged for here were plenty light enough to enable her fish to strut its stuff. Her 5-inch plug also must have been tailor-made, although at first I thought a 3-incher, more nearly the size of sand eels on which local bass normally feed, would be better. When she scored a second time, however, I wasn't about to argue over fish that were undeterred by a few extra inches.

Fortunately, they were equally fond of my 3-incher. Before action tapered off ten minutes later and we decided to huddle over hot coffee and talk strategy, I had two chances to test my rinkydink rig. The first one I flubbed because I hauled back on the fish's strike as hard as if I were using the 8-foot rod and 20-pound-test line I'd been accustomed to. Keep this in mind when using your a-lot-lighter-than-normal gear. Unless you keep reminding yourself and rehearsing how you're going to react, you'll probably overdo it as reflexively as a kneejerk.

A soft drag, of course, will enable your line to survive a hard yank, and, in fact, I had had the foresight to loosen mine. Unfortunately I immediately overcompensated. With a little slack to play with, this fish rolled once, shook its head, and snapped my line.

One of the many attributes of baby bass, though, is that when you tangle with one, there often are others right behind it anxious to get into the act. A swirl behind the third cast I made with a fresh lure signaled another customer; a wary one, judging from the tentative way in which it made its pass; spooked, perhaps, by the thrashing and splashing of the fish I had just lost. I slowed my plug to a stop, letting it float and drift a second or two till it came abeam of a half-submerged boulder, then I twitched it twice, resumed reeling ve-e-e-ry slowly, and bingo! My rod bowed like a willow switch, my reel sang the sweetest music this side of Guy Lombardo, and I needed every bit of ingenuity I could muster to tucker out that 3-pounder enough to work it out of the current, through a patch of barnacled boulders, and onto the beach.

Before you get the idea that the ubiquitousness of small stripers makes catching them boringly predictable, let me point out that action stopped almost cold for Peg and me at this point. Except for the fish responsible for her dunking, neither she nor I caught another fish. Swirls we had, and chases, and twice a small popper had processions of fish pursuing it, so they were there. Trouble was, we had not yet learned what's different about baby bass. Things like these. . . .

Being bass, they often seek their prey in fast water, but being less strong than the bruisers that cruise right in the boiling body of a rip, they tend to stay along a rip's edges or in its less turbulent tail.

They sometimes prowl in shallow pockets where normally you wouldn't even consider casting a lure.

Because they're less battle-scarred, they tend to be more aggressive than grownups.

Their presence does not mean that bigger bass are absent, and, in fact, they seem to hit more readily when in competition with bigger fish.

There was no question in either Peg's mind or mine that Sunday as we headed over the dunes to our car that we had enjoyed superior sport, a test as demanding, a romp as delightful as any we'd ever experienced on any species regardless of size. But if we had harbored even the slightest lingering doubt, it would have been dispelled when we met a man in the parking lot who told us about the stripers two anglers had just caught less than 50 yards from our car.

"Four of them," he said, eyes bulging. "Biggest must have been over 20 pounds. See," he added, pointing to a pair of smooth trails leading over the dunes. "Right there, that's where they dragged 'em. How'd you do? Not so good, huh?"

Without an instant's hesitation, without a trace of envy, Peg and I dueted back, "Oh, we did fine, just fine."

Other Methods

Featherweight fishing and fly-fishing are only two of the variations that enterprising anglers have found for the traditional techniques of fishing the surf. Show a surfman a method that works well afloat and he will adapt it ashore. Jigging alongside a jetty is essentially the same from rocks as from a boat. A live bait maneuvered through a tideway looks much the same when walked from shore as when drifted from a skiff. Baitfish survive as well in a cage anchored in the shallows as in an aerated tank amidships.

If there should be a different way, the surfman will try it; if there should be a better way, he will discover it. When bluefish catches suddenly declined a few years ago along a riverbank where 10- and 12-pounders had been swarming during every dropping tide for two weeks, I watched a man heave a hunk of mackerel out among the swimming and popping plugs and, alas, get skunked. But a few yards up the shore a man who substituted a big bushy jig for his swimming plug connected right away. The first man concluded that the fish had seen too much of the same old artificials and that the mackerel meat he had caught bluefish on elsewhere would turn the trick. The second man figured that the fish were deeper and a bottom-bounced jig would reach them. One was right, one was wrong, but both were thinking.

With so much ingenuity afoot, what new methods could there possibly be for fishing the shore? How about this? You want to get your bait out beyond a distant bar. At 200 yards, casting is out of the question. If only there were some way to suspend a bait over that water, to skip it around a bit to attract attention the way they do with outriggers on charter boats. But outriggers have long arms. Your only arm is your rod. You'd need an airborne point of suspension. Hmmm. A radio-controlled model airplane maybe? Or . . . or . . . . What's that youngster doing up there in the sand? What's he holding? String? Yeah, couple of hundred yards of it, and at its end, flying as sweetly as you please, is a kite. Perfect! Why, a mullet or a menhaden tethered to the tip of that kite's tail . . .

Before you start searching for a patent application, let me point out that kite fishing has been around for a long time. Perhaps two thousand years! Pacific natives from the Celebes to the Solomons were flying kites from their canoes many centuries before Florida charter skippers adopted the technique.

From shore, your problems are more perplexing. Without wind and motion to aid in sending your bait-burdened kite aloft, land-based kite fishing is not likely to succeed with enough consistency to make it worthwhile. Unless . . . why not a balloon to help with the lift-off? Sure, why not? Or a gun to propel your bait to that distant ridge of white water? Or why not just swim out to the ridge and fish while standing on it? Or . . . ?

See what I mean?

There's always a chance you'll get dunked.

9

Safety in the Surf

CAN YOU GET HURT FISHING the surf? Of course.

Are you likely to? Of course not.

Precaution, restraint, common sense, plus enough humility to acknowledge that Dame Nature can deck you two falls out of three will enable you to fish without having to worry about anything more important than where your next fish is coming from.

To avoid the hazards of surf fishing, you first have to understand them: what they are; where they exist; how to avoid them; and if you should happen to get into trouble, how to get out of it. These hazards have six sources: land, water, weather, insects, fish, and you.

Land

The Parker River Wildlife Refuge in northern Massachusetts is a surf fisherman's dream: five marvelous miles of unpopulated beachfront backed by 4,650 acres of dunes, fields, and marshes. Deer graze along its brush-bordered fringes, foxes stalk rabbits and fieldmice and woodchucks in its grassy folds, and a dazzling array of wildfowl make it a birdwatchers' Mecca. The broad gravel road that bisects the refuge is amply punctuated with parking areas from which wide-open well-marked paths lead to many of the area's popular fishing spots—Kettle Hole, Polio Camp, Emerson Rocks— but you know how it is when you see those footprints leading off into the dunes midway between parking areas. Their owner, you are convinced, is right out there beyond the grasses mining the Mother Lode. Naturally you pull up, suit up, and head out too.

A lovely night: bright, crisp, clear, still. As you leave the road, a rich flowery fragrance billows from the bushes: beach roses, and roses have thorns. By the time you reach the water, your new light-weight plasticized waders are so perforated they'll give you about as much protection as a pair of pantyhose.

I emphatically do not suggest that you avoid this problem simply by steering clear of behind-the-bushes fishing. Hard-to-get-to places often offer the best prospects simply because you have them all to yourself. There may not necessarily be more fish there, but what there are will be able to concentrate exclusively on your lures.

What I do recommend is that you tote rather than wear your waders when you expect to have to trudge through brush and brambles enroute to the water. The extra load will be more than offset by the ease with which you can walk. The conserved energy will be a big help on your way back when you have all those fish to carry.

Once a rock almost cost me a hundred dollars. What happened was, I was trying to catch my first striped bass in two days and two nights of plugging the stony shore of Cuttyhunk Island, south of Cape Cod. Dragging my duff three miles to the Island's East End, I pulled my self onto one of the hundreds of weed-draped boulders that had been bared by the receding tide and started skipping my popper through the creamy combers as they came tumbling toward me out of the fog.

On my third cast a fish struck my plug in 2 feet of water and spent the better part of the next five minutes airborne before I slid it into the shallows 7 or 8 feet below. I couldn't hoist it, because that might break my line. Besides, there wasn't room enough for it on the rock. Instead I slid down and carried my first fish in fifteen hours of casting to the crest of the steep stony shore 50 feet away, kissed it, and lay it gently at the base of a big boulder.

Then I turned and had no idea which rock to return to. They all looked the same: big and wet and weedy. But, hey, with all those bass out there, I wasn't about to waste time deliberating. Hitching up my waterlogged chinos, I hustled toward one at the water's edge that looked high enough and flat enough for a casting platform, yet low enough for me to haul my 160 pounds onto without delay.

I reached the rock between waves. Across my sneakered feet a clear foam-flecked wash of water carried pebbles, shells, strings and swatches of seaweed, and—as alien as a bagel in a Casbah—a roll of twenty-dollar bills. There were five in all; coincidentally, I thought, the same number I had securely tucked away in my left-rear pocket for settling my account at the inn where I was staying. They were, in fact, one and the same. Apparently I had squished them out of my pocket while sliding off the rock.

But most rock-caused accidents are physical rather than fiscal. On another trip to Cuttyhunk, Mrs. Fallon almost fractured her face when she lost her footing on the apron of smooth slippery stones that cover much of the island's shore. Rocks like these are treacherous. Worn smooth by the sea's ceaselessly heaving them up a beach and dragging them down again, they offer no flat solid surface for your feet. When wet, it's as if they're glazed with ice.

By treading carefully in sneakers with corrugated soles, I have been able to remain upright most of the time, but I'm lucky. I've been blessed with a good sense of balance that enables me to react instantly and readjust my weight to counteract a rock that rolls or a foot that slips. Unless you have the equilibrium of a tightrope walker, you're better off avoiding this kind of shoreline until you've developed a set of surflegs, but if the water beyond the boulders should be too tempting, take the time to tie on a set of cleats or creepers. Lacking them, crouch as low as the waves will allow, proceed carefully, and walk softly; tread as tenderly as if those stones were eggs.

Rough rocks, of course, can cut you up a lot worse than smooth ones. If Peg had nosedived onto a cluster of barnacles instead of a smooth stone, her pretty pink cheek would forevermore have resembled minced ham. Fortunately, rough rocks are easier to stand on. This is because, being firmly secured in the ground or too big for the sea to budge, they can't roll and grind themselves smooth. Still, it's best to wear cleats or creepers for traction. These rocks, like the one that stole my bankroll at Cuttyhunk, are wet. You seek them out because they're right out there among the waves where they can enable you to cast farther, to watch your plug more closely, to see the flash of a fish before it strikes, to fight a hooked fish more efficiently. But the price you have to pay for these advantages is fishing from a slimy-slick surface.

Jetties are a special case. On the first third to half of jetties that I fish regularly, individual rocks are set carefully to form gently slanting sides topped by a broad flat surface with few intervening gaps. Straight, solid, and secure, this surface is as well suited for fishing as it is for walking. Except in abnormally high seas, it doesn't even get damp.

But don't be deceived. Approximately at the point where the water becomes intriguingly fishable, the jetty becomes perilously unwalkable. Abruptly, as if the jetty's construction contract had been about to expire, rocks have been dumped haphazardly instead of deposited deliberately. To fish beyond this point, you must crawl across, crouch on, slide down, and cling to slick sloping slabs of granite separated by great gaping sea-filled gulfs.

So all right. I exaggerate. Maybe it just seems that way because I do so much of my jetty fishing after dark. Maybe also it's because

Jetties enable you to get right out there where the fish hang out, but slippery sloping surfaces can make walking hazardous.

I remember those frogmen bobbing among the boulders for the bodies of two fishermen who didn't take the jetty seriously.

The obvious hazard of wading a weed-filled shoreline is the ease with which you can slip. By walking carefully, stepping deliberately, making sure your forward foot is firmly planted before advancing your rear one, you should be able to stay upright.

But thick weeds also can trip you. I recall one moon-bright night when I was inching along a rocky ridge to get within casting distance of the downcurrent edge of a broad sprawl of sand, and I spooked a 2-foot eel. Its sudden slithering across my ankles made me jump. When my rear foot became snagged in a clump of kelp, I almost lurched sideways into a sluicing current, but by bending my knees, tilting my head, and shifting my forward foot a few inches, I wound up with nothing more serious than a wet nose.

The tranquillity of a tropical shore can be deceiving. What could be nicer? A balmy tropical afternoon, a vast mudflat full of tailing bonefish, and all the time in the world to stalk slowly, cast carefully, play precisely, and when you've finally persuaded a bone to yell "Uncle," slip out your hook, pat the fish on its sleek silvery butt, and make a date for another day.

Nothing could be nicer, so you slip into your trunks, jog along the beach till you see a flash or detect a shadow or spot a tail amidst a milky underwater cloud, and then slink into the shallows. Next thing you know, you're in the local outpatient clinic having your tootsies treated for coral lacerations or punctures from sea urchins.

Sneakers are a must where coral or shells can cut your feet. A barefoot romp through a Maryland mussel bed many years ago not only shredded my soles but tucked enough mud into the cuts to nurture a couple of raging infections.

Coral also can inflict nasty abrasions on unprotected legs. Graze your thigh on a clump of coral and you'll think you've brushed against an emery wheel, sparks and all. When bathing suits or Bermuda shorts are uniform of the day, navigate accordingly.

Mud was the Waterloo of a promising plugger named Renaldo Cavalieri. Renaldo is the quintessential Italian. Pasta-portly with a full crop of jet-black curls crowning a spumoni-sweet smile, he laughs incessantly, loves ubiquitously, and brightens every place he goes with his own special brand of mozzarella pixie dust. He also frightens easily.

Well, not easily, really. I guess he could handle some modest terror like a vampire bat in his bedroll or a sleeping bag full of snakes. It's just that getting stuck hip-deep in mud in the middle of the night makes him start yelling funny things like "Heeelp!"

It wasn't as if he were alone out there on that clamflat, although I suppose it must have seemed that way to Renaldo. One minute he and I were sloshing side by side through the soupy edges of a shrouded marsh heading for a cluster of rocks silhouetted against the slightly-less-black sky, and the next, "Heeelp!"

I suppose I should have waited, but it was, after all, only 50 yards. And besides, those rocks are exposed for only about ten minutes on either side of low tide. A pair of casters were out there already, and after an hour-and-a-half drive, I was anxious to make the most of what little time we had left.

You could blame it on the waders, but remember, I gave Renaldo his choice.

"Too big, or leaky," I told him, "take your pick."

I was glad when he left me the leaky ones, because at least they were my size. Even with water oozing in, my feet pretty well stayed put in their boots when the going got gooey and I had to lean forward, grab myself by the groin, and he-e-eave.

Not so with Renaldo and his seven-league boots. When he heaved, he heaved his foot; the boot stayed put. Except, that is, for the other boot, the one he put his considerable weight on while heaving. That boot squished deeper and deeper into the goo.

"Heelp!"

"What's that?" asked one of the casters on the rocks beside me.

"Probably the wind," answered his friend.

"Yeah," I said, "probably just the wind."

Renaldo was not laughing incessantly or sprinkling pixie dust when I slogged alongside him in response to his next summons. Even his love supply was turned, if not off, then down very very low. Nor did my assurance that he could not possibly have died a slow and lonely death, swallowed by a dark dispassionate sea, restore the bloom to his cheeks or the gleam to his eyes.

"All you'd have had to do," I told him, "is unstrap your waders."

"Take me back."

"Slide right out and dogpaddle through the shallows back to shore."

Getting mired in a mucky mudflat at night can be a terrifying experience if you're not prepared. I don't know whether my friend Renaldo could laugh now at John Jr.'s cartoon or not.

"The parking lot," mumbled Renaldo, "take me back."

The surest way to avoid an experience like Renaldo's is to take the longer way around. There's always a longer way. By following the slowly curving crest of the bank that edged that clamflat, Renaldo and I eventually would have reached those rocks. But, hey, that would have used up ten more minutes. "Time and tide" and all that, you know.

Waders that fit his feet would have helped Renaldo. So would leaning forward while he walked, and advancing before his feet got dug in too deep. But it's no use reminding Renaldo of how he might have avoided his ordeal. Renaldo does not subscribe to my counsel these days. Now that he is laughing incessantly again and loving ubiquitously and anointing the world with his pixie dust, Renaldo Cavalieri, the quintessential Italian, maintains that there is but one sure way for surf fishermen to avoid an early death.

"Never," admonishes Renaldo, "but *never* go fishing with a crazy Irishman."

Beware of sudden dropoffs. As a drunk who stepped out of the airplane said when they found him unhurt in the haystack, "It wasn't bad except for the first step."

I felt the same way when I took off across a dusk-dimmed marsh toward a pod of busting bluefish and immediately plunged up to my chest into a 2-foot-wide tidal trench. Overgrown with grass and obscured in shadow, it had escaped my attention. The dunking cost me two cameras, but I was consoled by the realization that if I had built up a little more momentum, I probably would have snapped my leg.

Most marshes are laced with these booby traps. Even on the darkest nights you can discern them if you watch where you're going, but seeing them solves only part of your problem. Be sure also, when leaping across, to shove off from solid ground, not mushy grass, and test the solidity of where you plan to land by poking it beforehand with your rod tip. Sure, you might have been a great broadjumper back in high school, but in those days you were wearing track pants, not waders.

Beaches also have holes. At low tide, note their sloughs and wrinkles, dips and depressions. Serious surfmen will learn the location of every one of these undulations, not only to help them lay their baits and bounce their lures more productively, but also to enable them to stay out of trouble.

Water

Even in an open ocean in all but the worst of weather, waves should pose no problem. Normally you can see them coming, brace yourself, time your jumps. Before they become too high to handle, you will have backed off onto the beach.

Occasionally an extra-high wave can catch you off your guard if you've left yourself no route for a quick getaway. A once-cocky caster told me how he got religion one night after inching his way down a rocky bluff to a platform of boulders about 8 feet off the water.

"Nicest looking location I'd ever fished," he said. "Couldn't understand why I never saw anyone there. Then I looked up, and

Waves have a way of catching you off your guard when you're preoccupied with landing a fish.

here comes this big white wall roaring at me out of the darkness. To this day I don't know how I clawed my way up that cliff in time, but whenever I start taking that ocean for granted, I remember that sight. Two or three seconds slower and I'd have been sucked right out."

Flooding tides can trick you by sneaking in and cutting you off when you're not looking. Not so with ebbing tides. In fact, they have a built-in safety factor because they bare *more* bottom, not less. When a tide is on the way in, anticipate how long you'll be able to stay safely on the jetty, sandbar, or marsh you'll be fishing, then leave plenty of margin in case you might have miscalculated.

A strong undertow on a steep beach can yank your legs right out from under you, but there's really no advantage to entering the water when a shore slopes off sharply. You can cast just as far and a lot more comfortably from solid ground.

Weather

Fog obscures hazards, robs you of reference points, denies you the sight of breaking bait and swirling fish, and generally signifies clam conditions that are considered poor for fishing. But don't let that stop you. The same number of hungry fish are out there. With no bait being stirred up, your lure will look like the only girl at the prom.

In fog, sounds can position you as well as sights; you can hear the foghorn, the chugging of the piledriver on the anchored dredge, the lapping of waves; you can see the lighthouse's flash, the parking lot's glow, the high dark bulk of a bluff or a building. Once while wading 50 yards off a shallow shore, a cotton-candy fog enveloped me so fast that I had no chance to get my bearings, yet finding my way back to the beach was easy. The tide, I recalled, was coming in. That meant a right-to-left flow, so I knew how to face toward shore. For reassurance, I listened carefully, and sure enough, I could hear wavelets breaking on the beach.

Cold and heat are not real hazards. Extremes in either direction are taken care of by proper dress up to the point where frostbite or sunstroke become possible; by then you probably will have headed home anyway.

In cold climes be sure to bring all the clothing you possibly might need. Those extra socks and jacket might stay almost all season in the trunk of your car, but better there than your bedroom bureau when a cold front suddenly moves in and temperatures plummet. A good slicker and waders will keep you dry, but for the rips and drips that you can't predict, keep a fresh outfit in that trunk, too, so you can be sure at least of driving home in comfort. Soggy skivvies make poor seat cushions.

Sunburn is buffered by ointment, glasses, long sleeves and pants, and broad-brimmed or at least long-visored headgear.

When lightning starts flashing, smart fishermen hightail it for cover. Usually I do, too, but sometimes I succumb to a foolish but irresistible weakness for staying. Surf fishing has an elemental excitement about it to begin with. When this is orchestrated by great rumbling crashes of thunder and startlingly brilliant flashes of

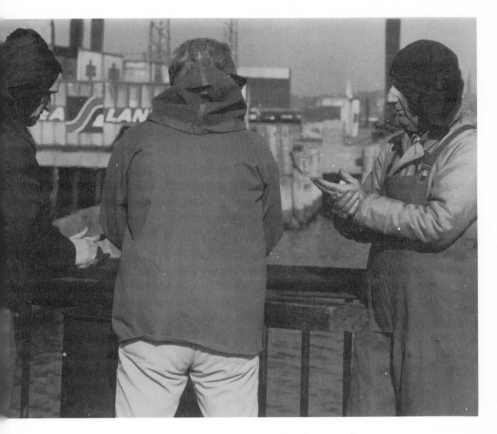

When there's fishing to be done along the ocean's edges, anglers
will find a way of coping with the cold. (Photo: Terry McDonnell)

lightning, some atavistic attraction draws me to it, demands that I
become part of it.

No, I don't advise fishing in lightning storms, because there *is*
danger. But if ever you should feel compelled to keep right on casting, be sure to stand close by a tall object that's almost certain to
shortstop any bolts before they reach your level.

Insects

Movie moguls could pare production costs on those sci-fi films
in which insects take over the world simply by doing their shooting

at the seashore. By exposing a single square inch of skin on a balmy breezeless evening, they could cast a whole mob scene. Midges, mites, mosquitoes, black flies, sand fleas, greenheads, no-see-ums; swarms of them, clouds of them, flights, wings, escadrilles of them. They nip, they gnaw, they pinch, they prick, they bite, they burrow. Burning stinging, itching, they can put you out of action in seconds, out of commission in minutes. "Insect bite" is a familiar entry in the logs of outpatient clinics.

But a lot of surf fishing is done despite bugs by anglers who either keep the critters away or fish where they ain't. Warm windless shores are likely to be buggy, especially if marsh and brush abound nearby. I do much of my surf fishing from a narrow peninsula that fronts the ocean for 5 miles. On its sound side, a high bluff buffers me against an east wind; on its ocean side, dunes do me the same favor when winds are from the west. No, I don't always fish the breezier side when insects are on the offensive, but you can be sure that this is one of the elements that I crank into my decision.

Not one of the major elements, though, because bugs, while always an irritant, rarely interfere with my fishing. With an effective repellent, a strong cigar, and the right clothes, I can keep most of them at bay. The occasional kamikaze that gets through to the unanointed inch behind my ear or the loose fold in my collar is just part of the very modest price I feel I have to pay for fishing the surf.

There are so many repellents on the market these days that industry sometimes seems to be spending more research money trying to make us smell bad than good. Sprays, oils, salves, pads—I've tried them all. Applied liberally and replenished frequently, they do an adequate job of keeping bugs at bay, and what they can't accomplish, a stinky stogie can. A night of puffing on a dime's worth of stewed tow rope makes my mouth feel like a municipal incinerator, but, as I say, the price is modest.

"So okay," said a friend with whom I discussed repellents recently, "if you can't recommend a brand, how about a method of application?"

"Easy," I answered, "one where the goo doesn't get all over my hands."

Fishing, not fastidiousness, inspired this answer. While I haven't done enough experimenting to confirm this conviction, I am sure that much of what repels bugs also repels fish. It stands to reason.

Gamefish have supersensitive sniffers. They depend heavily on smell and taste to find food and detect danger. In shallow water, where they can be cornered easily while seeking a meal, all of their senses must be ultra-alert. Dr. Clarence Idyll of the University of Miami's Division of Marine Sciences reported, "If a quart of water in which a human hand or the paw of a bear has been dipped for a minute is poured into a stream, it can cause migrating salmon to stop climbing a fish ladder a hundred yards away," and I decided then and there to play it safe. First, I make sure not to apply repellents to parts of my hand from which it can be transmitted to lures and bait. Second, I keep anointed areas out of the water. And third, I squish plenty of mud between my fingers before handling lures.

Clothing is as important as potions in your battle against bugs. Neck, wrists, and ankles should get as much attention from you as from the insects that seem to sense the juicy epidermal acres that lie beyond these barriers. When you've buttoned the collar and cuffs of your shirt and tucked the cuffs of your pants into your socks, apply a double dose of repellent to these fabrics. If your shirt does not have a collar, do what my son Jack taught me: soak a kerchief in bug spray and tie it around your neck.

Headnets keep bugs at bay, but they make me feel as though I'm fishing from inside a cage. Ten minutes tops and I have to tear them off. Maybe I'm claustrophobic, but I prefer scratching to screaming.

Fish

Chances are remote that you ever will be attacked by fish in the surf. On steeply sloping beaches you rarely will wade out far enough. On flats that barracuda frequent, you seldom will need to worry unless you're foolish enough to wear something flashy, whose glitter might trigger a 'cuda's wrath. Even on flats where you could step on a ray and have it whip its needled tail into your ankle, you normally are protected by vibrations: the beast skedaddles in a puff of mud long before you reach it.

But notice how I hedge in the previous paragraph? Words like "remote," "rarely," "seldom," and "normally" are little consolation to the wader watching blood gush from a freshly inflicted bite or grimacing in agony as he squeezes his poison-puffed leg. Authorities reassure us that even vicious and venomous sea creatures are scared of people and do their best to stay out of a wader's way, statistics are overwhelmingly in favor of surf anglers' being safe from attack, yet there's always that chance, however remote, that a startled or cornered critter will choose fight rather than flight.

If for any reason—high-risk waters, lack of confidence—you feel there's real cause for concern, you shouldn't be wading. If you find yourself concentrating extra hard on avoiding assaults, you're not concentrating hard enough on fishing. But keep in mind that in familiar waters you're always close to 100 percent safe from attack. The right clothes and reasonable caution will make up the difference.

Strange waters are another story. I still get the willies when I

Jim Tallon (left) normally enjoys this kind of fishing in the Sea of Cortez surf, but on one occasion a scorpionfish turned his night into a nightmare. (Photo: Jim Tallon)

reread this account of how Jim Tallon got stung almost fatally by an ugly and, incidentally, very common scorpionfish in the Sea of Cortez surf.

"It was a hell of a way to end a fishing trip. Like perhaps dying. The Mexican night sheathed us in damp blackness, and I lay face down in a jumble of reef-rock, coughing in nausea and gasping for air with a failing respiratory system. Pain raked my left leg from ankle to groin. Excruciating pain. Pain like I didn't know existed. Cold sweat popped out on my forehead; I began to shake.

" 'Put a tourniquet on it, Jess,' I choked. 'There's a nylon line on my fish stringer . . . in my pack.'

"Jess lit a match. It illuminated two red punctures in my ankle. Just a minute before, after some fantastic surf fishing, Jess and I had waded across a rocky, starlit lagoon toward the beach. Bits of phosphorescence glowed beneath the surface and we had stopped to examine them. Something like a chilled ice pick rammed into my ankle. Some aquatic creature scurried away, creating a silent wake in the oily, night-shine of the water. In three seconds pain lanced across to the opposite side of the ankle as though it had pierced the bone; in fifteen seconds it had coursed from ankle to thigh, like a thermometer in an open flame. Poison in the blood stream? If it reached my heart I knew that I would die. . . ."

Jim is an ace-angler, wise in the ways of surf fishing and an old acquaintance of scorpionfish, but frightened fish play no favorites. Jim, however, will not get jabbed again. "There'll be no more sneaker-and-levi-wading in the surf for me," he writes in the final paragraph of "Riddle on the Reef" (*Salt Water Sportsman,* November, 1973).

Sharks are more the concern of offshore boatmen than waders of the surf, but they cannot be ignored. A close-to-shore feeding spree by other fish sometimes will toll them in, especially in tropical territories. So will bleeding or struggling fish tethered to a stringer. When you start landing half-eaten fish, sharks probably have moved in; it's time you moved out.

Yes, I know that only a small percentage of the world's shark population are maneaters. Sure, I'm aware that very few of these are likely to attack without provocation. I also know that unloaded guns can't hurt you, but a lot of people get hurt by them anyway, so when it comes to guns and sharks, I treat both as if they're loaded. Show me a triangular fin slicing through the shallows and I'll show you a hastily vacated set of waders.

Most jellyfish are harmless. A few will inflict irritating stings on bare flesh that brushes against their tentacles, but only one is a real menace to U.S. surfmen. This is the Portuguese man-o'-war, a false jelly whose blue bladder, inflated by the breeze like a balloon spinnaker, propels it through tropical seas, and whose tentacles, trailing as much as 50 feet astern, can do a man in from heart failure or respiratory paralysis. Immediate treatment of a man-o'-war's sting is essential. Waders or long pants will protect you against the man-o'-war, but as an added caution, always give a wide berth to those blue balloons, especially when passing behind them.

Many species of fish have venomous spines that can inflict painful but not fatal punctures. I have seen a man's hand still swelled to almost double size a week after being stabbed by a common spiny dogfish. The man had handled hundreds without a slip. An honest guy, he acknowledged culpability. A little more care, he admitted, would have averted the injury. Even nonpoisonous punctures can be painful; if allowed to become infected, they can be serious. When a freshly caught striper unfurls its dorsal, it isn't waving goodbye. Those spikes in that fin are meant for you.

A fish on the beach can get in its last licks before expiring. Blues always seem to have a few chomps left, as well as sharp enough close-range eyesight, even out of the water, to aim them accurately. It's always wise to billyclub a blue out of business before extracting hooks. Also kneel on its body so a final farewell tremor won't jam a barb into your hand. For the same reason, any big fish should be pinned down while you're removing hooks.

You

Your biggest hazard in the surf can be yourself. That small firm voice that keeps prodding you to take one more step can prod you right behind the eightball. No need to be overcautious. Those few extra feet often can put you into fish. But if there's any doubt about depth or about solidity of the bottom, test with your rod tip before advancing.

It's the soloists who run the biggest risks. With a friend alongside, you have few worries. At night, however, especially when a noisy surf can drown out a vocal S.O.S., agree beforehand on how you will summon one another by flashlight in case of emergency. A series of rapid flashes is easiest; no pattern, no code, just flashes. Under no circumstances should you use this signal for anything other than a genuine emergency, and this includes announcing that you're into fish.

A drunk is in more danger in a cold, dark, sizzling surf than behind the wheel of a car. In traffic, other drivers dodge and honk, and there's a good chance that a patrolman will arrest him before he kills himself, but a high wave over a booze-woozy wader's head can put him down for the count. When a wave slams and tosses and tumbles, a man must move fast to avoid rocks and to reach air; with his reflexes anesthetized by alcohol, he probably won't move fast enough. Even beer is *verboten* where risks are high and the slightest dulling of one's senses could make a difference. Save the sixpacks for celebrating when you bring back the big one.

Safety for the Catch

And now that you have fished safely and successfully, what are you going to do with those fish you've caught? Will you be like the man on a pier to whom I once gave my leftover seaworms? As I turned to go, I noticed his catch. Five flounders, their hides stiff as leather, their flesh soft as dough, lay rotting at his feet. Seagulls would be scavenging them before evening.

Thank God for gulls. Without them to clean up discarded carcasses of once-beautiful fish, our seashores would reek constantly of decay. But then, of course, we would be more conscious of our wanton wastefulness. Revulsion might succeed where reason has failed.

But I suppose the man to whom I gave my worms can hardly be condemned. Criticized, yes, for being stupid, negligent, lazy, unimaginative, improvident; but not condemned. He was a poor man, couldn't afford a cooler. He knew that to leave his fish strung in the water would invite crabs and cunners. Better a barely edible fish than no fish at all.

But why not an onion sack dangled in the water? Or a bed of

Keep your fish cool and clean them promptly. Suggestion: Try cooking some on the spot. (Photo: Terry McDonnell)

weeds between layers of damp newspaper? Carelessness, not callousness, was the culprit.

With fish currently in the same lofty price bracket as beefsteak, few fishermen can afford to watch dollars decay. And no fisherman, rich or poor, can afford to abet the accelerating decline of a dwindling marine resource, but this argument doesn't pack the same wallop as a "$1.55 per pound" price tag on a trayful of flounder fillets.

For the stay-put fisherman, there's no excuse for wasting fish. Weeds, newspapers, and gunnysacks are free, and coolers are common. The same cooler that chills your beer can keep your fish fresh.

"But slime gets all over my sandwiches."

"Pack your fish in a plastic trash bag."

"But fish take up too much room."

"Fillet them."

"But I don't know how."

"Learn, dammit."

The only shore-fishing situation in which you might have a genuine problem in keeping your catch fresh is when you're on the prowl. This is stripped-down fishing, essentials only, every excess ounce eliminated. A single extra pound toted across soft sand on a hot night can burn you out precious minutes early.

I've seen some strange methods used by perambulating surfmen for storing their catches. One guy used to bury his fish in wet sand, marking the spot well and returning before an incoming tide reclaimed them. Careful timing was necessary, but after a busy session he could unearth a half-dozen or more catches along his favorite 2-mile stretch of beach. Then one night he got into a prolonged tug o' war with a big fish way out at the end of his route. By the time the fish broke off, all of his earlier catches were underwater.

Another guy used to slip striped bass into his waders, although only when he saw a stranger approaching.

"Any luck?" the stranger would ask, almost beseechingly.

"Nope," my friend would mumble.

Once a fresh fish wiggled right around his home plate and the "Nope" came out "No-e-e-EEE!"

The strangest stash I've heard of is supposed to have been perpetrated by an ambitious young outdoorsman-on-the-make named Ernie Callahan. I don't know how true this tale is, but the fellow who told it to me kept a straight face. Well, maybe wrinkled a little.

It occurred on a Florida beach, said my reporter, where Ernie had made a date to meet the immortal Zane Green. Green, a stranger to the area, had sought guidance at the first tackle shop he came to. Ern was buying bait.

"Sure," said Ern, always happy to share his knowledge, "meet me on the south beach at midnight. Right in front of the lighthouse."

When the stranger identified himself, a quiver coursed through the Callahan frame. Not from nervousness—Ern relaxes amidst royalty—but from anticipation. Destiny, he knew, had scheduled this meeting. His future was clear: big-league bylines, enriching endorsements, the Callahan name emblazoned across prestigious mastheads.

To make sure all would go well, Ern arrived early. Lantern, sand-spikes, tackle box, bait, a well-stocked cooler—all were arranged with meticulous care well back from the water. Then he baited up and cast to the inside edge of an offshore bar, where his bait was immediately snatched by a very large fish. The struggle was brief, remarkably so for so big and strong an adversary, but Ern didn't dare risk losing this battle. Here was incontestable evidence to impress the great Green, to ensure the fame and fortune that destiny had so clearly decreed.

The fish was a spotted wrasse, of the family Labridae, tropical cousin of our smaller commoner tautog. Though not renowned for its acrobatics, there are few fish more powerful than a 20-pound wrasse, especially of the rare spotted variety. Ern's fish was easily over 40.

Green would not be arriving for twenty minutes. What to do with his prize? With characteristic resourcefulness, Ern dug a hole, deep and broad and long, in which the fish finned while he resumed his casting. He was reeling in for the fourth time when he saw Green sloshing across the broad flat beach in front of the lighthouse.

"Nice spot," said the illustrious author-angler, "real nice. Anything doing?"

Composure was out of the question. On the brink of angling immortality, Ernie fairly erupted his announcement: "Doing? D-d-doing? I'll say there's something doing. I've just caught me a 40-pound spotted wrasse."

"Good Lord," exclaimed Green, "where is it? Show it to me. I've been trying all my life to catch one over 20. Forty pounds! That's probably the most sought-after fish in the sea."

"Follow me," said Ern exultantly, sloshing toward shore. Fifty feet in front of the lighthouse he paused, pointed, and proclaimed proudly, "There."

At that instant the lighthouse's beacon swept the beach, revealing, alas, only an empty hole. The tide had flooded so fast across the slowly sloping sand that Ernie's fish had swum free.

Agog, aghast, Ern could only point to where his fish had been, while his mouth worked wordlessly. The more he gurgled, the angrier Green grew.

"Callahan," the great Green finally fumed, "one thing I can't stand is a dumb fisherman. I wouldn't fish with you if . . . Good Lord, man, you don't know your wrasse from a hole in the ground."

As I say, I can't vouch for the truth of this tale.

Maybe those anglers huddled out there in their boats are enjoying some action too. But I'll take the shore.

10

Great Surf Spots

ADVENTURE, BEAUTY, SOLITUDE, TRADITION, CHALLENGE, ECONOMY—all are parts of the reason why men go down to the sea in waders. There is a pristine purity to the surf's wide-open fishing for major-league fish, on the fish's own turf, on the fish's own terms. There is an elemental man-against-the-elements intimacy: thundering waves, grinding gravel, screeching reels, in the same primordial no-man's-land where life began a billion years before. And there is peace, a special kind of cosmic quiet that only the remotest of lakes and streams can provide. Ponds used to offer a bonus of nighttime quiet. It was a compressed kind of quiet, with shoreline shapes sharply defining the limits of silence. But even that is gone. The splashing of bass and the croaking of frogs no longer can compete with the Top Ten's braying brashness.

Surf fishing is the complete recreation. And in the true sense of the term: a re-creation of body, mind, and spirit. To ignore knotted arms, throbbing back, burning eyes, chattering teeth, and cramped fingers and keep right on casting is to proclaim that you are still boss over your own body. Despite flab and looseness and cholesterol, you're still in control, still able to romp in the marsh hay with that great lusty mistress whose breasts billow in the far mountains, whose butt bounces in the rolling dunes. Dame Nature awaits you at the ridge of every sandy rise, on the slope of every ocean shore. She is elusive, she is coy, she is demanding. She pounds, sprays, drenches, sears, scratches, and with her Circe-song of changing tides and cycling seasons, she summons you constantly to new trysts,

241

new encounters. But when you catch her, whether in the passionate embrace of a pounding night surf or the soothing caress of a soft dawn sea, she shows you what physical fulfillment can be. Some broad!

Mentally there is distraction in surf fishing—a temporary respite from the demanding dullness of routine—but it is not a TV-type distraction in which dull fantasy is substituted for dull fact. Fact *is* fantasy when you are up to your rump in sizzling suds, and breaking fish are starting to work bait within plugging range and you are computing casting distance, lead angle, retrieve speed. Brains never are in neutral in the surf. Wind, time, tide, weather, season, plus a hundred other dynamic inputs must be cranked in constantly. Walk alongside a weatherbeaten old warrior as he wades the waves and stalks his quarry, and you'll hear wheels whirring, switches clicking.

All of a surfman's senses are exhilaratingly alert. The Manhattan cabbie, deafened by day from honking horns and screeching brakes, immediately detects the almost inaudible splash of a fish feeding down a darkened shore. The Norfolk waiter whose nose is constantly assailed by a hundred indistinguishable aromas promptly discerns the melon-smell of feeding bluefish. The Galveston editor, bleary-eyed from proofing manuscripts, has no trouble spotting the almost imperceptible wrinkle of a swirling fish. The Long Beach laborer's callused hands and knobby fingers dextrously tie knots and untangle lines in the dim light of dawn.

And while his senses are as alert as sentries, the surfman's psyche is being sanded smooth by soft days and quiet nights, by shared joys and birdsong and the reassuring rhythm of the tides. "There are no atheists in foxholes," wrote Ernie Pyle. Nor are there any among men who fish the surf seriously.

"But," you protest, "what about us landlocked guys who can't get to the ocean without blowing our budgets and AWOLing our responsibilities? What good is the surf if it's too far away to fish?"

First, my sincere sympathy. I cannot conceive of a full life so far from the ocean that I couldn't reach it regularly. If you don't feel this same craving, then stay put. If you can acquire all the emotional mortar you need from fishing your lakes and ponds and reservoirs, rivers and brooks and beaver bogs, then you don't need the surf. But I warn you, be careful about dropping by sometime when you just happen to be in the neighborhood. First thing you know you'll have a rod in your hand and an arrow through your heart. Back-home waters will be just as wonderful as before—Lord knows, I love mine as much as ever—but you'll feel restless, unfulfilled, easily distracted. Sound familiar? Sure, it's the same way you felt after a few dates with your one-and-only when work or school or parents pried you apart.

But if you'd really like to lock horns with a fish in the surf, don't let your dream simmer on the back burner till it boils down into a thick pasty impossibility. The ocean's edges may be a lot nearer than you think. A new highway has opened the Sea of Cortez' fabled shores to southwestern anglers. There are bridges to the Florida Keys and North Carolina's Outer Banks. Nantucket and Martha's Vineyard are reached easily and at reasonable cost via plane and ferry. By pooling resources, sharing expenses, researching carefully, and writing ahead to learn the right places and the right times, you and a few pals might launch a lifelong love affair with the surf that will make everything that's happened previously seem like practice. North, South, East, West; day, night, rain, shine; from beach, bridge, jetty, and pier; on clear sandy flats and slippery tide-tossed reefs; wherever an ocean embraces a shore adventure awaits.

The Southern Atlantic Coast

The cobia's nose is halfway up the man's back as he walks this Beaufort, S.C., highway toward his car. This is not an unusual sight in a country so laced with sounds and creeks that it's known locally as Venice, but the sight of the fish's tail dragging in the midsummer dust settles it for you: this is the bridge you're going to fish.

A good choice. This is the Fripp Island Bridge you'd heard about at breakfast and again at the bait shop where you bought your eels. With the tide flooding, you have a good chance of bagging one of these big brown bruisers. And then you wonder: what in the world would I ever do if I should tie into a 50-pounder? And then you think: but wouldn't it be wonderful to find out?

The bridge is busy, but not congested. Plenty of room beside this sheepshead fisherman. His smile says a lot of "Welcome," and a little "Hey, how do you like my five fat sheepshead? Not bad, eh?"

"Cobia, huh?" he asks.

"Yes. Seen any?"

"Oh, they're always around this time of year. Little hard to see

King-size cobia from a Beaufort, South Carolina, bridge:
a real test for any angler.

'em when the water browns up like this, but on this tide you might
spot some of them feeding." Then, glancing at your eel, he adds,
"Good bait. Expensive, but good."

You feel a flush of confidence, realizing that this is what the man
in the bait shop had said.

"Might as well buy the best insurance," was his advice.

From the looks of the bridge's barnacled pilings and the river's
shell-raked shoreline, he wasn't conning you about the need for a

stiff rod with at least 50-pound line and a heavy wire leader, either.

With no fish showing, a deep bait seems best. A half-dozen egg sinkers above a barrel swivel pull your eel down; when you dip and jerk your rod, the sinkers run up your line, then slide down again with a series of clicks. The noise has tolled in nosy fish for you before.

But these Beaufort cobia don't seem to be nosy. Or hungry. Or even here. The only thing unusual that you've felt after nearly an hour of eager attentive fishing is this gentle pressure that seems to be easing your eel toward the pilings.

Probably just a weed, you think, but it's pulling against the current.

Probably just a sheepshead, you think, but on a 14-inch eel?

By rights you never should hook this cobia. Normally it would drop your bait as soon as it felt the pressure you're applying so prematurely, but this is a hungry fish, a confident fish, and when it feels your pull, the eel already is in its gullet. By the time you get your mind resynchronized with your muscles and haul back on your rod, the fish has hooked itself.

Later, your main memory of this battle will be that it was the most awkward you've ever experienced. Details are blurred, but one in particular endures: you astride the railing, clinging with your left hand while straining with your right against a rod that's bent clear under the bridge, and a pair of incredulous strangers holding onto your belt and mumbling things about "crazy damn Yankees."

Warm-Water Flats

You'll wade for these Florida bonefish. Sure, boats let you see better, but what you lose in visibility you'll more than make up in control: proceed at your own pace, casting carefully to every suspicious shadow, covering an area completely, with no wind or current to coax you along.

The water is warm, the bottom solid. Comfortable in your chinos, secure in your sneakers, you can concentrate on trying to spot the ephemeral hints of the bonefish's presence: tails, shadows, muds, glints from their silvered hides. But despite the unruffled water, they will be hard to spot with all these scattered clouds mottling the shallows. Your polarized glasses will help, but remember to look deep, concentrate on the bottom, be alert for shadows.

Stalking bonefish on shallow flats requires a tiptoe tread, pinpoint accuracy, and shatterproof nerves. (Photo: Mark J. Sosin)

This bright, balmy, coined-in-the Keys evening makes back-home blizzards seem as remote as Mars. A half-hour of fruitless stalking makes Florida bonefish seem equally remote: not a strike, not a sign.

Time for a change in strategy. Spinning instead of fly-casting. Pork chunk on a weedless hook. Save your shrimp flies for a cloudless sky, an unmottled bottom.

A rising tide is flooding the flat when you spot the school. Too far for a careful cast. You're tempted to try, but you have waited too long to risk wasting this opportunity. When your lure lands, it will land gently, 10 feet in front and upcurrent of the fish. Can you intercept them?

Yes. They're edging in. Crouching, you tiptoe slowly parallel to the shore till the grazing school moves within range. You're trembling. Pl-e-ase, no bonefish fever. Not now. But your cast is short. In front of the school, all right, but barely 5 feet. Bye bye bones.

But they don't spook. The chop on the water, gentle as it is, must have muffled the splash. You raise your rod, crank your bail closed, and reel a turn; pause; another turn; pause. The gap has closed to three feet; two and a half; two.

Now what are you doing? Why are you raising your head, looking up, smiling, winking? What is that you're whispering?

"Thanks," that's what. With less than two fast-dwindling feet between you and your first chance to bag the bonefish you've been dreaming about since you first read of their incomparable rocketing runs, it just seemed like the right thing to do.

A second later, after you've seen the dorsal, felt the take, set the hook, and are holding your rod high while bonefish #1 shows you how the breed has earned its reputation, could that be a whispered, "You're welcome," that you're hearing in the chuckle of the water and the sizzle of your reel?

The Gulf

Its solid cemented surface makes the 600-yard jetty at Texas' South Padre Island secure and comfortable enough for you to concentrate exclusively on fishing. No distractions from steep slippery slopes, no casting with one eye on the water and the other on leg-breaking gaps between jumbled boulders. With a calm sea complementing a clear late-autumn sky, you're wearing shorts, shirt, and a puzzled frown.

The puzzle is what to fish for. Tarpon, you know, probably are waylaying mullet in the rough water off the jetty's tip; redfish and spotted seatrout should respond to cast spoons or live shrimp beneath popper floats; feathers jigged close and deep could dredge up big black or red drum. But today, you decide, is not a day for figur-

The redfish is among the most popular of the many species that inhabit the Texas surf. (Photo: Russ Tinsley)

ing odds and fashioning strategies. Today is a day to relax and let things happen, to toss out one of the small menhaden you've netted from a canal among the marshes and let fish help themselves—redfish, whiting, bluefish, sharks; you couldn't care less. Today a common croaker or a sheepshead will be as welcome as a prize pompano or a snook.

When you feel the first tug, you're momentarily irritated. You've just settled your sinker securely on the bottom, taken in slack, fingered your line, and sighed contentedly in anticipation of enjoying your afternoon. Then this inconsiderate line starts tugging . . . hey, that's a fish! And like a billion buck-fevered beginners before you, you leap upright, crank your bail shut, and yank your bait from a bewildered fish's mouth.

No one snickers. All up and down the jetty are fishermen who have done it themselves; most will do it again. The only laughter is from that family of Mexican Americans 50 yards to your right, and theirs is a friendly laughter.

So you cast again, and when your line starts slipping from your bail, you wait—on-n-ne, two-o-o, three-e-e, fo-o-our—and when you set your hook, it finds flesh. Your rod dips as the fish runs, jerks as the fish shakes, but the battle is brief. When you reel, a beaten fish responds, yielding to your rod's relentless pressure.

It's a redfish, long and bronzed and beautiful, a respectable 5-pounder. Two exciting hours later, it has three more reds, two trout, and a flounder for company, and as your line once again starts streaming from your spool, you wonder what this fish will be. Let's —on-n-ne, two-o-o, three-e-e, fo-o-our—find out!

It's a ray, an enormous, powerful, bat-winged creature that continues to cruise down the channel as if totally unaware of the arm-aching pressure you're applying. There's nothing you can do except lean back and think humble thoughts and wait for the inevitable "Pop" to signal that your 200 yards of 20-pound monofilament are being towed like a flimsy kite tail into Laguna Madre.

And so, with eyes popping, chest heaving, back throbbing, and legs trembling, you conclude your quiet afternoon on a Texas jetty.

The Sea of Cortez

The Big One! You decided long ago that surf fishing is for you. Now, with a few years of local action under your belt, you're ready for more exotic waters.

Where to? Bermuda for bonefish? The Bahamas for permit? Blues from Nantucket's beaches? Snook from Florida's Gulf Coast? When you define what you're looking for, the answer is easy: fair weather on vast unpeopled shores; smorgasbord of species; guaranteed action on good-size fish with the ever-present possibility of tying into something special. These spell the Sea of Cortez, that

600-mile-long finger of Pacific Ocean separating Mexico from Baja California.

But what part? A man could spend a lifetime sampling just the frosting. Your time is tight, your budget sparse. El Golfo, you conclude, is ideal. Less than 60 miles south of the border and a paved road all the way: travel will be fast and trouble-free. Still not heavily fished, despite its popularity with California and Arizona anglers, its accommodations will be adequate and reasonably priced.

Best of all, it's spring. Here around the mouth of the Colorado River, that means grunion, and during those brief magic moments when these small silver baitfish swarm ashore almost at peak tide to spawn in the sand, the mighty totuava, also on their annual northward spawning run, crowd in close behind. Totuava! Elsewhere they may be just plain croaker, but here in the Sea of Cortez where they sometimes exceed 100 pounds, they rate a name that resounds with the roaring of waves pushed by chubasco winds.

A sullen calm has settled on the sea's vast shallow shelf as you approach it. Its utter blankness seems to be defying you to find fish. Not a bird, not a boil, not even a ripple mars the monotony; except for that dark patch, which suddenly rustles the water, which suddenly erupts as a thousand squirming anchovies leap to escape pursuing predators.

Your silver spoon skittered across the anchovy school fools a

The Sea of Cortez almost guarantees action on good-size fish and offers the ever-present possibility of tying into something special. (Photo: Jim Tallon)

fish first time through. Your 7-foot rod and 8-pound line handle
it nicely. A corvina, El Golfo's seatrout. Three pounds. No totuava,
but totuava aren't expected. Tonight is for totuava. Today is warm-
up fishing, fun fishing, and there's plenty to keep you hopping all
day long. Bait breaks a dozen times as the tide floods the shallow
flats, then quickly recedes, and when no bait is breaking, you continue to catch fish anyway. More fish than you've ever caught before. More than you can keep track of. Pompano, Spanish mackerel,
a 1-pounder that looks like a bonefish's baby brother, plus two or
three species you couldn't identify. You wonder if, after all this
action and your long trudge back to your lodging, you'll have
enough steam left to take on totuava.

A couple of Margaritas and a delicious pompano *en papillote*
restokes your boiler. When Manuel arrives, you're ready. (Yeah,
Manuel. Really. Bright eyes, broken English, parchment skin. Right
out of a travel folder via Ernest Hemingway.)

Manuel knows his way across the Colorado delta to Isla Mon-
tague. A full moon makes it easy, but you're sure he would have
no trouble guiding his outboard blindfolded.

"There, Señor," says Manuel, beaching his boat at the mouth of
a narrow inlet. "Very good there."

"There" looks pretty much the same to you as everywhere else,
but "there" is where you lay your big bright balsa-wood plug, and
"there" is where, less than a half-hour later, you are rewarded with
a grabbing yank and a powerful surging pressure that tax your 9-
foot rod and 20-pound line to their limit.

Patience is as important as power when you're eager to see your
first totuava. Care and concentration ultimately will beat even a
brute like this in obstruction-free water, but it takes time. And
shallow water, remember, is not the totuava's normal domain. Once
when you think the battle is over, panic triggers a last-act lunge
that nearly rips your rod from your cramped fingers.

"Fine fish, Señor."

Manuel awards you his laurel wreath. Twice more he says it before dawn as you slide smaller totuava onto the sand. Twice when
you lose fish, he tactfully says nothing, but in his cigarette's glow
you can see him smile.

Adventures like this always end too soon. Seems you've barely
met the Sea of Cortez when it's time to leave. As Manuel's outboard cleaves the dawn-dappled surface, bringing you back to

breakfast and goodbyes, you gaze south across the Sea's other 590 miles and you think of grouper, sierra, pinto, jack crevalle, red snapper, cabrilla, roosterfish . . . and you know you'll be back.

The California Coast

San Francisco Airport. A two-hour wait between planes. What to do?

Fish, of course. It's warm, the tide is full, and the molten sun settling behind the mountained peninsula that separates San Francisco Bay from the Pacific Ocean spreads a shimmering sheen across the quiet surface. And in that waist-high water that covers a broad bait-rich sprawl of mud, there just have to be striped bass feeding.

Waders? Who needs them? Sneakers and chinos will do. Wring them out afterward and pack them in the plastic trash bag you've brought along just in case you should happen to find a place to fish.

You're glad you decided on a fly rod. It's light, its two-piece construction has been convenient for carrying, and its 9 limber feet will enable you to lay your weight-forward floating line right out where the bass ought to be dining. During the hour and fifty-two minutes before your nine-thirty departure, you'll be able to cover a lot of water.

Popping bugs first. Your favorite way when the surface is sunset-slick, when these bushy little floaters can be splashed and blupped with a racket that affects feeding stripers like a dinner bell. Nothing like taking a striper topside. A ringside seat for the chase, the swirl, the slap, the hit, A hundred times you've seen it, and your next will be as exciting as your first.

But these are West Coast stripers. Same species as back East, sure, but mightn't they have picked up a few peculiarities since their 1879 transplant? Feeding habits, for example. These sparsely dressed white bucktail streamers that you'll be using later on when it has become too dark to see your popper, these are designed to imitate sandeels. Will they also resemble anchovies to a selective striper?

With poppers, though, appearance makes little difference. It's size and noise and action and, to a minor degree, color that count.

With a little imagination and planning, you can catch stripers between flights close by the San Francisco airport. (Photo: Larry Green)

Cast your popping bug accurately, drop it softly, skip it like a frightened baitfish, and hungry bass will come a-running. West Coast or East, this should be the same.

The accuracy of your cast is all right: about 30 degrees to the right of straight out so that the slight left-to-right current will keep your bug under perfect popping pressure as it swings through a slight arc. A-plus you get for accuracy; for delicacy, D-minus. Your bug lands like a thrown stone. Okay, so you're overanxious, but on a shallow flat bass feed with their guards up. A sudden splash can send them scooting toward the security of deeper water.

Maybe your retrieve can make up for it. Start it immediately, without an instant's hesitation. A fish spooked by the splash might hear the follow-up commotion and figure he's missing out on an easy meal. Skip, pause, "Blup," silence—a fast, steady predictable rhythm.

Your bug is halfway back now, your line at 45 degrees to shore. Can't be more than a couple of feet of water beneath your bug. Time to raise your rod, pluck your bug, and false-cast for another try.

Your bug has barely left the water when there's a boil behind it. Easy, now. Careful. You've got an interested fish. A little more of the same and he'll be back. Up goes your rod, back goes your bug, down goes your rod, and ugh: a sickening tug in the seat of your pants. You've caught yourself by the keester.

All in a night's fishing. It has happened before. In seconds, the bug is back in business, chugging, blupping, BLASTING! With nowhere to go but up, the bass cartwheels, writhing and shaking to shuck the hook that you can see is set firmly in its jaw.

Even a strong determined 8-pounder is no match for your tight line and unyielding rod. A few hard boring runs, and the fish lies on its side gasping at your feet. You stoop to admire it and thank it and release it, and as you kneel on one knee watching it swim slowly away, you glance up at a plane that's just taking off. Could it be dipping its wing?

The Pacific Northwest

Washington State. A jumbled cluster of barnacled boulders, wet yet rough enough for secure footing. But only ten more minutes with this freshly flooding tide slipping in behind you. That dip between you and shore will fill in fast. At worst, you'll get wet, maybe lose a little skin on the rough rocks. Small price for a couple of extra casts into prime lingcod country.

Hard to explain why you're so optimistic. It's your nature, sure, but three hours without a fish should have dampened your enthusiasm. Must be the memory of that lone run of the morning. Not much at first, just a couple of fast jabs, but when you sank that hook, the strength of that fish was astonishing. Your light rod offered little restraint; when the ling reached its rocky sanctuary, your 12-pound monofilament frayed and snapped. But you have learned your lessons: let the fish swallow your herring so you'll hook it deep and tire it quickly; work the fish from the rocks sideways instead of across their tops so you'll avoid wear on your line. Now you want to put these lessons to work.

You cast to your left instead of straight out, reeling in slack as your bait swings slowly with the current. If a ling should hit, you'll be able to apply sideways pressure as you work your way back toward shore. This takes care of the tide problem.

When the tug comes, you're ready. No knee-jerk yank like the last time. This time you wait. Two tugs, three tugs, four. By the fifth, you have leaned forward, rod extended, tip toward the fish, and reeled in slack. Strike!

Your ling is hooked. A big rowdy roughneck, judging by the bow in your rod, the pull on your reel. As predictable as a sub skipper in an air attack, it dives. Once it has taken up station behind a rock

In Washington State you might want to take on a big rowdy roughneck of a lingcod. (Photo: Larry Green)

with your line over the top, there's no budging it. Time to work your way toward shore.

The dip, of course, has long since filled; few things in fishing take only ten minutes. But there's no problem. Hold your rod high, wait till the dip drains between swells, then leap across and resume your sideways pressure. Simple.

But few things in fishing are simple, either. How, for example, could you have predicted that when you raised your rod and bumped its handle on a rock, the vibration would send the fish scurrying? Or that you would have been off-balance when the fish yanked? Or that the dip would have been filling instead of emptying at the time?

Later, sitting on the shore soaked, scuffed, and totally contented, you admire the strong body, mammoth mouth, and fanglike teeth of your evening meal, and you wonder if Bobbie Burns, the auld Scot bard, could have had a ling fisherman in mind when he penned, "The best laid plans of mice and [fisher]men . . ."

Hawaii

You're a convert now, a devoted surfman who evaluates every trip, business or pleasure, in terms of its surf-fishing potential. If an early arrival, a delayed return, or a sleepless night can buy you even a few hours in the brine, your long tubular rod holder comes along. And nobody touches it. You'll willingly relinquish your best suit, your monogrammed shirt, your favorite tie to the baggage rack, but your rod remains in sight. No diplomatic courier ever was more protective of his pouch.

Especially on this trip. On this once-in-a-lifetime visit to Hawaii, you want everything to be perfect for your right-from-the-rocks encounter with papio, the junior member of the local jack tribe. The limber tip of your 9-foot two-piece rod should be perfect for whipping your half-ounce bucktail through the rocky wash. And for the clincher, you've brought along a couple of jars of porkrind. Back home the tantalizing tail-wagging of porkrind drives bluefish wild, and what, after all, could be tougher to tame than a 10-pound bluefish in a boiling tide rip?

A 10-pound papio from a boiling pocket of Pacific Ocean, that's what. Especially when this pocket is studded with coral heads and lava outcrops that sever 12-pound mono like so much spider's web. Cast and pray, that's all you can do, and be grateful that you brought along two dozen jigs.

Checking first for a quick-getaway route in case of a sudden out-

Coral clumps and lava knobs make Hawaii's shoreline hazardous, but papio make the effort worthwhile. (Photo: Jim Rizzuto)

size wave, you slip into the warm thigh-high water and let fly straight out, a careful and comfortable 50 yards.

"Let it settle," you remember your bluefish mentor telling you ten years ago. "Wait just a second or two till it touches bottom, then yank and crank, yank and crank."

Reflexively you follow his advice, ignoring the obvious: Hawaiian combers treat a lure differently from a Martha's Vineyard tide rip. Before you can yank, your jig has snared a coral clump.

One cast, one jig.

Next cast, your line snarls. By the time you straighten it, your hook is fast to a lava knob. Two jigs.

Your following two casts cost you no jigs, but your retrieves are so fast and frantic that no papio could catch your lure if it wanted to. But then you snap off two jigs in a row trying to drop them beyond the breaking waves.

As you're sitting a half-hour later contemplating the futility of traveling halfway around the world to deposit thirty bucks worth of bucktail jigs in a Hawaiian surf, you don't notice the handsome jet-maned gent alongside you until he heaves back on his rod and hits pay dirt. For ten minutes you watch him weave an 8-pound papio through a minefield of lava and coral, currents and waves. When he lands his fish, he looks up.

"Hi. What are you sitting there for? C'mon down and join in the fun."

This is Jim Rizzuto, Mr. Fishing Hawaiian Style, but you have no way of knowing. All you see is a nice guy who might be able to salvage your day. You're about to explain how you're all out of jigs, when Jim points to a box in the water.

"Help yourself," he says. "Jumping jacks. Got here before first light and filled the box."

So you rig one of these ultra-uglies and cast it and retrieve it in accordance with Jim's suggestions, and by the time you have to part company—"Can it be noon already?"—you have hooked five papio and, amazingly, landed four.

"Aloha," says Jim as he drops you outside your hotel. "Come back."

And you will, you will.

This is the way a couple of my daughters started—and almost every surfperson has some such early memory of a sunny day and the beginning of a lifelong pleasure.

11
Getting Started:
How the Experts Did It

HOW DOES ONE GET STARTED fishing in the surf? There must be almost as many answers as there are fishermen. Recently when Mrs. Fallon returned from an afternoon at the beach she told me of an elderly gentleman she had met.

"It was raining," she said, "and there he was standing all by himself. He wore waders and a slicker and a sou'wester hat, and he had a single small flounder. You could tell from the eager way he watched and waited and held his rod that he *knew* another fish would be right along, and you could tell from his smile that if it took a minute or a month, it wouldn't make much difference.

"This was his first year in the surf, he told me. Just went out one day with a freshwater rod, tossed out a clam, and caught a flounder. Been at it ever since; rain or shine, day or night, every chance he gets."

At the other end of the spectrum is the man who accompanied my friend John Hovnanian on a recent August night casting live eels for striped bass. John had caught a 12-pounder the night before and was confident that even without sleep he would be able to surpass that.

"One fish," John told me when he phoned next morning, "and this guy catches it. Thirty-one pounds. First striper he ever caught, but you can be darn sure it won't be his last."

Some surfmen start late, others are blessed with being born to it. A parent, a pal, a summer vacation, a chance meeting, a dare, a shot in the dark—all have started people fishing the surf. Most have like it, many have loved it, and a few have never come back.

"Too arduous," they have complained, or "too complicated" or "too uncomfortable." (Never "too dull.")

No question: surf fishing is not for everyone. Yet I can't help feeling that those who have found the surf unsatisfying might have fared better if they had been guided by someone who knows the ocean's infinite moods, who has stalked and fought and beaten—and been beaten by—fish that occupy its endless edges. There's just too much variety in surf fishing for there to be many dissatisfied customers.

With this in mind I have asked veteran surf fishermen to share their experiences with readers of this book. "A few words about how you got started," I wrote, "a few suggestions about how today's tyros might do as well." Here are their replies.

FRANK WOOLNER *is one of the originals. Invading the Cape Cod surf after his return from WWII, he lay the keel for a career that has included a shelfful of books, countless articles in all the major outdoor magazines, and longtime editorship of* Salt Water Sportsman. *His* Modern Salt Water Sports Fishing *was described by H. G. "Tap" Tapply, Associate Editor of* Field & Stream, *as "the most comprehensive book ever written on the subject."*

Frank Woolner.

Like so many others who engaged in a lemming march to the sea in 1946, it was during that blessed spring of new peace that I waded into the suds. Previously, the only sand in my shoes had been from a beach called Omaha White in Normandy—where nobody had time for sport.

Surf casting was relatively easy for me, because I'd cut milk teeth on a variety of tackle combinations, including revolving spool used on inland black bass. Stepping up to the big rod, therefore, involved little more than a two-handed grip: it was the same discipline, albeit beefed-up.

Historians will discover that, for some reason yet inadequately explained, saltwater angling became camp in '46. At that time legions of hinterlanders swarmed to the seaboards; many of them were expert freshwater mechanics, so they revolutionized ancient tactics. Citizens residing right on the coast were somnolently wedded to conservative tradition: they were not the innovators.

To those of us from inland pastures, it was a tremendous challenge, a glorious adventure, and a new world to conquer. We had to learn much about tides and currents, moon phases and favorable winds. We got saucer-eyed at the power of a bursting surf, and we got knocked on our duffs with chilling regularity.

Compared to Ike Walton's description of stream fishing as "tranquillity," this new sea sport was better described as "elemental fury." I have always viewed it this way. Still do, even though it is worth noting that the centurions of 1946 were both young and tough, most of them just back from four or five years of grinding warfare.

By today's standards the tackle was sorrowful: Burma cane rods and Cuttyhunk line, tin squids and a few plugs. Most of us lacked the ready cash to buy expensive split-bamboo rods and, even if we were well heeled, the well-built natural cane of that time was more efficient. Sure, they splintered at the worst possible times—but so did the touted split bamboo. Cane was always questionable, but a good stick offered action roughly comparable to today's best tubular fiberglass.

There were good reels. Penn Squidder and Surfmaster models were considered supreme, although many of us started with less efficient winches, such as the old Ocean City bay types with their heavy metal spools. Spinning had yet to invade the salt-chuck, and the first of these coffeegrinders were immediately self-destructing.

In the beginning of it there were few beach buggies: most of us walked, and if we chose to fish all night, then we dug foxholes in the sand to sleep for a few hours when the tide was foul. This wasn't any reversion to wartime practice, simply a means of escaping cold wind. On Cape Cod, even in midsummer, the breeze can be mighty sharp during a starlit mid-watch.

My first striper was a 9-pounder out of the Cape Cod Canal, caught the first time I fooled around with a surf rod. Nothing remarkable, other than the fact that it was hooked on an eelskin rig I'd sneakily altered. All skins at that time (and most of them now) were reversed or turned inside out. A maverick, it seemed to me that a bass would prefer the natural outer skin color, so I experimented.

While it worked and I thought I'd discovered a secret, honesty dictates confession that it never worked very well again. That first striper fought hard, but fooled me because it tumbled so easily. Like all amateurs who luck-in, I felt that *Roccus* was a true patsy. After a while I learned better.

For newcomers, like me, the whole business was pure magic. On weekends we pounded eastward over narrow, perilous road nets in humid summer nights, almost believed (under the yellow lights of the Cape Cod Canal) that reels were made of solid gold. Shortly we gravitated to the outer beaches where the high surf taught us new and vital lessons.

So we were young then, and tough, but we took some terrible chances. Sleep was an abomination, since fish were available around the clock. We fished—until we were almost comatose with fatigue—and then we climbed into our cars and drove back home. Too often I have seen the road ahead begin to funnel, slapped my face to remain awake—and still dozed off. The God that takes care of fishermen and damned fools always intervened at the last moment, and then I'd be wide awake with fear after a near miss with another car or a tree. A few of my close friends were not so fortunate.

Old-timers like to say: "At least, we saw the best of it!" And that's a relative matter. In 1946 striped bass were plentiful, but small even by today's standards. A 30-pounder was a real trophy, and the newspapers reported about gentlemen who caught "bull bass," defined as critters weighing 20 pounds or better. During my first full season, in which I caught a lot of fish, only one was a "bull."

Bluefish, at that time, were at the bottom of their cycle and hardly worth mentioning. Those we caught, always in late summer, were midgets of 3 to 6 pounds. Bass were the big deal, and almost every one of us sold our rod and line catch at anywhere from ten cents to a hoped-for twenty cents per pound. A few always went home to grace the family table. As every herd animal will say, we had a lot of fun, but we didn't make much money. We also suffered to enter Paradise.

On the credit side, the surfman of '46 faced a minimum of restrictions: practically all of the beaches were wide open to the general public, day or night. No-trespassing signs were almost unknown. We ranged our searim like latter-day corsairs, camping on the dunes in makeshift tents or catnapping fully clad in those aforementioned foxholes. The beach buggy really arrived in 1947 and, by 1948, had become an in thing, so popular that sand drivers organized (in 1949) to protect their own interests and keep the beaches clean. By that time there was a low rumble of discontent from coastal residents who had begun to fear this strengthening invasion by "outsiders."

For me, much of the old black magic remains, but it was sweeter at first encounter. I recall such crazily divers things as fishing with the legendary Arnold Laine during a vicious midnight electrical storm—and we caught a pile of bass while the heavens exploded. I remember a night when my brother Dick and I were both tumbled and thrown far up on the beach at Orleans by a wave that came from nowhere—and we wiped the sand out of our ears, went back, and cast for stripers.

Many things—bass slicing through emerald-green combers on a crystal morning at Monomoy Island; an arctic tern furiously snapping at my fingers while I released him after he tangled in my line at dawn; fire in the water, tremendous surf pushed by hurricane winds, and days when the sea breathed as easily as a healthy child. Finally, a glorious association with dozens of wonderful old surfmen who were the best in their respective time slots.

Hooded of eye, and growing a mite old myself, I now regard the new challengers—and think them pretty naive. But I also think: *They'll be better than we were!* Things progress.

I have been fortunate. As editor of *Salt Water Sportsman* it has been my pleasure to fish the high surf on both coasts of the United

States, and well down into Central America. You want to know something?

Surf fishing is an ultimate. It is man against the sea, with nothing but basic tackle and intelligence. It is exaltation and fury and high adventure. No matter how the ball bounces, there'll always be a new searim to conquer.

GEORGE HEINOLD *is familiar to* Outdoor Life *readers as that magazine's Salt Water Editor. His love affair with surf fishing, launched way back when Pearl Harbor was just an obscure wrinkle in the Hawaiian shoreline, still is going strong. George has fished most of the meccas from Maine to Oregon and beached many remarkable fish, but the man's real measure in my eyes is the infectious delight with which he still describes something so comparatively minor-league as catching porgies from a jetty.*

I first became seriously interested in surf fishing back in the late 1930s and early '40s. Those were the days of Calcutta and Burma cane rods, Cuttyhunk linen line, and wide-spooled conventional reels. It was the era when Rhode Island surfmen used either rigged or strung eels, and metal squids for daytime fishing. One had to have an educated thumb, especially when casting eels. Only a few surfmen were using plugs, which most veterans sneeringly referred to as "broomsticks."

My apprenticeship was served on the shores of Jamestown and Narragansett, both rocky shores. We did a lot of night fishing. Before my thumb became educated I went through my share of back-lashes and bird's-nests, and I was pretty discouraged. But the veterans (the Clarks, the Kings, and the Potters) were picking up fish up to 40 pounds.

During about my tenth trip, I made a cast with an eel that put me into a 32-pound striped bass. From then on, I was a convert. Though surf fishing is less rewarding in fish, it offers the challenge of high sport. One is alone. Whatever he catches is due to his own efforts—no captain or mate to steer him into fish.

The largest fish I ever caught in the surf (other than sharks and rays) was a 52 1/2-pound striped bass in Maine; my largest blue a 21-pounder; and my largest weakfish an 11-pounder. Though I am now well into my sixties, I still fish the surf whenever possible. It is the challenge and feeling of self-accomplishment that keeps me at it.

In the 1950s I began making regular trips to the Outer Banks of North Carolina and the Eastern Shore of Virginia for channel bass (red drum) and bluefish, and thus became acquainted with the sandy-shore technique. I learned how to spot sloughs and holes between the waves. My largest red drum was a 59-pounder and my largest black drum a 63-pounder. I have also enjoyed some fine "trout" and bluefishing in this area. At my age, I find the mild climate down there and the fact that most fish are caught on bait a great advantage, though I still sling a pretty mean metal squid when the fish are on top.

In 1953, I had my first surf fishing on the West Coast. In those days, no one used artificials out there, depending mostly on bait. Using a squid, I caught my first stripers out there on squids—at Humbug Mountain, Oregon. I also caught some more in California. I wrote an article in 1954 about it in *Outdoor Life* entitled "Yankee Squid in the Pacific." I like to think that in some small way I contributed to the use of artificials in the Western surf.

MILT ROSKO *is one of those lucky guys who learned early what he liked best and has been doing it ever since. And doing it supremely well: Milt's byline is a staple on bookshelves and magazine racks wherever fishing literature is sold. After cutting his teen-age teeth on New Jersey stripers, blues, and weaks, Milt racked up almost all the sporting species on all three coasts, offshore as well as on. Despite these exotic experiences, he retains a special fondness for working a night tide along the Jersey shore with his teen-age son, Bob.*

Back when I was a teen-ager, World War II had most of the surf and jetty fraternity away doing a stint for Uncle Sam. Locally my dad and I would occasionally frequent the beaches at Sea Bright and while away an afternoon catching fluke, weakfish, and croakers. From time to time we'd visit friends at Point Pleasant, N.J., and I always brought along a vintage double-built split bamboo rod and an old Ocean City reel without a star drag. It was on the beaches at Point Pleasant that I was introduced to a block tin squid, which was given to me by an angler who'd landed a mess of weak-

Milt Rosko.

fish, at a time when they ignored my squid bait on the bottom. Soon I managed to land several on the shiny metal squid, and along with several fluke that I had caught earlier in Manasquan Inlet I had a nice stringer of fish.

So it went in my very early teens. Nothing spectacular along the surf and jetties. But it was enjoyable, and the beauty part about it all was that it didn't cost a thing! I just took along my tackle and could go fishing at my leisure. Gradually I met quite a few good fishermen, and as an eager teen-ager I wasn't bashful and asked lots of questions, and so I learned a great deal. In those days there was a superb caliber of fishermen along the beach, and practically everyone was a regular. This was before spinning and the increased popularity of beach sport, and I'm happy that I lived through that era of learning with people who loved surf and jetty sport for what it was in those days, and continues today, just tough fishing, where you enjoyed being out on the beach or climbing around a slippery rockpile whether you caught fish or not. The fish were a bonus that simply added to the enjoyment.

I was sixteen years old when I caught my first striper. It was while casting from a rock abutment alongside Highlands Bridge in the Shrewsbury River. I used a basic bottom rig and tapeworm as bait, and from that time on I was really a fanatic. Because of school and eventually working, most of my surf and jetty sport was done at night, and to this day I still most enjoy after-dark sport, simply because there's no one around and you can really enjoy the solitude that the beaches and jetties offer.

I kid you not that as a teen-ager, young working man, and then a married man, the cost of fishing was a major consideration.

Frankly I didn't have a lot of money to use for fishing. Before I owned a car I used to take the Central Railroad of New Jersey to Highlands. I rented a boathouse locker in which I kept my fishing tackle, and I used to fish as far as I could walk, and because of this I got to know the area extremely well. I worked the Sea Bright rock wall, the wooden groins that extended out from it, and the couple of old rock jetties in the area, along with the stretches of beach. I caught my share of bass, and then some, on practically every lure imaginable. It was from the top of that wall that my wife, June, caught her first striper while we were dating, a 7-pounder that walloped a block tin squid and porkrind shortly after daybreak.

That cost factor mentioned earlier kept me from doing some of the fishing I would like to have done, but because of it I became a better surfman and jetty jockey, simply because I concentrated on the fishing at hand. I learned many things by trial and error, but thank the regulars along the seacoast for taking me under their wing. I might note that there were many of them too.

Things really haven't changed much along the coast today when compared to when I began. True, there are more fishermen, and it's harder to find the solitude I once enjoyed. But the fish are there, and I suspect there are more of them now than ever. I've found good fishing from the surf on all three of our coasts, and have included many species in my catches, most notably the striper, blues, weakfish, channel bass, and a host of other stalwarts.

Today my economic situation is quite a bit different from what it was thirty years ago. I've had the opportunity to catch blue marlin, striped marlin, and white marlin, sailfish, and the many tunas, and I have fished all three coasts offshore and on, and many exotic ports of call. But still I fish the surf and jetties regularly, and hope to continue to be able to do so for many years to come. For unlike boat fishing, along the surf and jetties everything depends entirely on the angler. There's no captain to run the boat, mate to rig the lines, or guide to point out the fish to cast to. When I'm on a rock-pile or along the beach it's one on one. Me versus the fish. When I score it's because I did everything right, not because someone else did everything right.

My son, Bob, began surfing and climbing around rockpiles with me very early in life, and now at fifteen he's an accomplished young angler. He loves it as much as I do, and while he accompanies me when we head offshore to the canyons to search for the marlins and tunas, he's always anxious to climb around coastal rockpiles with me for blues, stripers, and weaks. It's fun, too, just the two of us working a night tide together, and very satisfying to see him outfish me on oft occasion. These youngsters learn fast today, faster than I did. I like to think it's because I taught him that way.

A word of advice to someone just starting along the surf and jetties. Don't figure that if you try it alone you'll eventually catch on. If you take this approach, you're going to spend many frustrating years before you master the sport. First get to know the proprietor of a good old-fashioned coastal tackle shop. Even though it may cost you a few pennies, purchase your tackle from him, and ask and heed his advice on where to go and what to do. Most often you'll be able to meet some good fishermen in the shop, and if you're polite and genuinely interested one might take you under his wing and let you drag along with him a couple of nights. One night with such a regular will result in your learning more than if you spent a season on the beach alone. Above all, be consistent. Nobody ever became a good surfman or jetty jockey going fishing once a month.

In these days of high costs, where offshore fishing has become prohibitive from a cost standpoint, jetty and surf fishing is still the best bargain going, and surprising as it may seem, often you'll catch more as an experienced surfman than many inexperienced boatmen catch. Indeed, when I look over my personal logbooks of many years, on an hour-for-hour basis I've outcaught many of my fellow anglers who do their fishing from boats!

It's difficult in an article or book to tell you just what this fishing is all about. Only once you've experienced standing on a windswept jetty in the dark of night, with waves crashing across the rocks and the salt spray blowing onto your storm suit, can you appreciate the exciting surroundings in which you'll be fishing. Then, when a 20- or 30-pound striper grabs your rigged eel, and gives you fits as it tries every trick in the book to secure its freedom, and finally you sink a gaff into it, only then can you appreciate why I say nothing can compare with this most exciting of sports. It's you against the sea, and here your skills will show. When you reach the status of being called a regular along the seacoast, it's a reputation you'll have earned, and one that you will cherish through all the days of your life.

FRANK DAIGNAULT *was a little late in making his debut in the surf, but he has wasted no time in catching up. A frequent contributor to* Salt Water Sportsman, *he also has published articles and photos in many national and regional periodicals. In his beat along the Rhode Island shore and the outer beaches of Cape Cod, Frank is renowned for fishing harder, longer, smarter, and usually better than anyone around, except occasionally for his lovely wife Joyce.*

It was an autumn weekend that changed the whole course of my life some fifteen years ago. Opening of the hunting season was approaching and at the time it seemed that there was little for an outdoorsman to do, so I accepted the invitation of a friend to try the Rhode Island shore for migrating stripers.

I didn't even own a saltwater outfit, however, and had to make do with a freshwater rig filled with 8-pound-test line along with a bag of surface plugs intended for largemouth bass. On the beach at Charlestown, we came upon a large group of people all casting feverishly and we joined them. Bluefish—I had to ask what they were—were strewn about the shore and about every twenty minutes others would pass. Rods would arc in sequence as they approached until I hooked up and then I would lose track of the blitz as I marveled at the raw power; nothing I had ever hooked among lily pads had felt like this.

In spite of the number of lures I either broke off or had bitten off, I took a fair number of blues and just at dark caught a 10-

Frank Daignault.

pound striper. The lineside was decisive in causing us to phone wives and nap on the seats of our auto that night.

With the next dawn we sweated and chased, clubbing out blues with rocks, giving up every pickerel spoon we owned to a sea filled with teeth. And I know now that we were taken in by the excitement of blitz fishing. For me there was no going home. We haggled about when we should leave, my poor partner fearing domestic reprisals from a wife already dismayed by one phone call; I just wanting to fish more and more. When he dropped me off in the street outside my home with my duffle and share of the catch, my understanding wife was pleased that I had enjoyed myself. A little rest that afternoon and I felt compelled to go back.

Columbus is a hero at that time of the year, good for a day off. After three days and nights of blitz fishing only a pig needs another day off. Oink.

Phoned in sick Tuesday.

I thought then that I had done it all, having sampled every type of inland hunting and fishing New England has to offer. Nothing I had experienced growing up with my dad in the field could compare, could be as compulsive, as the autumn surf. Oh, I had bought a hunting license with the real intention of going, but the pheasants were pretty well shot up by the time the fish were gone; grouse were hawky. The one Saturday I tried to hunt it was like being away and in love. Not that I loved hunting less; something else had taken over. I spent that day trying to decide where I belonged: with the sound of dry leaves or with a pounding surf? And the haunting possibility that this would be the day that stripers and blues would go on a feeding binge. Would I be able to endure the account of what I had missed from the many familiar comrades I had met on the striper coast? It was my farewell to arms.

A couple thousand surf nights and many a season have passed since then, and while I'm supposed to be telling you how I got started, it might be more of a service to the American culture to teach you how to stay away. That first passionate autumn in the high surf affected a greater change in my life than anything I've ever experienced. Broke as I was, I cashed a bond for my first surf rod and the family auto had its tire pressures lowered to become my first beach buggy. My domestic life was a little strained until the kids were old enough to come along; now my wife is as mad about the surf as I am. Mine joined me and has her own waders, but I could give you a very impressive list of fisher-persons who lost a tide in divorce court; their marriages went up in the mist of a skittering Reverse Atom.

Regulars around me have come and gone, a few having fished around the bend; one while fighting his last striped bass. Others have risen to almost incredible legendary heights. Take "Pergo" and Eddie Felice, Eddie "Detra" Mekule, Whitney, Woolner, and a spectacular group of surfmen from New York that is too long a list. Then there are those who leave the surf and go to boats for more fish. They are fishing, but they join a far less spirited group, often composed of our losers from the beach. And I can't help but wonder if they realize that they have quit something.

But the real good ones mentioned above, and oh so many more that helped cut that first beach trail, are carved into my memory. Nights, on mid-watch hunt for striped bass, I can almost see their faces in the surf. That's where we all begin, with the old-timers who had a common ground that kept them happy their whole lives—a devoted worship of the striper coast; in love with the Nauset surf, the hard moving rips of the Provencelands, or the bursting suds of Narragansett. Why? Maybe it's the smell of melon, and tooling a machine along the surf line to the call of diving birds, and the feel when something out there comes to life exploding on your plug and goes.

JIM RIZZUTO'S *childhood apprenticeship in the New Jersey surf (a pretty shaky one, as the following paragraphs will show) has flowered in Hawaii. Through Jim's articles a lot of anglers have enjoyed a vicarious sampling of Hawaiian surf fishing and have had their appetites whetted for experiencing it firsthand. For island anglers, his "Fishing Lines" column is required reading.*

I wince with embarrassment as I recall my first trip with a long rod. It is now twenty-five years later, and I still cannot discuss it without blushing.

That first "surf" trip was to fish for blacks (tautog) from the Manasquan rock jetty some thirty miles from my former home in New Jersey. Dad had prepared me for everything—except what to do when the rig got stuck on the bottom. That, unfortunately, is the most common thing that can happen as the sea surges back and forth across the snaggled black teeth of the ocean floor.

When I was stuck solidly, I just reached for the knife and cut the line off at the reel. As I recall the moment, vivid purple flashes come to mind, and I realize they mimic the livid color of Dad's face when he discovered how much of my newly purchased twisted-linen line had disappeared in a half-hour of fishing.

Who had ever taught me that initiative could substitute for ignorance? What damnfool conceit had kept me from seeking help with my problem? Even as I bore up to the well-earned rebuke, I knew that more misjudgment would mean an end to my fishing career, at least temporarily.

Yet, somehow, I was fated not to avoid it. I became *persona non grata* for future trips when Dad discovered that I had followed all of his careful directions for locking up the car, but had left the keys inside our '39 Olds. He had to break one of the wing windows to get us home, where I was to stay until I learned to use my head for "something besides a hat rack."

Fortunately, it wasn't long before he had to start taking me fishing again out of self-defense. Some of his lesser-skilled friends had found that it was always worthwhile taking me along on their jaunts because I had learned the secret spots where Dad had scooped the sand for beach lice, the mole crabs that blacks will eat when everyone has given up because the rocks are "fished out."

No matter what problem you've got, somebody else has already had it before, so don't be ashamed to ask for help. Study every aspect of the sport as you go along—who knows to what strange use you may put what you learn?

Fishing information is very much transferable from place to place. Those same beach lice that caught me blacks in New Jersey are the "sand turtles" that catch me o'io (bonefish) and papio (jacks) in Hawaii. The same through-the-eyes hook-up I used with 3-inch killies to catch fluke in Barnegat Bay works with 3-pound bonito baits that take Pacific blue marlin. And when I take my own kids fishing, I keep the car keys in my pocket.

KEN LAUER *is a guide—or maybe it's more appropriate to say the guide—for anglers patronizing that great foamy fishbowl along the Outer Banks of North Carolina. His famous Outer Banks Safaris is headquartered in Buxton. Angler's News readers are kept advised of what's doing along the Tarheel coast via Ken's colorful column.*

In the paragraphs that follow, he distills the wisdom of better than a quarter-century of serious surf fishing.

Surf fishing is a second career for me. I spent twenty years in the Navy Medical Corps, and by the time the eighteenth rolled around it was quite clear that whatever else I did, medicine was not going to be part of my post-retirement plans. The only other interest I had was fishing, and Hatteras didn't have anything to offer the visitors, novice fishermen or pros, in the way of guiding service, so . . .

Surf fishing and I came together in 1946 after a move from Pennsylvania to Virginia Beach, Va. I'd been something of a freshwater fisherman up to that point, but the sudden infusion of salt water proved to be a little too much. I got sand in my shoes the first day at the beach and it's been there ever since. Thanks to my military service, I had a chance to fish in most of the really good places, as well as some that weren't so good, but taken as a whole it was a really invaluable experience.

How did I become a surf fisherman? Not by any conscious effort on my part; at least not any I could discern. For a number of years I fished whenever and wherever I could, always watching and listening; watching the experts, or at least those I considered to be experts (which was damn near anyone who caught more fish than I did) and giving a listen to what they had to say. I never read any books on the subject of surf fishing, but I did have a chance to talk to several who wrote the books and a few others who should have. It was a gradual process of learning that took several years, but with only one hobby, I had lots of time to devote to the piscatorial arts. To me, fishing is like any other sport: to be really good you've got to practice. And I love to practice.

Most anyone can be a surf fisherman, but to be really good there are a few very important points to observe and steps to follow. For instance, when fishing new ground, some place far removed from your home waters, you might find the same kinds of fish, but the technique can be entirely different. Pay a visit to the local tackle shop, ask a few questions, eat a little humble pie, and keep the eyes and ears open. When you hit the beach, observe the other fishermen carefully. If there's a blitz going on, it won't make any difference, but if there isn't, you should be able to find the 10 percent that's catching 90 percent of the fish. If you're like me, you're gonna want to try your own style of fishing first to see if it's adaptable to strange territory. When that doesn't work, it's always nice to be aware of what will.

OK, fine, but what exactly do we look for? Well, let's start with the assumption that you're among a group of fishermen and a couple of guys are really dragging in the fish while the rest have to be satisfied with one now and then. Now's the time to use your eyes. What are they doing that you're not? Is the bottom rig different? Are the hooks closer to the bottom than yours? How about the bait—is it different or possibly fresher? It's been clearly proved that fresh bait is far superior to bait that is a couple of days old, even if the older bait has been well iced and looks good. When I say fresh, I mean bait that's been netted the same day it's being used. I know you can't always be sure your bait is that fresh; that's why many of the smart fishermen carry a throw net with them. If you net your own, you can be damn sure you've got the best.

Distance. Now there's something that can and often will mean the difference between success and failure. Sometimes the fish can be found close to the beach, other times the guy who gets that extra 10 or 15 yards is having a field day while you're still fuming. Distance is governed by many factors: length of rod, test line, weight of lure or sinker, and finally the skill of the fisherman. If you're not getting the distance you need, watch somebody who is. Take a close look at what he's doing, and ask a few questions. Above all, ask questions. Not, I hasten to add, during the height of a blitz; busting fish demand all of a man's concentration.

Don't shoot rabbits with an elephant gun. It's not necessary to heave heavy mono to catch big fish. Remember, heavier line means less distance, and to me distance is very important. Covering larger stretches of water can only increase your chances of catching that lunker, especially if he's lying on the outer edge of the bar and your heavy mono's been keeping you on the inner edge.

Tangled lines are pretty much a part of the fishing game, but there is something you can do to decrease your chances of fouling another line, or being fouled. This method works particularly well among a group of lure-chuckers. You know how far you can cast, right? OK, pick out a couple of guys who are casting farther than you; or not as far, doesn't matter which. If you are the long caster, wait till they've cast and then shoot over them. Time your retrieve so that you don't catch their lines on the way in. Works nearly every time. Even if they cast before you've completed your retrieve, chances are you'll be far enough in, it won't matter. If you are the short caster, wait till the guy next to you is part way in, then cast. I guess what it boils down to is having a little consideration.

Finally, practice. If you really want to be a successful bring-home-the-bacon surf fisherman, practice. Work with different weight lines and find out what's best suited for you. Don't hang up that rod in winter. There must be a football or baseball field you can use to sneak in a little casting. Be one of the 10 percent. Welcome to the club.

LARRY GREEN *is West Coast Editor for* Field & Stream, *a renowned writer/photographer, and a consummate surf fisherman. Larry's special blend of angling prowess and wry rascality came through loud and clear in a recent letter in which he wrote, "My back yard has so many striper scales on it that it looks as though it's paved with ice chips." Then, fully aware that stripers had long since left my New England shores, he concluded with a tantalizing "Gotta catch a tide." "A hernia," I wrote back, "that's what you should catch." "Already got one," he replied in his next letter. "Also 28-, 26-, and 24-pound stripers on that tide I was catching."*

When Jack asked me to do a little reminiscing about what got me started surf fishing, I slid back in my big easy chair, stared at my collection of surf rods hanging in my den, and almost instantly

Larry Green.

began to feel that tingle of excitement enter my tail bone and creep up my spine toward my brain.

No, not there . . . WAY UP.

I'd ridden my old balloon-tired Elgin bicycle over the hill to the Pacific surf from my home in San Bruno, Calif. Eight hundred and seventy-three rubber bands held an old battered surf rod and reel across my handle bars. I was twelve years old then and all aglow about being a seasonal perch fisherman. Already I was hoarding spots in the tide pool as if I owned them outright, especially those pools where big rainbow perch of a pound or better finned contentedly, unaware that I stalked them with all the cunning of an osprey hovering over a trout that ventures too close to the surface.

With a badly molested little rock crab dangling from the end of my rusty hook, I probed the depths of that pool. Little did I suspect that a huge striped bass lay in those depths awaiting one wrong move by one of those perch.

The bass ate my crab. Thinking I was snagged, I pulled enough to irritate the striper. As my line rose to the surface, I saw the biggest fish I'd ever seen move out of the tide pool and into the breaker line of the surf, dragging with him that poor molested crab and some 20 feet of rotting 45-pound-test braided Dacron that sizzled from my reel before it snapped off the spool. I chased that damn striper right into the surf, but came up with nothing more than four pockets full of sand and a mouthful of kelp. Or maybe it was four pockets of kelp and a mouthful of sand. Whatever, wet, shaking, and dazed by the sight of a bass over 20 pounds, I could remember only one thing: the bass had gone back home. And if the surf was where fish like this lived, then that is where I'd fish from there on out.

Though I could never convince my folks of it, I think that bass had everything to do with me flunking the sixth grade. Instead of multiplication, spelling, and such boring italics, my workbook was filled from cover to cover with drawings of the striped bass that cleaned my reel.

From that spring day forward, I've been chasing striped bass with an almost insane momentum, looking for . . . who knows? But I can tell you it ain't that rusty hook and that molested crab. I really hope that I never find what I'm looking for, so the hunt can go on and on and on and on. That is what surf fishing is really all about.

Glossary

anadromous   Living in the sea but spawning in fresh water; refers to fish such as shad, Atlantic salmon, and most striped bass. *Catadromous* fish such as the American eel live in fresh water and spawn in the ocean.

angler   A person who fishes for sport. The name is derived from *angle*, a term still used in many countries to designate a hook used in fishing.

angleworm   An earthworm used for bait. Although they soften and leech quickly in salt water, angleworms are a satisfactory substitute for the more expensive and harder-to-get seaworms.

backing   Heavy line wound directly on a spool underneath lighter, less coarse line used in casting. A linen line, for example, though poor for casting, is strong enough to restrain a running fish that has taken out 150 to 200 yards of monofilament and also stands up better against abrading by close-to-shore rocks. Economy was a consideration when monofilament was new and expensive; by filling part of your reel spool with cheap linen line, you could save several dollars with no loss in casting or playing capability. Modern mass-produced monofilaments enable you to fill your entire spool at reasonable cost, so on lines of 20-pound-test or stronger, backing is used less than in the past.

backlash   A tangled line resulting from the overrun of a revolving-spool reel.

barnacle   A small hard marine crustacean, approximately hemispherical in shape, that clings to solid surfaces such as rocks, boats, and pilings when they are exposed to salt water.

bass bug   One of the many freshwater lures that can work as well on saltwater species. Designed originally to be manipulated with a fly rod across the surface of largemouth-bass waters in imitation of frogs, mice, and large insects, bass bugs are equally effective against striped bass.

beach buggy   A motor vehicle for transporting surf fishermen along sandy beaches.

billfish   Fish such as marlin, sailfish, and swordfish whose upper jaws are elongated into a point. These are deepwater species, usually caught while trolling from boats.

bitter end   The outside end of a line.

blitz   One of those glorious occasions when a school of furiously feeding fish hits everything you throw at them.

blue plug   Probably the earliest plug used for stripers in the Cape Cod Canal. Actually, a muskie lure with its faceplate bent down so it would kick up a commotion on the surface.

bobber   Any of several plastic or wood devices used to keep bait a desired distance below the surface. The bobber's jumping or sudden submerging signals a fish's biting your bait. Also called a float.

bridge gaff   A device for lifting a hooked fish to a high elevation such as a bridge, pier, or cliff on which the fisherman is standing. Normally these are simple grapnels on the end of a long heavy line.

broomstick   Any early surf-casting plug fashioned from a length of broom handle with its face beveled to plow up a wake during retrieve.

buck   A male fish. The term normally is used to differentiate between the sexes during spawning. Also called **Jack.**

bucktail   Originally, the term denoted hair from the tail of a male deer, but now also denotes substitutes such as nylon. The term often is applied to the combination of these fibers and the hook to which they are tied. Bucktails can be used by themselves on single or treble hooks, or as trailers on plugs and spoons.

bulldogging   Swinging of the head by a hooked fish.

catadromous   Living in fresh water but spawning in salt water; refers to fish such as the American eel. *Anadromous* fish (shad, Atlantic salmon, most striped bass, etc.) live in salt water and spawn in fresh.

chop   Light waves caused by wind and tide.

chopper   A name applied to adult bluefish.

chum   Ground fish food used to attract gamefish. Scraps tossed into a tideway every few seconds entice fish to follow the food supply to its source. A perforated container can be tethered to the belt of an angler standing in a tidal flow to attract topwater feeders or anchored close to a beachfront to toll in bottom-dwellers. Oily fish such as menhaden are especially effective, but almost any fish, as well as clams, crabs, and mussels, can be used.

chumpot   A perforated container for dispersing chum when immersed in water.

cow   A large female fish.

cut bait   A piece of fish used for bait.

demersal   Living on or near the ocean floor.

dextral   Right-sided; having both eyes on the right side of the head, as in the winter flounder.

doodlebug   A small barrel-shaped cork float attached a few inches behind a baited hook to keep it suspended off the bottom, thus avoiding bottom-scrounging bait-stealers.

doormat   A large summer flounder.

drag   A brake or clutch on a reel for controlling tension under which fish take out line.

drail   A torpedo-shaped sinker with offset neck for attaching line; designed for trolling, but can be used from shore.

dropper loop   A loop tied in the line for attaching an additional lure above the one tied to the end of the line.

eel bob   A lure in which an eel's head is cut off and a lead weight sewed under the forward skin.

eelskin rig   A lure in which the forward end of an eel's skin is slipped over a lead collar that has a pair of hooks attached to it in series by a wire leader.

estuary   Water in the general area of where a river meets the sea.

false-casting   In fly-fishing, swishing the line back and forth before casting in order to extend more line beyond the tip top.

fathom   A unit of nautical measurement equal to 6 feet.

feather lure   A lure made from or dressed with feathers.

ferrule   A plug-and-socket combination on matching ends of a rod so they can be fitted together. Can be either metal sleeves or part of the rod's fiberglass body. Always lubricate male ferrules with oil from your hair, forehead, or behind your ear to avoid sticking.

fishfinder   A bottom-fishing rig which enables a fish to run with your bait without having to pull your sinker. The term also applies to electronic sounder used on shipboard for checking depth and locating fish.

fly rod   A light rod that casts line rather than lure. In salt water, used with streamer flies and popping bugs.

forage fish   Small fish of various species with no sport or commercial worth but valuable as food for larger gamefish. Examples are sand eels, mummichogs, and many kinds of sculpin.

foul-hook   To hook a fish somewhere other than in its mouth.

gaff   A large unbarbed hook on a handle used for landing fish. Hand gaffs for surf fishing are about 2 feet long and usually are carried with a protective covering over the point. Retractable gaffs are available, as are gaffs with coiled flexible line for tying to an angler's waist. Pier gaffs are oversize barbless treble or quadruple hooks on heavy line that can be dropped the long distances from pier or bridge to snag a hooked fish.

gamefish   Any species sought for its sporting qualities.

green fish   A fish with plenty of fight left.

guide   One of the metal rings along the length of a rod through which line passes. Sometimes guides are lined with smooth hard material such as agate or special alloys to reduce friction and avoid grooves. The guide at the end of a rod is called a tip top. Also, of course, a person who is hired to help a fisherman find and catch a fish.

hardware   In rod making, those metal parts such as ferrules, guides, tip tops, and real seats. In fishing, metal lures such as squids and spoons.

horse   To fight a fish by force rather than finesse.

ichthyology   The study of fishes.

iron   A surf-casting colloquialism for metal lures.

jig   A piece of metal, usually lead or stainless steel, with a hook in one end. The metal can be spherical, flat and round, or otherwise streamlined. A jig's hook often is dressed with feathers or bucktail. Line is tied to an eye in the body of the metal head. In use, line is alternately yanked and relaxed while retrieving, thus imparting a fast-slow, rising-retreating action. *To jig* a lure is to use it in this fashion.

kite   A special kite used occasionally by shore fishermen to carry baits to distant fish.

knot   A unit of nautical velocity equal to one nautical mile, or about 1.14 statute miles, per hour.

lateral line   A thin longitudinal line along a fish's side that enables fish to detect vibrations.

leader   A length of wire or line attached to the main line's forward end. Usually these are wire or heavy monofilament for protection against abrasion from rocks and sand and against severing by sharp-toothed species such as barracuda and bluefish. In fly-fishing, long fine leaders bridge the gap between flyline and fly. Usually these are heavy at the butt end and taper to a slender tippet.

littoral   Pertaining to a shore or coastline.

live-lining   Employing live bait. Traditionally this term refers only to the use of swimming baits such as herring, mackerel, and mullet and to the techniques for employing them. Occasionally applied to drifting seaworms.

meat fisherman   A person who fishes with bait instead of lures. Also a person concerned solely with catching as many fish as possible.

memory   The tendency of stretched monofilament line to return to its original dimensions. Pressure caused by memory can crush reel spools.

milt   A white milky substance containing sperm that is ejected by a male fish to fertilize a female's eggs.

monofilament   A single continuous synthetic fiber, usually nylon.

mossbunker   A colloquial name for Atlantic menhaden, a small oily school fish of the herring family that often is ground for chum or used whole as bait for striped bass and bluefish.

mullet   One of various inshore fishes popular as both bait and food. There are more than 100 species in the world. In the U.S., mullet are most abundant around Florida, although they are found along our entire East Coast and the southern part of our West Coast.

mummichog   A popular small baitfish found in coastal shallows from eastern Canada to Texas.

panfish   Any small edible fish not big enough to be considered a big-league gamefish. Examples are the porgy (scup) of the East Coast and the many sea perches of the West Coast.

peeler   A crab just prior to shedding its shell. Also called *shedder*.

pelagic   Pertaining to the ocean's upper levels; refers to fish that spend most of their lives in this region.

plankton   Drifting microscopic animals that provide a valuable supply of food for small fish.

plug   An artificial lure, usually of wood or plastic, designed to resemble a baitfish in size, shape, and color. Normally a plug is armed with one treble hook in its tail and one or two under its body. A body hook sometimes is removed to increase sport, but this should be done only with careful consideration of the effect it will have on the plug's balance and hence its action. A plug's body can be jointed as well as solid. Popular plug types are the popper, swimmer, diver, and darter.

plug bag   A container for carrying lures. Can be either fabric or hard plastic, carried on back or shoulder, and usually is compartmented.

poach   To take fish illegally. Also to cook fish by a method similar to boiling but in a special bouillon.

popping   A jerky topwater retrieve with a lure whose concave face makes popping sounds.

popping bug   A floating fly-rod lure of hair or cork that makes a popping noise during a topwater retrieve.

porkrind   A strip of pig's hide used as a lure. Also used to denote plastic substitutes. Often these are attached to the hook of another lure, such as a leadhead bucktail jig, although they can be used by themselves on bare hooks.

priest   A small billy club, usually weighted, for knocking out freshly caught fish. Always use a priest on sharp-toothed fish such as blue-fish, barracuda, and sharks.

promontory   A high point of land projecting into a body of water.

puppy   A small red or black drum.

purse seine   A large net for catching schooling fish. With its bottom weighted and its top floated, the seine is strung in a vertical posi-tion around a school. A line through rings spaced along the seine's bottom is drawn tight, closing the net like a purse around the fish inside.

race   Churning water where currents collide.

rat   A school fish of barely legal size.

reel seat   A metal sleeve attached to the shaft of a rod which is de-signed to receive and lock onto the foot of a reel.

rip   A condition of turbulence in salt water where tidal currents col-lide with one another or with wind, rocks, or underwater undula-tions.

roe   Fish eggs.

roll cast   In fly-fishing, a cast in which the line is rolled out like a hoop. Useful when brush or trees make a backcast impractical.

salinity   The proportion of salt in water.

sandspike   A tube stuck in sand and used for holding a rod. Normally these are made of aluminum and their bottoms are cut at an angle for easy insertion into the sand.

sea trout   A sea-run brown trout, found mostly in rivers of Canada and eastern United States.

seatrout   A popular saltwater gamefish of the drum family similar to the weakfish.

shedder   A crab just before shedding its shell. Also called *peeler*.

shoal   A shallow area, as over a sandbar.

shock leader   A length of tapered monofilament with the heavy end tied to hook or lure. Protects action end of line against abrasion from rough-bodied fish such as tarpon.

shooting head   The front level section of a weight-forward flyline.

sinistral   Left-sided; having both eyes on the left side of the head, as in the summer flounder.

sinker   A metal weight, usually lead, that can be made in various shapes and sizes and is designed to pull your bait or lure to a de-sired depth.

skimmer   A large surf clam used for bait.

slammer   A term sometimes used to refer to large bluefish because of the way they often seem to slam into a lure.

slick   A smooth oily layer on water.

snapper   A young-of-the-year bluefish. Also, a family of warmwater fish (red, mutton, gray, etc.).

snell   A short line, usually monofilament, with a hook at one end and a loop at the other. Because the snell usually is heavier than the line to which it is attached, it provides protection against abrasive rocks and fish's teeth.

snowshoe   A large winter flounder.

solunar tables   Data tabulated originally by the late John Alden Knight and currently published by his daughter-in-law, Mrs. Richard Alden Knight, for predicting daily feeding times of fish and game. Maintaining that best fishing is likely to occur in fresh water as well as salt when the moon's tidal pull is weakest, Mr. Knight calculated these times for locations throughout North America and devoted many years to confirming his calculations.

sound   To measure the depth of water. Also, of a fish, to dive deeply. Also, as a noun, a long broad inlet of the ocean generally parallel to the coast.

spinner   A lure consisting of or containing a revolving or spinning metal blade.

split shot   A small spherical or cylindrical lead sinker that is split and opened so it can be crimped on a line with pliers. Originally designed for one-time use, split shot now come with small tabs which when squeezed reopen the slot, releasing the line and enabling an angler to reuse the shot.

spool   Cylindrical portion of a reel on which line is stored.

spoon   A lure with the general shape of a spoon. A spoon wobbles or flutters during retrieve.

spreader   A device which permits fishing with two baited hooks side by side without their leaders becoming tangled. The leaders are tied to eyes at the ends of a horizontal piece of stiff wire. In the center of the wire is a piece of metal, usually a swivel, with two eyes, one above the other. The sinker is attached to the bottom eye, line to the top. The spreader is especially effective when fishing for flounders from an anchored skiff, but it also works well in the surf.

star drag   An adjustable drag developed by William Boschen and introduced in 1913. Named for the star shape of its adjusting wheel.

streamer fly   An artificial fly designed to resemble a small baitfish.

strip bait   Bait made from a strip of the flesh of a fish. Also used occasionally to denote porkrind or its imitations.

stripping   In fly-fishing, the act of pulling line from a reel when preparing to make a cast. Also, retrieving line in fairly fast and regulargly spaced intervals. In fish culture, the act of forcing eggs or milt from ripe fish.

swivel   A device, usually of brass or stainless steel, for connecting line to leader or leader to lure, whose purpose is to prevent line twist. The barrel swivel has a closed eye at either end, while the snap swivel has one eye and one safetypin snap. For bottom-fishing, a three-eyed swivel is often used, one eye for your line, one for your sinker, and the third for the leader to your baited hook.

teaser   A secondary lure used in addition to the main lure to increase chances of a fish striking.

tides   Movement of the ocean toward and away from land because of the moon's and sun's gravitational pull. Tides flow in and out twice daily, with a given tidal condition ordinarily occurring about fifty minutes later each day in accordance with the rising of the moon. In certain mid-Pacific locations such as Tahiti, tide always is low at sunrise and sunset, high at midnight and noon.

Tides are important in determining where and when fish will feed. Although no rule applies everywhere under all conditions, one that usually applies is that on an ebbing tide fish wait off the mouths of rivers and creeks for food. Suggestion: examine shorelines at low tide to locate holes, sloughs, sandbars, rocks, wormbeds, etc., where fish may be found when a flooding tide covers them.

A flooding tide moves in, an ebbing tide moves out. Slack water is that infinitesimal instant between flood and slack when flow seems to cease. Spring tides are unusually high and occur twice each month, at full and new moons. Neap tides, occurring midway between spring tides, are abnormally low. Because many mudflats are not exposed at times of spring tides, a good selection of mudworms is hard to find in bait shops.

tide tables   Tabulated times of high and low tides for every day of the year for key coastal locations, with corrections for intermediate points. Usually they contain data on moon phase and tidal flow as well. An invaluable aid for marine anglers. Often published as an advertising giveaway.

tippet   The fine outside end of a tapered leader.

tip top   The line guide on the tip of a fishing rod.

ultralight   Designation for spinning tackle where line is less than 3-pound-test and rod less than 3 ounces.

waders   Waterproof footwear of either hip-high or chest-high style.

wetland   Coastal area that is wet at high tide, dry at low.

Index